SEX DIFFERENCES IN SOCIAL BEHAVIOR: A SOCIAL-ROLE INTERPRETATION

SEX DIFFERENCES IN SOCIAL BEHAVIOR: A SOCIAL-ROLE INTERPRETATION

ALICE H. EAGLY
Purdue University

LEA   LAWRENCE ERLBAUM ASSOCIATES, PUBLISHERS
1987   Hillsdale, New Jersey   London

Lawrence Erlbaum Associates, Inc., Publishers
365 Broadway
Hillsdale, New Jersey 07642

Library of Congress Cataloging in Publication Data

Eagly, Alice Hendrickson.
  Sex differences in social behavior.

  (John M. MacEachran memorial lecture series ; 1985)
  Bibliography: p.
  Includes indexes.
  1. Sex role. 2. Interpersonal relations. 3. Sex
differences (Psychology) I. Title. II. Series.
[DNLM: 1. Role. 2. Sex Factors. 3. Social Behavior.
BF 692.2 Ells]
HQ1075.E24 1987   305.3   86-32921
ISBN 0-89859-804-4

Printed in the United States of America
10 9 8 7 6 5 4 3 2 1

For Bob, Ingrid, and Ursula

JOHN M. MacEACHRAN MEMORIAL LECTURE SERIES

Sponsored by The Department of Psychology, The University of Alberta in memory of John M. MacEachran, pioneer in Canadian psychology.

Contents

Preface

It is an honor to contribute to the series of volumes based on the MacEachran Memorial Lectures sponsored by the Department of Psychology at the University of Alberta. I delivered my lectures in October, 1985, and in the ensuing months prepared a book manuscript based on the lectures. The opportunity to present a preliminary version of the manuscript to an interested audience at the University of Alberta is very much appreciated. Professors Brendan Rule and Eugene Lechelt were responsible for the many arrangements that were made for my visit. I am grateful for their efforts as well as for the hospitality of the other faculty and the graduate students at the University of Alberta.

For some time I had thought about writing a book presenting a social-role theory of sex differences and incorporating some of the new meta-analytic work in this research area. I had not undertaken such a project because I was always in the midst of one project or another that seemed essential to developing my understanding of sex differences. Because the invitation from the University of Alberta fortunately came at a time when several of these projects were nearing completion, I was able to respond to the invitation by preparing the overview that this book contains.

Part of this book presents my own research, which I carried out in collaboration with several persons when they were graduate students. Wendy Wood and Linda Carli were my main collaborators on this research when I was on the faculty of the University of Massachusetts, and Valerie Steffen was my main collaborator during the more recent years when I have been on the faculty of Purdue University. Maureen Crowley, Patricia Renner, Carole Chrvala, and Mary Kite also made important contributions to this research while I have been at Purdue. The efforts of these individuals are greatly appreciated. I have also been fortunate to have support from the National Science Foundation for my research on sex differences and gender stereotypes. I held Grants BNS-7711671, BNS-7924471, BNS-8023311, and BNS-8216742 while I carried out the research described in this book. Chapters 2 and 3 are based on parts of this research that were published in the *Psychological Bulletin,* copyrighted by the American Psychological Association, and adapted with their permission (Eagly & Crowley, 1986; Eagly & Steffen, 1986a).

Some weeks after delivering the lectures at the University of Alberta, I produced a draft manuscript that a number of people read in part or in its entirety. The comments that these people provided contributed to the quality of the final manuscript. For this help I express my appreciation to Shelly Chaiken, Kay Deaux, Judith A. Hall, Michael Harvey, Blair Johnson, Tom Johnson, Mary Kite, Donald Kuiken, Martha Mednick, Brendan Rule, Sandra Tangri, Barbara Wallston, and Wendy Wood. During the project, I also benefited from James Franklin's competent assistance with library work, Holly Norman's excellent secretarial help, and Anna Fairchild's painstaking help with proofreading.

My husband Bob has been very supportive during this project, both intellectually and personally. He has listened patiently as I gave frequent reports on the progress of what was first the lectures and then the book. In addition, he read the entire manuscript and gave many valuable suggestions for improved exposition. My enthusiasm for producing an overview of modern research on sex differences in social behavior was also shared with our daughters Ingrid and Ursula. In fact, their insights about sex differences have stimulated my interest in the topic over the years. There was, for example, the day I told Ingrid (who was then 15) about the main findings of the research review on sex differences in aggression that is reported in Chapter 3 of this book. Ingrid calmly stated that, "Everyone already knows that" and thus provided yet another illustration of one of the main themes of this book—that gender stereotypes and actual sex differences are not nearly as discrepant as most psychologists have been assuming that they are.

I hope that the quantification used in this book for synthesizing research on sex differences will not place a barrier between this presentation and some potential readers. Although I believe that the quantitative methods illustrated in this book represent an important advance in the social sciences, these methods are not a sure route to the truth. The findings they generate should be carefully scrutinized and judged for robustness by comparing them with the findings that emerge from using other methods. Methodological diversity has much to recommend it—for the study of sex differences as well as for other topics.

A. H. Eagly
Purdue University

Prologue

In the mid-1970s a consensus about psychological sex differences began to emerge in the writings of research psychologists. A central tenet of this consensus held that sex differences are usually either unproven or nonexistent, even for those attributes that are popularly believed to be more characteristic of one sex than the other. It was also claimed that those few sex differences that had been adequately documented in the psychological literature are quite small in magnitude and therefore relatively unimportant in natural settings.

While this assessment of sex differences was evolving, a research literature also grew up concerning popular beliefs about women and men. This research on *gender stereotypes* (see Ashmore, Del Boca, & Wohlers, 1986) forced psychologists to confront the fact that non-psychologists believe that women and men are different. Faced with evidence of widespread gender stereotyping, sex-difference investigators of the 1970s were often cast in the role of crusaders against the misguided societal stereotypes that portrayed women and men as differing in their skills, personalities, and social behaviors.

In the first half of the 1980s, the assertion that sex differences are minor and perhaps even better termed *sex similarities* has been reiterated by a growing number of psychologists (e.g., Belle, 1985; Deaux, 1984; Hyde, 1981; O'Leary & Hansen, 1985; Wallston & Grady, 1985), some of whom suggested that it is puzzling and surprising that gender stereotypes have persisted among the general public in the face of an apparent absence of research support for sex differences in the psychological literature. The major response to this seeming disparity between scientific evidence and popular beliefs has been an increased emphasis on biases and rigidities in

1

processing social information. The contention was offered that the views of the general population were wrong, because of biases in the way that information is processed (e.g., Hamilton, 1979; Jones, 1982).

It is now time to reconsider the average person's view of women and men. Perhaps it is not entirely reasonable to dismiss as misguided the beliefs held by the majority of the people in a society and to suggest that these beliefs be replaced by generalizations ostensibly based on research findings. A more valid view of sex differences may give more credit to people as largely accurate observers of female and male behavior and incorporate a more sophisticated awareness of the limitations of psychological research and of the methods that traditionally were used to draw conclusions from large research literatures. The apparent mismatch between research findings and popular beliefs may originate, not primarily in the biases of the perceiver, but much more importantly in the narrow focus of experimental research and the nonsystematic methods used to summarize research findings.

Maccoby and Jacklin's pivotal review, *The Psychology of Sex Differences* (1974), was the touchstone for diagnoses of sex differences in the 1970s. This influential review shaped the consensus about sex-difference findings. Because of its central position in the literature, the Maccoby and Jacklin work is inescapably the central focus for criticism of the 1970s approach. This criticism has its scientific basis in the new scholarship that has sprung from dramatically improved methods for aggregating and integrating research findings.

Despite my current stance as a critic of 1970s scholarship on sex differences, I count myself among the many psychologists who offered descriptions of sex differences that, like the Maccoby and Jacklin (1974) work, reflected the Zeitgeist and the tools of analysis of that decade (Eagly, 1978). To understand these descriptions, scholars should focus on the shared interpretations that developed among psychologists who possessed a given set of methods that they conscientiously applied in a particular historical context.

In this book, I confine my analysis to social behaviors. This focus is narrower than that of Maccoby and Jacklin (1974), who attempted to review the entire psychological literature on sex differences and thereby included cognitive abilities and social behaviors in a common framework. However, there is good reason to believe that descriptions of sex differences should be different for the two domains. Because cognitive abilities are generally assessed by a limited number of standardized tests administered under highly controlled conditions, these sex-difference findings should be relatively stable (see Linn & Peterson, 1985). In contrast, social behaviors are assessed in diverse ways in far more varied settings. Therefore, sex differences in social behaviors are likely to be inconsistent across studies, and accounting for variability between studies becomes a fundamental aspect of integrating research findings. Because the definition of the situation in which behavior occurs must be considered in order to account for this variability between studies, the theoretical analysis for social behaviors should be somewhat different than it is for cognitive abilities.

To account for sex differences in social behaviors, social psychology is favorably situated: As a field that deals with social interaction, it should offer important insights. Yet most social psychologists have not paid much attention to the subject, despite the great popular and scientific interest in it during the past fifteen years. Moreover, many investigators in the inner circles of social psychology regard the study of sex differences as theoretically uninteresting.[1] This opinion is not capricious but reflects the focus of contemporary social psychology on cognitive processes. True enough, sex differences in social behaviors have been uninteresting in terms of most of the cognitive theories that have been popular in social psychology during the past fifteen years (see Fiske & Taylor, 1984; Markus & Zajonc, 1985). Social psychology's current view of the person as an active and constructive information-processor, who creates social realities from the information at hand, does not, in and of itself, yield effective analyses of sex differences. Disappointingly, the main currents of contemporary social psychological theorizing have so far contributed relatively little to this research area.

To provide a credible analysis of sex differences in social behaviors, I have found it necessary to reach back to earlier theoretical traditions. I have drawn upon certain concepts provided by social-role theory and theories of social influence. Within this framework, selected aspects of recent theorizing about social cognition and attitudes prove useful. Yet, the overall emphasis of this analysis is on the person as a recipient of social pressures, albeit a person who actively collaborates in creating and reacting to these pressures. Although the emphasis of my analysis on social pressures and norms tends to go against the constructivist grain of contemporary social psychology, I think the analysis is eminently appropriate for the study of sex differences. Thus, to account for differences in the behavior of social groups, it is necessary to determine what the members of each group possess in common. Once it is realized that they share a certain position within a social structure, the social pressures that group members experience begin to become evident and emerge as the most likely source of their distinctive social behaviors. This book examines differences in the social position of the sexes and contends

---

[1]In this book the term *social psychology* refers primarily to the varieties of social psychology that are practiced in departments of psychology. Sociologically trained social psychologists have somewhat different intellectual and methodological traditions (see Stryker, 1983).

that these differences expose women and men to systematically different role expectations.

The analysis of sex differences provided in this book is *not* eclectic, even though explaining sex differences is a task that may seem to lend itself to considerable eclecticism. Many theories of sex differences have been proposed, based on biological factors, early childhood socialization, and other perspectives. Yet the class of explanations that seems most compelling to me—explanations based on the social roles that regulate behavior in adult life—has so far not received a sufficiently unified and forceful presentation to make it a distinctive theory of sex-typed behavior. Even textbooks in the psychology of women (e.g., Hyde, 1985; Williams, 1983) do not acknowledge such a social-normative perspective as a general theory of sex-typed behavior. On account of this lack of recognition of the importance of this class of social psychological explanations, I decided to interpret sex differences in social behavior in terms of a single social-normative perspective. Although this viewpoint accounts for a considerable range of research findings, it inevitably oversimplifies the complex realities of sex differences to some extent. Some simplification must occur in the service of achieving a coherent conceptual representation. I hope that the benefits of stating a consistent theory of sex differences will include the stimulation of new research that displays the theory's predictive power and reveals its limitations. Greater understanding of sex-typed behavior should emerge from the interplay of this theory with competing theories.

The idea that women and men manifest distinctive social behaviors may make many psychologists anxious because of what they perceive as the risky social consequences of acknowledging group differences or even discussing them at all. The controversial nature of debates about racial differences (Herrnstein, 1973; Jensen, 1973) is still very much in the minds of many psychologists. Yet if investigators avoid scientific scrutiny of issues with far-reaching social and political consequences, the science of psychology would have to ignore many concerns that people regard as important and risk losing relevance as a discipline. Moreover, avoidance of the controversies taking place in our society over the nature of sex differences leaves the debate to be waged mainly in terms of ideology. The ideological alternatives are already spelled out: Many traditional ideologies foster belief in sex differences rooted in biology, and feminist ideologies typically either minimize sex differences or foster belief in certain of them as indicators of women's oppression or superior moral qualities. Psychological research cannot supplant ideological debates about sex differences. Nevertheless, in the long run, maximally valid descriptions of sex differences should follow from the application of the scientific method. In the short run, the scientific method may yield incomplete and even misleading descriptions, but these are generally corrected as tools of analysis are refined and scientists criticize each other's theories and research methods. In fact, the objectives of this book include the criticism of some of the conclusions that psychologists have offered about sex differences.

Discerning the social consequences of new generalizations that social scientists provide concerning sex differences is no doubt an impossible task because it would require understanding of future as well as present social conditions. Therefore, it is incautious to presume that acknowledgment by social scientists of existing sex differences invites discrimination against women or any other particular consequence. Even in the case of generalizations that may be regarded by some people as unfavorable to women, it is difficult to predict whether such generalizations would foster change-oriented compensatory education, discriminatory treatment, or some other reaction. In my view, the links between research findings and social policy are varied, often complex, and seldom very direct. Nevertheless, the chances that societies evolve sensible and humane social policies are usually increased by social scientists' presentation of valid, scientifically derived descriptions of social reality. The presentation of such descriptions of sex differences is a central purpose of this book.

Finally, a comment is needed about how the words *sex* and *gender* are defined in this book. Following usage suggested by Unger (1979) and Deaux (1985), *sex* refers to the grouping of humans into two categories—females and males. This grouping is based on biological differences between the two categories of people and is culturally elaborated in all societies. When female and male behavior differs, I refer to this difference as a *sex difference*. Consistent with the traditional usage of the term *sex difference* by psychologists, the term denotes that females and males have been shown to differ on a particular measure or set of measures. The term should not be taken to imply any particular causes of such differences. Although in recent years some psychologists have suggested that *sex difference* refer only to biologically caused differences and *gender difference* only to environmentally caused differences (e.g., Macaulay, 1985; Sherman, 1978), issues of causation are far from settled and should be left open for investigation.[2] Such issues cannot be solved or even usefully addressed by merely labeling a behavioral difference as biologically or environmentally caused. Moreover, the fact that my use of the term *sex difference* does not imply biological causation should be very clear on the basis of this book's consistent social psychological perspective about the causation of sex differences.

---

[2]In agreement with this preference to avoid prejudging the causes of sex differences, Sherman (1978) proposed and used the term *sex-related differences*. Although I share Sherman's intent, I prefer to adopt the simpler term *sex difference* and to make clear that the term has no causal implications in this book.

The term *gender* is useful and in this book refers to the meanings that societies and individuals ascribe to female and male categories. Thus, I refer to the social roles a society defines for women and men as *gender roles* and the stereotypes that people hold about women and men as *gender stereotypes.* These concepts are appropriately defined in terms of the meanings ascribed to the sexes.

1 The Analysis of Sex Differences in Social Behavior: A New Theory and A New Method

This book presents a body of new scholarship on sex differences in social behavior. The theoretical orientation that is proposed considers sex differences to be a product of the social roles that regulate behavior in adult life. In the process of examining the empirical implications of this new theoretical perspective, new methods are employed for integrating sex-difference findings from the large research literatures on social behaviors. This combination of theory and method is illustrated by applying it to some classes of social behaviors, and it is shown that the new approach makes sex differences substantially more predictable and amenable to interpretation than they have been in the past.

The study of sex differences has not been an area of rapid progress. Although slow progress may not be atypical in psychology (Meehl, 1978), some specific features of research and theory in this area may have made it difficult to develop an understanding of the conditions under which the behavior of women differs from that of men. First of all, progress might have occurred more quickly had psychologists not relied primarily on theoretical perspectives with only indirect relevance to adult behavior. In particular, approaches based on childhood socialization have provided the most popular interpretations of sex differences (e.g., Chodorow, 1978; Huston, 1983; Jacklin & Maccoby, 1983; Maccoby & Jacklin, 1974). To be sure, sex differences have interesting developmental histories that are worthy of study in their own right. Yet, understanding development does not necessarily enlighten us about the factors that maintain a sex difference among adults. Biological theories have also proven to be popular (see Bleier, 1984; Fausto-Sterling, 1985), but also feature causal variables that for the most part are not directly relevant to sex differences in adult social behaviors.

A second and perhaps equally important barrier to understanding adult sex differences stems from the timing of psychologists' interest in sex differences. It was the mid-1970s when sex-difference findings came under the most intense scrutiny by psychologists. Somewhat ironically, this timing meant that influential diagnoses of the state of the evidence were formulated just a few years before an adequate technology for summarizing and integrating large research literatures became widely available to psychologists.

A third barrier to progress is that most of the research that psychologists have regarded as relevant to sex differences in adult social behaviors has been conducted in a particular type of social context—one in which research subjects interact with strangers, primarily in short-term encounters. This feature of research methods, which has typified social psychological research more generally, has limited and continues to limit the insights that the sex-differences literature can provide. This constraint raises the issue of whether psychological research strips behavior of its context and thereby distorts knowledge about sex differences—a point argued by several feminist critics (e.g., Parlee, 1979; Sherif, 1979).

The work described in this book has overcome to a great extent the first two of these barriers—(a) the focus on causal variables only indirectly relevant to adult behavior and (b) the absence of an adequate technology for integrating research findings. Thus, the theoretical approach that I propose speaks to the indirect relevance issue by employing adult roles as the major predictors of adult sex differences. The methodological advances that I describe speak to the research integration issue by implementing the statistical methods of quantitative reviewing. However, the third barrier, the use of a limited range of social contexts in research, has not been overcome: The research in the core literature on adult sex differences has been carried out almost exclusively in a social context of short-term interactions with strangers. This fact raises questions about the validity of psychologists' generalizations about sex differences. These questions are addressed in detail in the final chapter of this book, after I have described research on a number of types of social behavior.

SOCIAL ROLES AS
DETERMINANTS OF SEX DIFFERENCES

The theory that I present has emerged from my own research on sex differences (e.g., Eagly & Carli, 1981; Eagly & Crowley, 1986; Eagly & Steffen, 1986a) and gender stereotypes (e.g., Eagly & Steffen, 1984; Eagly &

Wood, 1982), as well as from other social psychologists' work on sex differences (e.g., Deaux, 1976; Hall, 1984; Henley, 1977). This approach emphasizes the numerous ways in which the social behaviors that differ between the sexes are embedded in social roles—in gender roles as well as in many other roles pertaining to work and family life. According to this theory, the contemporaneous influences arising from adult social roles are more directly relevant to sex differences in adult social behavior than is prior socialization or biology. Social roles are regarded as the proximal predictors of adult sex differences, although these roles may in turn be linked to other, more distal factors such as childhood socialization pressures and biological predispositions.

In implying that sex differences reflect the differing social positions of women and men more strongly than differing beliefs and values that may be instilled during childhood socialization, the social-role account illustrates the type of explanation of group differences that House (1981) has termed *structural*. House has distinguished between a *structural* approach to explaining group differences in personality and behavior and a *cultural* approach. Structural explanations emphasize that members of social groups experience common situational constraints because they tend to have the same or similar social positions within organizations and other structures such as families. In contrast, cultural explanations, deriving from the familiar socialization interpretation, emphasize that members of social groups acquire common beliefs and values because of the socialization pressures they experience during childhood. Although structural and cultural approaches are not entirely incompatible, theories of group differences tend to emphasize one or the other of these types of explanation, and the cultural approach has dominated the study of sex differences. In contrast, the social-role account of sex differences presented in this book is primarily a structural theory of the behavioral tendencies that distinguish women from men.

Social roles have already received some attention from social scientists as causes of sex differences. Shorthand explanations of sex differences have often focused on "sex roles" or "gender roles," without much specification of the content or functioning of such roles. More interestingly, one aspect of roles—their status within a hierarchical social structure—has been explored in some detail as a possible cause of sex-typed behavior (e.g., Henley, 1977; Lockheed & Hall, 1976; Meeker & Weitzel-O'Neill, 1977; Unger, 1978). In addition, both Henley (1977) and Hall (1984) have noted some of the ways that nonverbal sex differences may be a product of various aspects of females' and males' differing past histories of role occupancy. For example, females' superior ability to decode nonverbal cues (see Chapter 4) could arise in part from their greater likelihood of having occupied nurturing roles, which tend to require nonverbal sensitivity. Building on such ideas about the behavioral consequences of women's lower status vis-a-vis men and other sex differences in role occupancy, this book provides a systematic analysis of social roles as the source of those pressures that have caused women and men to behave differently in the studies that psychologists have carried out.

Psychologists' Definitions of Sex Differences

Before explaining how social roles account for sex differences in social behavior, I must describe the type of comparison that psychologists make when they infer sex differences. Psychologists have typically examined whether female and male behavior differs, given presumed equivalence in all contemporaneous factors other than sex. Although holding other factors constant can be a difficult goal to achieve in some specific research settings (see Parlee, 1981; Wallston & Grady, 1985), it is a typical goal of research design. Investigators attempt to hold other factors constant in order to interpret an observed difference as a sex difference and not as a difference due to some extraneous variable correlated with sex. As a part of this strategy of holding other factors constant, female and male subjects are ordinarily exposed to equivalent stimuli. For example, in an aggression experiment examining sex differences, female and male subjects are exposed to the same eliciting stimuli. Comparisons between women and men are also usually controlled for differences in demographic characteristics such as age and social class. And, most importantly for the present analysis, women and men participate in psychological research as occupants of the same social role. This role equivalence is of crucial importance. Both female and male research participants are assigned the same, rather ambiguous role of "subject." Even though women and men are differently distributed into social roles in natural settings, the research setting is generally as free as possible of specific role constraints that derive from subjects' daily lives.

Research settings are designed to be free of specific natural-setting roles in order to rule out differing roles for women and men as an alternative interpretation for observed sex differences. For example, in a study of sex differences psychologists would seldom compare male engineers and female technicians, male physicians and female nurses, or even husbands and wives. Rather, subjects, who are often college students, are exposed to equivalent stimuli in a laboratory or field setting that is minimally affected by the constraining role obligations of daily life that are associated with occupation and family. Therefore, when psychologists study some form of social interaction, they generally have their research subjects interact with an experimenter, a confederate of the experimenter, another subject, or a computer or other laboratory apparatus that simulates social interaction. As a consequence, most of the social interaction that is monitored in research occurs in the context of short-term encounters with strangers (or simulated strangers).

These methods not only allow psychologists to rule out certain types of explanations for sex differences but also greatly increase experimental control, especially when subjects interact with a confederate or with the standardized responses provided by laboratory apparatus. However defensible these research methods may be, they must be kept in mind in interpreting psychologists' generalizations about sex differences. For example, when Maccoby and Jacklin (1974) wrote that there is no clear evidence that females are more nurturant than males, they meant that they could not find evidence that female and male research subjects, when faced with the same eliciting stimuli, behaved with differing degrees of nurturance. On this basis, they concluded that evidence did not favor a general or underlying tendency for women to be more nurturant than men. The fact that women are much more likely than men to occupy roles that require nurturant behavior and therefore provide more nurturance in natural settings (Robinson, 1977) is irrelevant to Maccoby and Jacklin's assertion about nurturance. Assertions of this type, which violate common sense because they contradict observations of behavior in natural settings, can be understood only in the context of research methods that attempt to hold constant all contemporaneous factors other than sex.

This aspect of research methodology suggests that one implication of the claim that social roles underlie sex differences has not been of much interest to psychologists. This implication is that women and men often behave differently because they are carrying out dissimilar organizational and familial roles. For example, in a business office, men may, on the average, behave differently than women with respect to tendencies such as assertiveness and helpfulness, because men more often have roles such as executive and manager whereas women more often have clerical positions. Yet differences between men and women who occupy different roles have not been regarded by psychologists as relevant to sex differences, although they have been of considerably more interest to sociologists (e.g., Kanter, 1977; Williams, 1985).

An exception to psychologists' lack of interest in comparing women and men as occupants of different roles is found in research on close relationships (Huston & Ashmore, 1986; Peplau, 1983; Peplau & Gordon, 1985). Nevertheless, the diverse sex comparisons reported in this research have not been treated as a basis for generalizations about sex differences in behavioral tendencies such as aggressiveness. This reluctance may stem from uneasiness about determining whether sex differences manifested in close relationships are merely due to the effects of the differing specific roles (e.g., husband and wife) occupied by men and women.

At this point in my analysis, the claim that social roles are the underlying basis of sex differences is offered within psychologists' conventional framework of controlled comparisons between the sexes. Role differences are assumed to be responsible for the differing behavioral tendencies that women and men manifest when confronted by equivalent stimuli in typical research settings. The mechanisms through which roles bring about sex differences in such settings are of considerable interest from a social psychological standpoint. Two types of mechanisms are considered. The first type involves conformity to gender roles. The second type involves the transmission to individuals of (a) skills relevant to social behaviors and (b) beliefs about the consequences of social behaviors. These skills and beliefs, which affect behavior, are indirect manifestations of social roles because they are acquired through prior participation in roles.

Gender Roles as Determinants of Sex Differences

Psychologists have often claimed that people have a social role based solely on their gender. Gender roles are defined as those shared expectations (about appropriate qualities and behaviors) that apply to individuals on the basis of their socially identified gender. Gender roles are germane to explaining the sex differences that occur in typical research settings because these roles cannot be ruled out by investigators' efforts to hold constant all contemporaneous factors other than the fact of being female or male. Merely by avoiding organizations and families as contexts for research, investigators can avoid comparing women and men when they are directly under the influence of their organizational and familial roles. However, researchers cannot rule out comparisons of women and men when they are under the influence of their gender roles, because gender roles do have direct impact on the social interactions that occur in typical research settings. Therefore, conformity to gender roles, but not to other social roles, provides a potential explanation of the sex differences observed in controlled research settings.

Gender roles differ in a number of ways from roles based on obligations to particular others. The greater *scope* or extensiveness (Sarbin & Allen, 1968) of gender roles is one such difference, because one's gender role is potentially applicable to a large portion of one's daily life, including that portion that may occur in research settings. Others to whom one incurs gender-role obligations can be many of the people with whom one interacts rather than just particular others. Gender roles also have greater *generality* (Sarbin & Allen, 1968) in the sense that many expectations about women and men apparently exist at the level of general qualities or characteristics, akin to personality traits, rather than at the level of specific behaviors. In contrast, the main content of role expectations for many positions, such as those in bureaucracies, is a detailed specification of required behaviors as well as penalties for failing to behave in the specified ways.

In their greater scope and generality, gender roles are similar to age-based roles such as *old person* or *teen-ager* as well as roles such as *handicapped person* that are based on physical attributes. For convenience in contrasting gender roles with roles of lesser scope and generality, I refer to roles based on obligations to particular other people as *specific roles.*[1] Of most interest in this analysis are specific roles based on family and occupation.

The most direct empirical support for the idea that people have expectations about female and male characteristics is found in the literature on gender stereotypes, which has documented that people perceive many differences between women and men (e.g., Bem, 1974; Broverman, Vogel, Broverman, Clarkson, & Rosenkrantz, 1972; Rosenkrantz, Vogel, Bee, Broverman, & Broverman, 1968; Ruble, 1983; Spence & Helmreich, 1978). Yet these expectations are more than beliefs about the attributes of women and men: Many of these expectations are normative in the sense that they describe qualities or behavioral tendencies believed to be desirable for each sex. Thus, according to classic definitions in social psychology, social norms are shared expectations about *appropriate* qualities or behaviors (e.g., Newcomb, 1950; Newcomb, Turner, & Converse, 1965; Sherif & Cantril, 1947; Thibaut & Kelley, 1959). The tendency to regard many stereotypic sex differences as appropriate has been established by research showing that these differences are perceived as desirable. For example, Broverman et al. as well as Spence and Helmreich demonstrated that ratings of the ideal woman and man parallel those of the typical woman and man. Such findings show that people tend to think that women and men ought to differ in many of the ways they are perceived to differ.

The idea that normative expectations are *shared,* which is part of the definition of social norm, implies that consensus exists about appropriate characteristics and that people are aware of being consensual. Relatively high consensus about perceived sex differences and the desirability of these differences has been shown repeatedly in stereotype research (e.g.,

---

[1] A term such as *general* or *diffuse* could be applied to roles based on sex, age, and ethnic group or on physical attributes such as attractiveness and various handicaps. However, because gender roles are the only type of such roles considered in this book, such a term is not needed in this analysis.

Broverman et al., 1972).[2] People's awareness of their society's consensus about sex differences was demonstrated in Williams and Best's (1982) stereotype research, which employed the somewhat unusual method of asking respondents to report the characteristics believed to be associated with each sex in their culture.

The findings I have cited from the gender-stereotype literature thus provide evidence that the three critical features of normative expectations are present for expectations about women and men—perceived appropriateness of expected characteristics, consensual nature of expectations, and awareness of consensus. The strong empirical support for the important idea that many aspects of gender stereotypes constitute social norms should be kept in mind. Social norms that apply to people of a particular category or social position constitute a social role. Consequently, the collection of shared expectations held in relation to women constitute the female gender role, and those held in relation to men constitute the male gender role.

A time-honored assumption of social psychologists, embodied in concepts such as *normative influence* (Deutsch & Gerard, 1955) and *self-fulfilling prophecy* (Merton, 1948), is that people often comply with other people's expectations. In general, people are assumed to communicate their expectations to others by a variety of verbal and nonverbal behaviors and to react positively when their expectations are confirmed. Yet decades of research have demonstrated that the processes by which one person's expectations result in another person's expectancy-confirming behavior are diverse and that the link between expectancy and behavior is contingent on various conditions (Darley & Fazio, 1980; Harris & Rosenthal, 1985; Snyder, 1984). Certainly it is not correct to view humans as automatons who passively acquiesce by always behaving consistently with social norms. Individuals differ in the extent to which they conform to norms, and situations differ in the extent to which they elicit conformity. Nevertheless, expectancy-confirming behavior appears to be common (Rosenthal & Rubin, 1978).

---

[2]In the social-cognitive literature on stereotyping (e.g., Ashmore & Del Boca, 1981), consensus about the attributes of a social group qualifies a stereotype to be considered a *social* or *cultural* stereotype. More importantly, in the present analysis this feature and additional features of gender stereotypes qualify them to be considered *normative beliefs* constituting a role. Thus, my argument is that aspects of gender stereotypes should be viewed as gender roles, because these stereotypes have all of the defining features of roles.

The reservations that Ashmore, Del Boca, and Wohlers (1986) expressed about whether gender stereotypes are consensual seem overly cautious given evidence of substantial agreement about these stereotypes between very diverse samples of college students, their parents, and other adults (Broverman et al., 1972), between college and community samples (Deaux, Lewis, & Kite, 1984), and between samples of college students in 30 nations (Williams & Best, 1982). Furthermore, individual respondents within these samples have been shown to agree with one another to a considerable extent (Broverman et al., 1972).

The power of expectancies to determine behaviors has been displayed in research on the *behavioral confirmation of stereotypes* (e.g., Snyder, 1981), including gender stereotypes. This research has provided impressive evidence that, at least under some circumstances, people act to confirm the stereotypic expectations that other people hold about their behavior. Stereotypes about women and men have yielded some of the most striking demonstrations of behavioral confirmation (e.g., Christensen & Rosenthal, 1982; Skrypnek & Snyder, 1982; von Baeyer, Sherk, & Zanna, 1981; Zanna & Pack, 1975).

Expectancy-confirming behavior should be especially common when expectancies are broadly shared in a society, as is the case for expectancies about women and men.[3] Under these conditions, all participants in an interaction are likely to hold roughly the same expectancies, because they are based on observations available to everyone (e.g., observations that in most natural settings men have higher status than women). Participants therefore often hold gender-stereotypic expectancies about their own behavior as well as others' behavior. Such participants should strive to manifest stereotypic qualities in their own behavior, even in the absence of contemporaneous external pressures. As Swann's (1983) research on self-verification processes has shown, people actively collaborate in bringing events into harmony with their conceptions of themselves. Thus, participants in an interaction not only communicate stereotypic expectancies to other participants but also may act to confirm the stereotypic expectancies they hold about themselves.

The Content of Gender Roles

To the extent that gender roles are a cause of sex differences in social behavior, it is crucial to understand their content. Researchers' predictions about sex differences could then be guided by their knowledge of the content of gender roles. Fortunately, considerable insight into this content can be gleaned from gender-stereotype research. Beginning with the work of Rosenkrantz, Broverman, and their collaborators (Broverman et al., 1972; Rosenkrantz et al., 1968) and continuing with the work of many other investigators (e.g., Bem, 1974; Deaux & Lewis, 1983; Ruble, 1983; Spence & Helmreich, 1978), gender-stereotype studies have shown that the majority of the beliefs that people hold about the differences between women

---

[3]Although some social scientists (e.g., Bem & Bem, 1970) argued that gender-role expectancies are such a pervasive and consensual aspect of social life that they are rarely examined critically or regarded as subject to redefinition, it is possible to overestimate extent of agreement about gender roles. The resurgence of the Women's Movement in the 1970s has been associated with considerable questioning of many norms about appropriate female and male behavior.

and men can be summarized in terms of two dimensions, the *communal* and the *agentic,* both of which define positive personal attributes.

The communal dimension of gender-stereotypic beliefs primarily describes a concern with the welfare of other people, and women are believed to manifest this concern more strongly than men. Examination of the attributes that comprise this dimension in various studies (e.g., Bem, 1974; Broverman et al., 1972; Spence & Helmreich, 1978) shows that caring and nurturant qualities predominate (e.g., affectionate, able to devote self completely to others, eager to soothe hurt feelings, helpful, kind, sympathetic, loves children). A few additional traits pertain to interpersonal sensitivity (e.g., aware of feelings of others), emotional expressiveness (e.g., easily expresses tender feelings), and aspects of personal style (e.g., gentle, soft-spoken). Because the most popular terms for describing this dimension (expressiveness, warmth-expressiveness, social-orientation, and femininity) do not adequately convey its main content, I prefer Bakan's (1966) term *communion* and label this dimension *communal.* According to Bakan, communal qualities are manifested by selflessness, concern with others, and a desire to be at one with others.

The agentic dimension of gender-stereotypic beliefs about personal qualities describes primarily an assertive and controlling tendency, and men are believed to manifest this tendency more strongly than women. Examination of the attributes that comprise this dimension in various studies (e.g., Bem, 1974; Broverman et al., 1972; Spence & Helmreich, 1978) shows that the majority of attributes pertain to self-assertion (e.g., aggressive, ambitious, dominant, forceful, acts as a leader) and independence from other people (e.g., independent, self-reliant, self-sufficient, individualistic). Some additional attributes pertain to personal efficacy (e.g., self-confident, feels superior, makes decisions easily) and aspects of personal style (e.g., direct, adventurous, never gives up easily). Because the most popular terms for describing this dimension (instrumentality, competency, task-orientation, and masculinity) do not adequately convey its main content, I prefer Bakan's (1966) term *agency* and label this dimension *agentic.* According to Bakan's definition, agentic qualities are manifested by self-assertion, self-expansion, and the urge to master.[4]

---

[4]Bakan (1966) discussed, not only the positive consequences of communion and agency, but also the negative consequences of a high level of either of these qualities, when not tempered by at least a moderate level of the other, presumably complementary quality. Bakan especially emphasized the dangers of a strong sense of agency, unmitigated by a sense of communion. Exploring the implications of this logic, Spence, Helmreich, and Holahan (1979) constructed scales of the negatively evaluated aspects of both communion (e.g., servile, whiny, fussy) and agency (e.g., arrogant, dictatorial, egotistical). Yet, consistent with the assumption that gender-role norms specify behaviors thought desirable in each sex, my analysis is formulated only in terms of the positively evaluated aspects of communion and agency.

In view of evidence that gender stereotypes encompass information pertaining to matters other than communal and agentic personal attributes (Deaux & Lewis, 1983), the rationale should be stated for the concentration on these personal attributes in this book. This decision to consider only personal attributes derives in part from research showing that such personal qualities or traits are by far the most prevalent form of gender-stereotypic belief (Berninger & DeSoto, 1985; Deaux & Lewis, 1983). Moreover, it is these communal and agentic aspects of beliefs about the sexes that have been shown to manifest the three critical features of normative expectations (see prior section). In addition, the focus of the present analysis on social behavior dictates the importance of these personal attributes. Social behavior can be predicted from the content of stereotypic beliefs about personal attributes because these attributes are themselves abstractions about social behavior (Canter & Meyerowitz, 1984). For example, because *aggressive* is an abstraction about social behavior, knowledge that aggressiveness is ascribed to men more than women and thought more desirable in men suggests that men behave more aggressively than women when gender roles are salient.

The Moderate Quality of Gender Stereotypes.   These gender stereotypes about communion and agency do not represent women and men as widely separated categories. People do not believe, for example, that all women are very gentle and all men very rough or that all men are very dominant and all women very submissive. Instead, consistent with behavioral data on actual sex differences (see Chapter 5), people's beliefs appear to represent the sexes as somewhat heterogeneous, partially overlapping groups, possessing different average levels of various attributes.

This qualified nature of gender stereotypes has been demonstrated by two methods. By the first of these methods (e.g., Broverman et al., 1972; Deaux & Lewis, 1983; Eagly & Steffen, 1984), respondents rate a prototypical member of each sex (e.g., "average woman") on rating scales that represent each attribute as a continuous scale. This scale is (a) anchored on one end by a high level of a trait (e.g., very dominant) and on the other end by a high level of the opposite trait (e.g., very submissive) or (b) anchored on one end by a high likelihood of possessing a trait such as dominance (e.g., extremely likely) and on the other end by a low likelihood of possessing the same trait (e.g., extremely unlikely). Research implementing this method has consistently shown that, whereas differing amounts (or likelihoods) of stereotypic attributes are ascribed to each sex, neither sex is rated extremely. By the second of these methods (e.g., Eagly & Kite, in press; Jackman & Senter, 1980), respondents estimate the percentage of each sex (e.g., women) possessing each attribute (e.g., dominance). Research implementing this method has consistently shown that, whereas differing percentages of women and men are thought to possess stereotypic attributes, extremely high or extremely low percentages are not estimated for either sex. Thus, both of these methods have shown that the sexes are believed to be different but not extremely different.

Despite evidence suggesting that gender stereotypes have a somewhat moderate quality, this point might easily be overemphasized in view of Jackman and Senter's (1980) research suggesting that the sexes are perceived more categorically than other social groups. This research examined the extent to which groups based on sex, race, and social class are perceived categorically rather than in the qualified way inherent in the notion of overlapping distributions. The sexes were rated more categorically than racial groups or social class groups, with the exception of the upper class, which is a relatively small, elite group. Yet, because Jackman and Senter examined perceptions on relatively few personal attributes, the hypothesis that stereotypes of the sexes are more categorical than stereotypes of other social groups deserves more detailed exploration.

The Internalization of Gender Roles.   The idea that people may apply stereotypic expectations to themselves suggests that people's own attitudes and values have the stamp of societal gender roles on them. In terms of available research, this hypothesis that people internalize gender roles can be examined at the level of social attitudes and at the level of the self concept. Demonstrating the internalization of stereotypic qualities in social attitudes, public-opinion research has shown that (a) women are somewhat more favorable than men on a variety of so-called compassion issues, which pertain to jobs, income redistribution, and other economic policies to help poor and disadvantaged groups, and (b) men are substantially more favorable than women on a variety of issues involving the use of force and violence (Shapiro & Mahajan, 1986). This partition between compassion issues and force and violence issues can be seen to reflect the partition between communal and agentic personal attributes.

Demonstrating the internalization of stereotypic qualities in the self-concept, research has shown that (a) self-reported traits and behaviors differ for women and men, and (b) the direction of these differences is toward greater communion in women and greater agency in men (Bem, 1974; Broverman et al., 1972; Canter & Meyerowitz, 1984; Feather & Said, 1983; Spence & Helmreich, 1978; also see Hall's, 1984, review of self-reported personality traits). In addition, much of this research has shown individual differences within each sex in the extent to which people describe themselves gender-stereotypically. However, these individual differences are only of tangential relevance to the task of integrating research on sex differences, because sex-difference findings are group comparisons—

aggregate female versus male comparisons that do not take these individual differences into account.[5]

The fact that some people do not internalize societal gender roles and others internalize them only to a limited extent does not, in and of itself, provide a basis for predicting that behavioral sex differences are typically minimal. It should be kept in mind that group averages representing the social attitudes and self concepts of women and men do differ along gender-stereotypic lines. Moreover, internalization of gender-role expectations is not a necessary prerequisite for stereotypic behavior because such behavior is rooted only to some degree in people's own attitudes and self-concepts. People often conform to gender-role norms that are *not* internalized, because of the considerable power that groups and individuals supportive of these norms have to influence others' behavior through rewards and punishments of both subtle (e.g., nonverbal cues) and more obvious (e.g., monetary incentives, sexually harassing behavior) varieties. Indeed, the extent to which gender-stereotypic behavior arises from a desire to behave consistently with one's attitudes and self-concept or from an effort to manage an impression of oneself to obtain relatively short-term gains is an issue of considerable interest from the standpoint of theories of social influence (Kelman, 1961; Schlenker, 1982) and social roles (Sarbin & Allen, 1968; Stryker & Serpe, 1982).

The Social-Structural Origin of Beliefs about Communion and Agency

A major assumption of the social-role interpretation of sex differences is that the perception of women as especially communal and men as especially agentic stems from the differing specific roles that women and men occupy in the family and society. The distinctive communal content of the female stereotype is assumed to derive primarily from the domestic role. The distinctive agentic content of the male stereotype is assumed to derive from men's typical roles in the society and economy.[6]

One type of support for this viewpoint is a functional argument that stems from Parsons and Bales's (1955) theory of role differentiation in the family. Parsons and Bales argued that within the family a differentiation of function is observed in which women adopt a primarily "expressive" role

---

[5]The focus of this book on group differences between women and men is in no sense meant to deny the existence of individual differences within each sex. Group means aggregate over individuals, who vary among themselves. Yet the analytic problem in research on sex differences is inherently one of group differences.

[6]A seminal precursor of this role distributional argument is Kiesler's (1975) discussion of why people expect greater success from men than from women.

and men a primarily "instrumental" role. As other scholars have pointed out (e.g., Aronoff & Crano, 1975; Crano & Aronoff, 1978; Laws, 1979; Leik, 1963; Sherman, 1971; Slater, 1961), the Parsons and Bales analysis is problematic in several ways. Some of the deficiencies of this analysis stem from Parsons and Bales's use of the expressive versus instrumental terminology, which, as already noted, fails to convey the main content of people's expectancies about female and male characteristics. In addition, the terminology greatly oversimplifies the content of female and male roles, even as these are defined in traditional families. Also problematic is their treatment of the division of labor between homemakers and breadwinners as a fairly strict separation between the private and public spheres of life—that is, between the internal affairs of the family and the activities that link the family to the external social system. This dichotomous description is not entirely in accord with empirical studies of people's everyday activities (e.g., Robinson, 1977; Walker & Woods, 1976). Had Parsons and Bales described the traditional division of labor in a way that accurately takes into account the wide-ranging obligations of homemakers and breadwinners, their analysis might have fared better over the years.

Despite the multiple problems of the Parsons and Bales (1955) version of the functionalist theory, one of the basic ideas of this analysis—that there is a link between the division of responsibility in the family and the general expectations held for women and men—deserves an open-minded hearing. This basic idea has been newly presented by Williams and Best (1982) in a form that takes account of the contemporary research literature on gender stereotypes.[7] Williams and Best maintained that the communal qualities valued in women are important for good performance of domestic activities, especially childrearing, and that the agentic qualities valued in men are important for good performance of behaviors enacted in the specific roles more often occupied by men than by women. The centrality of childrearing in those activities that foster communal qualities has also been argued by other social scientists (e.g., Chodorow, 1978). The activities that foster agentic qualities might be described broadly as those connected with paid employment. However, certain occupational activities that are highly male-dominated may be especially important in determining the qualities that are valued in men. Such activities might include competing for rank within various political hierarchies and fighting in wars. M. Harris's (1974, 1977) functional analysis of gender-role expectations has implicated the assign-

---

[7]This streamlined functional analysis drops some of the more problematic features of the Parsons and Bales (1955) analysis—for example, the ideas that (a) role differentiation along instrumental versus expressive lines is necessary for group effectiveness and adequate group morale and (b) specialization along either instrumental or expressive lines is easier for individuals than blending the two modes.

ment of military roles to men as the cause of societies' placement of a high value on aggressiveness and other agentic qualities in men. Indeed, Parsons and Bales's (1955) emphasis on homemaker and breadwinner roles in the family was somewhat narrow because it gave little consideration to the particular types of paid occupations that are disproportionately carried out by men or women outside the home. In societies with high levels of female labor-force participation, more attention should be given to the types of jobs held primarily by employees of one sex (see Eagly & Steffen, 1986b; Yount, 1986).

The link between the specific social roles typically occupied by each sex and gender stereotypes has also been explored by Yount (1986). She argued that gender stereotypes emerge from attributes generated by the productive activity of women and men. In this theory, productive activity includes the work of homemakers as well as employees because such activity encompasses all means by which people obtain their material subsistence. Because gender-stereotypic attributes reflect the social and physical conditions of the productive activity of the sexes, Yount regarded these stereotypes as instances of *work-emergent traits.* The conditions of production differ for women and men in a largely sex-segregated work force, and therefore the traits ascribed to women and men differ. When work-emergent traits are internalized and become components of workers' self-concepts, these traits help them to perform work tasks and to cope with the stresses they face in their work roles. Thus, according to Yount, gender stereotypes facilitate the productive activity typically carried out by workers of each sex.

Williams and Best (1982) emphasized that a division of labor assigning a disproportionate share of domestic activities to women and of other activities to men is found in all world societies (see Munroe & Munroe, 1980) and viewed this sexual division of labor as the cause of the stereotypes of women as communal and men as agentic. As they demonstrated, these stereotypes are held by citizens of a wide sample of modern nations. As I have argued, these stereotypes in fact constitute gender roles—prescriptions for appropriate male and female qualities. From a functional standpoint, gender roles derive from the division of labor, and, in turn, help prepare children and teenagers for the specific roles they are most likely to occupy as adults. Thus, when young people learn and then conform to gender-role expectancies that females be communal and males agentic, they manifest behaviors that are presumed to help them become successful occupants of the roles that are typical among adult members of their sex. As a consequence, gender roles tend to maintain the existing division of labor between the sexes. Quite clearly, the impact of gender roles is conservative.

The gender roles and stereotypes held in a society at any one point in time are rooted, not primarily in the society's cultural tradition, but more importantly in the society's contemporaneous division of labor between the sexes. Women are viewed as suited for the specific social roles that women typically occupy, and men are viewed as suited for the specific social roles that men typically occupy. This assumed linkage between gender stereotypes and the division of labor, which perhaps seems self-evident to the functionally inclined social scientist, was put to empirical test in research that Valerie Steffen and I carried out (Eagly & Steffen, 1984). The particular version of the functionalist idea tested in this research is that contemporary gender stereotypes about communion and agency stem from the current-day distribution of women and men into domestic and employee roles. In this research, subjects indicated the extent to which people described in various ways would have a variety of communal and agentic attributes. Subjects judged the attributes of women and men whose occupations were not indicated and of women and men whose occupational role was described as either homemaker or full-time employee. As expected, occupational role proved to be a strong determinant of judgments of communal and agentic attributes: People in the domestic role were regarded as more communal and less agentic than people in the employee role.[8]

If gender stereotypes are based on observations of women and men carrying out their occupational roles, the important observations for perceivers in the United States and many other industrialized countries are that mainly women are in the domestic role and somewhat more men than women in the employee role. Perceivers should therefore think about women's and men's characteristics as if women and men had different occupations. More specifically, because about half of all women are employed outside of the home in the United States (U. S. Department of Labor, 1980), American perceivers should regard women's personal attributes as between those of homemakers and employees. Because most men are employed outside the home, these perceivers should regard men's personal attributes as similar to those of employees.

In support of these predictions, our research found that average women and men whose occupations were not mentioned were perceived stereotypically: Women were seen as high in communion and low in agency compared with men. In addition, homemakers of both sexes were viewed as even higher in communion and lower in agency than average women; full-time employees, regardless of their sex, were perceived like stereotypic men (low in communion and high in agency). These and related findings suggested that the characteristics perceived to typify the domestic and paid

---

[8]This research operationalized the division of labor in terms of occupancy of domestic or full-time employment roles. Future research might explore the division of labor as a continuous variable: Hours of labor devoted to each role per week might be an appropriate index of relative obligation to each role. Whether an employment role is believed to require agentic or communal qualities could also be investigated: Some jobs are believed to require a high level of agency (e.g., business executive) and others to require a high level of communion (e.g., preschool teacher).

employment roles underlie contemporary gender stereotypes and roles (see Eagly & Steffen, 1984). In the language of social roles, people believe that women, more than men, ought to manifest the communal qualities that they think typify homemakers and that men, more than women, ought to manifest the agentic qualities that they think typify paid employees.[9]

Gender Roles and Social Status.   Another pervasive difference in women's and men's lives, in addition to the greater investment of women in the domestic role, is that the specific roles occupied by men tend to be higher in hierarchies of status and authority than the roles occupied by women. The domestic role itself has lower status than the role of breadwinner. Therefore, in the family, husbands generally have an overall power advantage for both routine decision making and conflict resolution, even though there are some areas of decision making in which wives have primary authority (Blood & Wolfe, 1960; Gillespie, 1971; Scanzoni, 1972, 1979). In employment settings, women and men are not equal on the average. Women are likely to be employed in positions that have relatively low status and that have little power and limited opportunity for advancement. As a group, male employees are more advantaged, with many men having jobs of relatively high status that confer power and offer possibilities for advancement and rising income. As far as supervisory and administrative roles in organizations are concerned, there is abundant evidence that women become progressively scarcer at higher levels (L. K. Brown, 1979; Kanter, 1977; Mennerick, 1975). Also, in task-oriented groups that are not part of large organizations, men generally have higher status than women (Meeker & Weitzel-O'Neill, 1977) and are more likely to be regarded as leaders (Lockheed, 1985) and to acquire leadership positions (Bartol & Martin, 1986).

A status and power difference as pervasive as the one that separates women from men is bound to have implications for gender stereotypes and roles. Although individuals' status within organizations does not appear to affect the perception of their communal qualities, higher-status people are perceived as considerably more agentic than lower-status people (Eagly & Steffen, 1984). Consistent with this greater agency, Eagly and Wood (1982) showed that high-status people in organizations are believed to exert influence more successfully and to be influenced less readily than lower-status people. Eagly and Wood also documented gender-stereotypic beliefs that men are influential and women easily influenced and obtained findings

---

[9]Eagly and Steffen's (1984) experiments on gender stereotypes merely elicited respondents' general concepts of women and men and of women and men identified by various specific roles. This research did not address the important issue of the conditions under which people apply their stereotypes to individual women and men in natural settings.

consistent with the functionalist claim that these beliefs stem from perceivers' observations of women's chronically lower status in natural settings. Therefore, not surprisingly, the status difference between the sexes may have particularly clear implications for the perception of the relative power and influence of women and men.

The idea that men's higher status leads people to expect men to be authoritative and dominant and women to be submissive and compliant is compatible with the perspective of sociologists working within the *theory of expectation states* (Berger, Rosenholtz, & Zelditch, 1980). According to this theory, sex functions as a status cue or *diffuse status characteristic* (e.g., Lockheed & Hall, 1976; Meeker & Weitzel-O'Neill, 1977). People utilize sex as a status cue because of their extensive prior experience in natural settings where they observed that sex was correlated with power and prestige. According to the theory of expectation states, people infer others' general competence and value from their sex because of its function as a status characteristic. However, as Eagly and Steffen (1984) have shown, status appears to lead to a somewhat narrower set of inferences than Berger and his colleagues have claimed—namely, to inferences about agentic qualities, which include dominance and submissiveness (Eagly & Wood, 1982).

Gender Roles and Physical Characteristics.   Whether communal and agentic qualities are to some extent inferred directly from perceived physical attributes of women and men, as suggested by ecological theory (McArthur & Baron, 1983), requires further evaluation. Deaux and Lewis (1984) found that physical characteristics, described in masculine (tall, strong, sturdy, broad-shouldered) versus feminine (soft voice, dainty, graceful, soft) terms, had considerable impact on the perception of communal and agentic personal qualities. Yet, with the possible exception of *soft,* these particular feminine qualities are not physical characteristics inherent in the female body. Thus, women are not inherently more graceful than men, although men have inherently greater height and upper-body strength. From a role perspective, qualities such as gracefulness come to covary with sex because they are expected to be manifested in many of the social roles that women disproportionately occupy. Such qualities thereby become markers of one's social position.

Another consideration in evaluating inferences from physical attributes is that words often are ambiguous in their reference to physical or psychological qualities. Thus, Deaux and Lewis's (1984) subjects are unlikely to have encoded the word *soft* only as soft flesh, or, for that matter, encoded the word *strong* only as muscular strength. For these reasons, research on inferences from physical characteristics to psychological attributes might well be pursued by varying drawings, photographs, or videotaped presentations of the human body (e.g., Beck, Ward-Hull, & McLear, 1976; McArthur, 1981).

From a role perspective, even physical qualities such as muscular strength that inherently differ between the sexes derive their implications for psychological attributes from the social roles to which men and women are assigned. These characteristics covary with role occupancy and may be underlying causes of role assignment, especially in pre-industrial societies (e.g., the assignment of men to military roles). Perhaps an example not involving a sex difference will clarify the way in which role occupancy can impart meaning to physical attributes. Among young men, muscular body type covaries with occupancy of athletic roles. On the basis of this observed covariation, perception of this physical characteristic in a young man may lead people to infer athletic competence, as well as traits such as persistence and sportsmanship and attitudinal qualities such as liking for sports.

Complexities in Gender Roles and Related Behaviors

Particularistic Content of Gender Roles.   The beliefs that women should be communal and men agentic provide an extremely general and abstract description of gender roles. At a more concrete level, these roles also include more detailed beliefs regulating particular classes of behaviors. This additional content of gender roles may be stored in several types of knowledge structures:

1. As psychologists (Ashmore, 1981; Ashmore, Del Boca, & Titus, 1984; Deaux, Winton, Crowley, & Lewis, 1985) and cognitive anthropologists (Holland & Davidson, 1984; Holland & Skinner, in press) have demonstrated, gender-role expectations may be stored in knowledge structures that might be termed gender subtypes or subcategories. These subtypes (e.g., hustler, nerd, Don Juan, slut, prude, dog) apparently often provide people with pejorative labels for categorizing individuals who deviate from norms defining appropriate male or female behavior.

2. Detailed expectations about how men and women should behave may sometimes be stored as concrete and specific sequences of behaviors. Knowledge structures of this type have been called *scripts* in the social cognition literature (Schank & Abelson, 1977).

3. People's expectancies about specific behaviors of women and men take features of situations systematically into account and thus may be

stored as rules about how women and men should behave in various types of situations.[10]

Consider, for example, how these three types of particularistic beliefs might be manifested for one agentic quality—aggressiveness. In addition to the belief that men are and ought to be more aggressive than women, people no doubt hold additional beliefs about male and female aggressiveness, and these beliefs function as more detailed social norms. For male behavior, these beliefs might include (a) gender subtypes labeling men who are overly or insufficiently aggressive (e.g., macho, bully, sissy, yellow-belly), (b) behavioral scripts detailing sequences of aggressive actions thought appropriate for men, and (c) rules such as chivalric rules specifying the conditions under which men should and should not aggress in particular ways. Because of the complexity and potential importance of such particularistic beliefs, investigators should examine them in detail when exploring the effect of gender roles on a specific class of behaviors. There is currently little understanding of how these diverse types of beliefs relate to one another or to the more general and abstract aspects of gender stereotypes that are described by agency and communion. Yet the rapid growth of social-cognitive research on various types of cognitive structures (see Kihlstrom & Cantor, 1984; Markus & Zajonc, 1985) offers promise for future investigators of these more complex aspects of gender roles and stereotypes (see Ashmore, Del Boca, & Wohlers, 1986; Deaux & Kite, in press).

It is likely that many of these detailed beliefs about appropriate male and female conduct are culturally transmitted, for example, through literature, legend, and film, rather than merely derived more directly from observations of the contemporaneous division of labor between women and men. Cultural productions provide a wealth of information available to form complex knowledge structures about qualities and behaviors thought appropriate in diverse historical periods and societies. Given, as I have argued, that people's own observations of their own society underlie their overall tendency to view women as communal and men as agentic, those particularistic beliefs that continue to receive widespread adherence in a culture may have to be consistent with the prevailing views of the communion and agency of the sexes. Many beliefs implicit in cultural productions come to be regarded as anachronistic or even as negative models because, I suggest, they are inconsistent with beliefs about communion and agency deriving from the current distribution of women and men into social roles. For example, female gender subtypes that were once positively evaluated,

---

[10]Findings given in Chapters 2 and 3 on respondents' estimates of the likelihoods of female and male behaviors show that respondents' beliefs do take situational contingencies into account.

such as "Southern belle" and "beauty queen," seem to be now regarded more ambivalently, especially by women, as women's roles have changed.

Variability in Behavior Related to Gender Roles. To the extent that gender roles are important causes of sex differences in social behavior, women and men should differ in a wide range of social behaviors, in social contexts in which gender roles are salient. For example, consistent with research showing that women are expected to be more communal than men, women would be more empathic and expressive than men, as well as more nurturant and caring. Consistent with research showing that men are expected to be more agentic than women, men would be more aggressive, assertive, and dominant, and less easily influenced than women. Thus, analysis of the content of gender roles and consideration of the demonstrated tendency of these roles to be confirmed in behavior suggest that social behavior tends to be stereotypic in settings in which gender roles are salient.

Although analysis of gender roles suggests that behavior tends to be stereotypic on the average, this perspective does not imply that sex differences would be of uniform magnitude. On the contrary, the analysis is compatible with a contextualist (Georgoudi & Rosnow, 1985; McGuire, 1983; Rosnow, 1983) perspective by which sex differences are affected by many aspects of the social context in which they occur. Many of these Sex × Situation interactions should prove to be understandable in terms of social psychological variables. For example, because conformity to role expectations occurs mainly when such expectations are salient, stereotypic sex differences should appear under social conditions that increase the salience of gender-role expectations. Although these social conditions are not yet thoroughly understood, they likely include the presence of other people since other people are usually thought to reward behavior in accordance with prevailing social norms.[11] The absence of counterstereotypic expectations based on other social roles is also very important for obtaining stereotypic sex differences, because in natural settings, other social roles are often far more salient and provide more explicit guides to behavior than expectations based on gender. For example, in employment settings, the role expectations associated with one's job are very important determinants of one's behavior.

---

[11]A number of complexities are evident in predicting the effects of an audience of other people on the tendency to behave stereotypically. For example, audiences would have greater power to reward individuals who are motivated to please them. Also, some audiences may be thought to reward behavior deviant from societal gender roles and would therefore decrease the tendency for behavior to be gender-stereotypic.

Skills and Beliefs Acquired in Social Roles as Determinants of Sex Differences

Prior enactment of specific roles can be an indirect cause of sex differences through the skills and beliefs that people have thereby acquired, provided that these roles have been disproportionately occupied by people of one sex. With respect to the skills learned in social roles, it is no doubt true that all roles require that incumbents learn a set of competencies in carrying out certain sequences of behavior for certain audiences (Athay & Darley, 1982). More narrowly relevant to the present analysis is the explicit skill learning required by many roles. This learning is sometimes quite elaborate. In addition, enacting a social role may affect a variety of attitudes and beliefs, because role incumbents gain information when they view events from the perspective of the role.

Skills as well as attitudes and beliefs are often transported from one setting to another. Women and men bring with them to research settings the skills, attitudes, and beliefs that they have acquired in natural settings. As a consequence, female and male behavior is likely to differ in research settings, even though women and men are treated equivalently and are assigned the same specific role (i.e., of research subject, questionnaire respondent, etc.). Indeed, role theorists such as Brim (1960) have argued that attitudes, beliefs, and behaviors learned in one role are often transferred to settings unrelated to the role. For example, aspects of an individual's employment role are sometimes transferred to family settings. Brim (1960, pp. 139–140) illustrated this phenomenon by referring to a business executive who "... begins to treat his wife as if she were his secretary and needs to be reminded of the fact that he is no longer at the office." Such spillover is especially likely in psychologists' traditional research settings, because these settings are usually not highly structured in terms of specific roles that would provide clear-cut guides for conduct. Consequently, research subjects may tend to "fall back on" the skills and beliefs they have gained in other social roles, as well as on gender roles.[12]

Skills and beliefs relevant to social behaviors are sometimes acquired,

---

[12]However, research settings may be structured in some respects. Thus, situational variables are often manipulated in experiments, and the cues that comprise these manipulations sometimes create strong demands to behave in particular ways (see Snyder & Ickes's, 1985, discussion of experiments as strong situations). Situational cues that constrain behavior would decrease individual differences, including sex differences. Yet, despite this characterization of research settings as sometimes highly structured, I suggest that these constraints are seldom as strong or as all-encompassing as the role expectations that are common in organizations and families.

via an anticipatory socialization process (Merton & Kitt, 1950), in special training roles in which pupils learn the skills and beliefs necessary for good performance in roles that will be occupied at a later point. For example, a lawyer attends law school, a new employee may temporarily be a trainee, and a teenager may baby-sit for young children. By such experiences, many skills and beliefs that facilitate good performance in adult roles are acquired prior to occupying these roles. Disproportionate distribution of the sexes into training roles brings about sex-typed skills and beliefs. For example, if baby-sitting jobs are held mainly by girls, women (compared with men) enter adulthood with a higher level of skill for nurturing young children as well as with different beliefs about child-care activities.

Sex Differences in Skills.   Although gender roles as well as specific roles may affect skills, the skill learning that occurs in gender roles is probably somewhat diffuse. Therefore, this analysis concentrates on skills that are acquired primarily by persons of one sex because they are more likely to have occupied specific social roles in which such skills were trained or required for role performance. For example, for these reasons of prior role occupancy, the skills involved in using firearms are more common among men, and the skills involved in carrying out clerical tasks are more common among women. As a consequence, if a research setting confronts subjects with firearms (e.g., Berkowitz & LePage, 1967) or clerical chores (e.g., Pandey & Griffitt, 1977), female and male subjects are likely to react differently.

Even the overall division of labor between women and men—the tendency for more men than women to be paid employees and for more women than men to be homemakers—may bring about sex differences in skills (Williams, 1985). Paid occupations, although somewhat variable in their demands, generally require systematic decision making, a certain emotional detachment from co-workers, and a focus on accomplishing defined tasks. Emphasis is placed on achievement through meeting organizationally relevant goals, commonly in competition with other employees. Rewards are ordinarily contingent on one's ability to meet these goals.

In contrast, the domestic role requires quite a different set of skills. Competent homemakers must progress toward multiple goals, often without much guidance concerning the specific tasks or procedures that facilitate progress toward these goals. Also largely absent are clear feedback and specific rewards related to the quality of one's role performance. In addition, homemakers work cooperatively with other family members, often subordinating their own personal goals to those of family members. They excel if they develop empathy and the ability to understand and anticipate the needs and problems of other family members. A certain degree of emotional expressiveness is also helpful in meeting others' personal and emotional needs. Such skills may be acquired nurturing roles such as preschool teacher as well as in the homemaker role.

Sex Differences in Beliefs about Consequences of Behaviors. Enacting a role brings about attitudinal learning as well as skill learning. In fact, the impact of role enactment on attitudes and beliefs has been documented empirically in a diverse array of research programs (e.g., Bandura, Blanchard, & Ritter, 1969; Festinger & Carlsmith, 1959; Janis & King, 1954; Janis & Mann, 1965; Lieberman, 1956). In particular, roles, including gender roles, may impart attitudes and beliefs that are relevant to behavior because they concern the consequences of behavior. For example, such beliefs would pertain to consequences that ensue if one aggresses against another person or helps another person. The centrality in my analysis of beliefs about the consequences of behavior follows from theory and research concerning the relation between attitudes and behavior. Thus, expectancy-value theorists (e.g., Feather, 1982; Fishbein, 1980; Fishbein & Ajzen, 1975) have often demonstrated that attitude toward a behavior is a major determinant of engaging in the behavior and is itself a function of the perceived consequences of the behavior.[13]

Because women and men are differently distributed into roles, they may acquire different beliefs about the consequences of important classes of social behaviors. For example, when people occupy military roles, they may acquire beliefs about the consequences of aggressive behaviors that tend to legitimize aggression (see Chapter 3). A sex difference in beliefs about aggression ensues because men more commonly have experience in military roles. Sex differences in beliefs about the consequences of a class of behaviors such as aggressive behaviors may then result in sex differences in behavior in research settings.

Social Roles and Sex Differences in Social Behavior

In summary, the social-role theory of sex differences implicates roles in

---

[13]The relation of attitudes and beliefs to behaviors has been explored in depth by social psychologists (e.g., Ajzen, 1985; Ajzen & Fishbein, 1977; Fazio, 1986), and much remains to be written concerning how these analyses pertain to sex differences in behavior. As a preliminary step, my emphasis on the perceived consequences of behavior builds on key aspects of these analyses. In addition, this emphasis is easily coordinated with certain psychological analyses of the presumed causes of sex differences. As illustrated in detail in Chapter 3, psychologists have sometimes argued that sex differences in classes of behaviors (e.g., aggression) are a product of the perceived consequences of these behaviors (e.g., the guilt and anxiety that are expected to follow from aggressing).

several ways. Gender roles directly induce stereotypic sex differences because these roles tend to be behaviorally confirmed. The distribution of the sexes into specific social roles indirectly supports stereotypic sex differences because this distribution is an important source of people's expectations about female and male characteristics.[14] Research has suggested that distribution into domestic and paid employment roles underlies expectations about communion and agency and that distribution into high and low status roles underlies expectations about dominance and submissiveness (Eagly & Steffen, 1984; Eagly & Wood, 1982). Another reason that the distribution of the sexes into specific social roles is indirectly relevant to sex differences in behavior is that experience in such roles imparts skills and beliefs that are relevant to social behaviors in a variety of settings, including research settings. To the extent that women and men are not proportionately represented in specific social roles, they acquire different skills and beliefs, which, in turn, may affect social behavior. Thus, the social-role theory of sex differences promotes a view of social life as fundamentally gendered, given current social arrangements. Women and men are subjected to somewhat different expectations, to which they conform to some degree, and they develop somewhat different skills as well as attitudes and beliefs. As a result, women tend to carry out social interaction somewhat differently than men do. These differences should be manifested in research data comparing women and men.

Figure 1 summarizes this account of sex-typed social behavior. The underlying cause of such behavior is the division of labor between the sexes. Although the division of labor is itself a product of a variety of other factors, the task undertaken in this book is analyzing the *consequences* of the division of labor, not its origins.[15] Whatever the ultimate causes of the division of labor, it shapes gender roles in such a way that women are expected to behave relatively communally and men relatively agentically.

---

[14]Although this analysis is stated at the molar level of the effects of the distribution of the sexes into social roles, it is largely compatible with Perry and Bussey's (1979) molecular, social-learning analysis of sex differences. Perry and Bussey maintained that children learn the behaviors thought to be appropriate for their sex by observing differences in the frequency with which male and female models as *groups* perform responses in given situations. Whereas the Perry and Bussey analysis emphasized the learning of specific responses, my analysis presumes that observations of the behavior of men and women affect people's ideas about appropriate male and female behavior (i.e., gender roles), and that these gender roles, along with other factors, are responsible for sex differences in behavior.

[15]Determining the causes of the division of labor is a task more appropriate for the analytical skills of a sociologist or anthropologist than those of a social psychologist. Yet, to share my speculations on this matter, I suggest that the requirements of the economy and social structure interact with the biological attributes of women and men and with the political ideologies of societies to produce differential role occupancy.

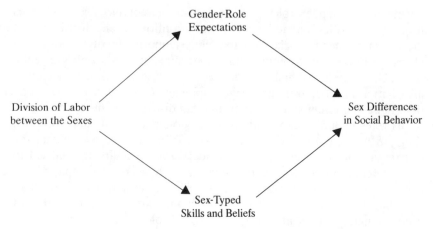

FIG. 1.1. Social-role theory of sex differences in social behavior.

By a variety of processes, these expectancies are often translated into stereotypic behavior. Furthermore, people's own occupancy of the occupational and family roles that comprise their own sex's component of this division of labor results in relatively sex-typed skills and beliefs, which themselves contribute to gender-stereotypic behavior.

The fundamental assumption of this theory of sex differences is that men's and women's differing specific roles in natural settings are the well-springs of sex-typed social behavior. Via the mediation of gender roles as well as sex-typed skills and beliefs, stereotypic social behavior results from these differing roles, especially women's greater commitment to the domestic role and lesser commitment to the employment role as well as women's lesser access to high-status roles. Only when these social arrangements change is there likely to be substantial change in the content of gender roles and in the sex-typing of skills and beliefs, and therefore in the extent to which sex differences occur in social behavior. The major shift of women into the paid work force in the United States in recent decades is a critical redistribution from this viewpoint. At first glance, it may appear that this redistribution should very seriously challenge existing gender roles and substantially reduce the magnitude of sex differences in skills and beliefs.

Despite the increase in the proportion of women in the paid work force, the overall tendency to perceive women as communal and men as agentic has remained intact (e.g., Deaux & Lewis, 1983; Eagly & Steffen, 1984). In fact, studies conducted in the late 1970s by re-administering items from stereotype questionnaires first administered in the 1950s and 1960s have found relatively little change in the content of the male and female stereotypes (Ruble, 1983; Werner & LaRussa, 1985).[16] According to the social-role account of stereotype content, gender stereotypes are understandably intact because the rates of paid labor-force participation of women (55%) and men (76%) still differ substantially (Bergman, 1986). Also, women, even if employed, spend more time in domestic-role activities than do men (e.g., Berk, 1985; Hartmann, 1981; Pleck, 1985). Consistent with the substantial amount of time that employed women devote to domestic activities, part-time work is much more common among employed women (30%) than employed men (12%, U.S. Department of Labor, 1984). Furthermore, within organizations, employed women tend to have lower-status jobs than employed men do. As explained earlier, these status differences also contribute to gender stereotypes. Finally, as suggested by the relatively small amount of research available on the ascription of gender-stereotypic qualities to particular paid occupations (Friedland, Crockett, & Laird, 1973; Hesselbart, 1977; Lifschitz, 1983; Shinar, 1978), women are disproportionately represented in paid occupations and specialities within these occupations that are perceived to require communal qualities and men in occupations and specialities that are perceived to require agentic qualities. In general, many aspects of the division of labor remain and must be taken into account, lest effects of the shift of women into the paid work force be overestimated.

The prediction that social behavior is sex-typed along gender-stereotypic lines by means of the mechanisms I have described can be made with confidence only in relation to settings in which specific social roles (e.g., occupational roles) are relatively unimportant. As already indicated, research settings favored by social psychologists typically fit this description. In natural settings some newly formed groups that lack a pre-established hierarchy (e.g., voluntary committees) may fit this description as well. In most other contexts, particularly in organizations and families, specific

---

[16]Self-concepts also have shown little change in their stereotypic aspects: Women continue to assign more communal qualities to themselves than men do, and men continue to assign more agentic qualities to themselves than women do. The size of these self-concept sex differences has apparently not changed, at least from the mid-1970s until the present (J. Spence, personal communication, April 22, 1986), although Heilbrun and Bailey (1986) reported a small decrease in differential endorsement of sex-typed traits when they compared three time periods (1958–64; 1970–74; 1977–82). Nevertheless, in the 1960s and 1970s, a marked attitudinal shift occurred in both men and women toward greater endorsement of equal opportunity for women in the workplace, equal access to political power, role-sharing in the home, and other forms of equality between the sexes (Ferree, 1974; Gurin, 1985; Helmreich, Spence, & Gibson, 1982; Kluegel & Smith, 1986; Mason, Czajka, & Arber, 1976; Thornton & Freedman, 1979). The disparity between this change in attitude toward aspects of role equality, on the one hand, and the lack of change in the communal and agentic aspects of gender stereotypes and self-concepts, on the other hand, deserves exploration.

social roles are probably of considerably more importance in determining behaviors. Because such roles may easily override gender roles, it is possible that women and men in the same specific role behave quite similarly. As I explore further in Chapter 5, the issue of the relative salience of gender roles and specific roles has not yet been adequately investigated. Psychologists have avoided the issue by choosing research settings in which specific roles (except for the research-subject role) tend to be relatively unimportant. This practice excludes from the core sex-difference literature most evidence of the direct impact of specific roles. An excellent opportunity is thereby created for observing the behavioral effects of gender roles and sex-typed skills and beliefs.

This book concentrates on the research literature that has ordinarily been interpreted by psychologists as providing evidence for the presence or absence of sex differences in social behaviors. This focus may strike sociologists as narrow. Yet, as explained earlier in this chapter, psychologists have been reluctant to infer sex differences in behavioral tendencies on the basis of applied literatures. Nevertheless, in this book relevant applied literatures are given some attention. Chapter 5 includes discussion of the hazards and potential gains involved in relating social psychological literatures on social behaviors such as aggression to more applied but potentially related literatures on issues such as crime and spouse abuse. Before turning to discussion of particular social behaviors, I describe the important methodological innovations that have improved reviewers' ability to integrate and aggregate sex-difference findings.

THE META-ANALYTIC REVOLUTION

A very large number of studies have been conducted on many classes of social behaviors, and comparisons between the sexes have frequently been reported in these studies. These areas of inquiry include research on aggression, helping behavior, social influence, nonverbal behavior, and various aspects of group behavior. Because many findings have been accumulated over the years, investigators desired to have some overall verdict about whether sex differences in such social behaviors should be regarded as established. Until very recently, this task of research synthesis was accomplished by the traditional reviewing methods that had long been used by psychologists. These methods, now often known as *narrative reviewing* (Glass, McGaw, & Smith, 1981; Rosenthal, 1984), generally consisted of the presentation of brief summaries of individual studies, followed by an overview of the general trend of findings in the set of studies. This method is problematic because of the lack of rigor in the reviewer's inference from the findings of individual studies to the general trend.

If the inference from the findings of individual studies to an overall generalization about a sex difference was not accomplished on an altogether impressionistic basis, it was often guided by a technique now known as the *box score* or *vote-counting* method. According to this technique, a simple count was made of the number of studies with significant findings in each direction and the number with findings that failed to reach significance. Reviewers' conclusions were generally guided by a majority rule, by which they declared as the truth of the matter the finding that occurred most often. An approximation to a box-score method was employed by Maccoby and Jacklin (1974), and some of the interpretive problems that their method created were noted by Block (1976) at an early point. More generally, Hedges and Olkin (1980) have elegantly demonstrated that the majority-rule procedure, which may sound altogether reasonable, is in fact a poor decision rule that under some circumstances becomes even poorer as the number of available studies increases. Majority-rule procedures ignore the fact that under the null hypothesis of no sex difference only 5% of the available findings (i.e., 2 $1/2$% in each tail of the distribution, given 2-tailed statistical tests) would indicate a significant result. Reviews of sex differences in social behavior have often found modest proportions (e.g., 30%) of the findings significant in one direction, few findings significant in the opposite direction, and a majority of findings nonsignificant (e.g., Hall, 1978; Eagly & Steffen, 1986a). Such distributions generally depart decisively from the distribution expected if there is no sex difference. Use of a majority rule for interpreting box scores has caused reviewers to conclude erroneously in favor of the null hypothesis of no sex difference under such conditions. This conservative bias appears to be a widespread problem in narrative reviewing (Cooper & Rosenthal, 1980).

The practice in narrative reviewing of judging study outcomes by their statistical significance is problematic in and of itself (Meehl, 1978) because it ignores the magnitude of effects and thereby uses only a portion of the information that is often available. An even more important limitation of the practice is its failure to take into account the statistical power of the studies. For example, one study may produce a significant finding and another study a nonsignificant finding because of a difference in sample size. Despite an inconsistency in statistical significance, the two findings may be consistent when judged by a metric that is unaffected by sample size. In such circumstances, it is misleading to claim that one study failed to replicate the other. In fact, it is rarely useful to compare study outcomes by their level of significance, the metric that reviewers traditionally applied and that many continue to apply (see Hedges & Olkin, 1985).

Starting in the late 1970s, several psychologists who were dissatisfied with the traditional methods of reviewing research on sex differences adopted quantitative techniques for aggregating and integrating research findings.

These techniques, known collectively as *meta-analysis,* provide explicit and statistically justified methods of drawing conclusions from the large numbers of studies that had been conducted in various areas of sex-difference research. In a meta-analysis, a quantitative summary is made of the results of studies testing the same hypothesis—in this instance, the hypothesis that there is a sex difference in a particular class of behaviors. Generally the magnitude of a sex difference is assessed for each study in terms of its *effect size* or *d,* which expresses the finding in standard deviation units. For sex-difference findings, *d* is defined as the difference between the means of the male and female groups divided by the within-group standard deviation (which is the standard deviation calculated separately with each sex and then averaged over the sexes). Alternatively, the magnitude of a finding can be described by a correlation coefficient—a point-biserial *r* that expresses the relation between sex, a dichotomous variable, and the dependent variable of interest. The magnitude of both *d* and *r* is independent of sample sizes of individual studies, although both statistics are of course more reliably estimated from larger samples.

Meta-analytic scholarship on sex differences began to appear in the literature in the late 1970s. In 1978, Judith Hall published a meta-analytic review of sex differences in decoding nonverbal cues (Hall, 1978). Other investigators carried out meta-analytic reanalyses of portions of Maccoby and Jacklin's survey (e.g., Cooper, 1979; Hyde, 1981). In the 1980s scholars have presented quantitative reviews of numerous areas of sex-difference research, ranging from cognitive abilities to social behaviors such as aggression, empathy, and altruism.

Criticisms and Technical Refinements. Controversy has followed in the wake of the introduction of meta-analytic methods in psychology and their application to numerous research areas (e.g., Cook & Leviton, 1980; Eysenck, 1978; Slavin, 1984). Simultaneously these methods have undergone rapid refinement. The methodologists and statisticians active in meta-analytic scholarship have explained the subtleties of good reviewing in several textbooks (e.g., Cooper, 1984; Glass, McGaw, & Smith, 1981; Light & Pillemer, 1984; Rosenthal, 1984). They have analyzed issues such as study quality and publication biases that have been important themes in critiques of meta-analysis. In addition, they have introduced increasingly more adequate statistical methods tailored to the analysis of effect sizes (Hedges & Olkin, 1985).

One of the most frequent criticisms leveled against quantitative reviews as a genre is that the quality of the studies is ignored (e.g., Basow, 1986). This criticism has an instant intuitive appeal because of the plausibility of the idea that reviewers should discard poor studies or at least not weight then as heavily as good studies. However, the criticism lacks force unless it is followed by specification of the particular sorts of flaws that would threaten the validity of the finding that is the focus of the reviewer's meta-analysis. It is these *specific* threats to the validity of findings that should be taken into account in the formulation of the meta-analysis, because global ratings of study quality are seldom informative. A study that is poor in some respects (e.g., has an inadequate manipulation of an independent variable) and thus fares poorly in a global rating of study quality may nevertheless provide a high-quality estimate of a sex difference.

A reviewer who assesses potential threats to the validity of sex-difference findings can determine whether studies that have presumed flaws have different outcomes than studies that are free from these flaws. Glass, McGaw, and Smith (1981) have claimed that presumed flaws, while perhaps in theory a source of invalidity, usually make little or no difference in study outcomes. Whatever the merits of this claim, meta-analysts' straightforward empirical approach to examining possible methodological problems has much to recommend it, given the many differences of opinion among psychologists about what constitutes methodological excellence in research. This approach injects considerable objectivity into the matter of judging study quality and evaluating its effects on research findings.

As will be seen in the context of the meta-analytic studies presented in Chapters 2 and 3, validity issues are taken into account in various ways in meta-analyses of sex differences. To make explicit to readers the methods for dealing with study quality, Chapters 2 and 3 include a series of footnotes explaining the ways that various techniques take study quality into account. In addition, Chapter 5 considers threats to the validity of the overall generalizations about sex differences that reviewers offer on the basis of aggregated findings.

Among the statistical innovations that help reviewers address some of the criticisms of quantitative reviewing are the tests of homogeneity proposed by Hedges (1981) and Rosenthal and Rubin (1982a). The homogeneity criterion permits reviewers to assess whether a set of studies, judged by their effect sizes, can be considered to have consistent outcomes—that is, outcomes sampled from a common population. This issue is vitally important in reviewing because rejection of the hypothesis of homogeneity shifts attention from the aggregated finding to a search for the attributes of studies that are correlated with the estimates of effect size. Thus, if application of the homogeneity criterion shows that a set of sex-difference findings are *not* sampled from a common population of findings, it makes little sense for the reviewer to concentrate on an overall aggregation of these diverse findings. Accounting for variability in effect sizes becomes the important goal of reviewing. Making prediction one's goal belies the criticism that meta-analysis consists of mindless aggregation of findings (Eysenck, 1978) or the combining of "apples and oranges." Studies are not merely combined but are disaggregated in various ways to discover which attributes of the studies are related to study outcomes. In this book, predictions about such relationships are derived from the social-role theory of sex differences.

The Importance of Meta-Analysis
to the Study of Sex Differences

Meta-analytic reviewing has rapidly become popular in numerous areas of psychology. Yet the suddenness of the shift from narrative to quantitative reviewing is especially striking in scholarship on sex differences. There are several reasons why meta-analysis has proven to be very attractive to scholars concerned with synthesizing sex-difference findings. One reason is that reviewers in this area are often faced with integrating large numbers of studies. The resulting information overload problem became severe in the 1970s as the Women's Movement focused psychologists' attention on gender, with the result that sex differences were more often reported and more carefully scrutinized in the psychological literature. When many findings are available, it is impossible for reviewers to systematically apply rules for drawing conclusions without using quantitative methods of some sort. Indeed, narrative reviewers offered generalizations about sex differences without providing explicit rules for drawing conclusions from the available research findings. In many such reviews, it is doubtful that any decision rules were applied consistently (e.g., see Block's, 1976, efforts to trace Maccoby and Jacklin's, 1974, decision rules). As Block's disagreements with Maccoby and Jacklin showed, reviewers' conclusions are unlikely to prove replicable by other reviewers as long as such methods are employed.

Another reason for the rapid shift to meta-analytic methods is that sex-difference research is often characterized by precisely the type of findings most likely to lead narrative reviewers to erroneous conclusions based on the intuitively appealing box-score method. As I demonstrate later in relation to several social behaviors, often the majority of sex-difference findings on a social behavior are small to medium in magnitude and sample sizes are only of moderate size. As Hedges and Olkin (1980, 1985) have shown, under such circumstances it is often true that a majority of findings fail to reach statistical significance. Evidence of this sort has usually led narrative reviewers either to fail to reject the null hypothesis or to conclude that findings are in disarray. Neither conclusion is warranted, but until recently one or the other conclusion has typically been drawn by reviewers.

Research on sex differences is especially appropriate for quantitative reviewing because of the relatively stable definition that the independent variable (female versus male) has across studies. Thus, the classification of research participants into female and male categories is accomplished in similar ways in the studies, and exceedingly few people classified as members of one sex in one study would end up classified as members of the other sex if they participated in another study.[17] In contrast, other independent variables, especially manipulated ones, are very often operationalized in very different ways across studies. Even variables representing other social categories (e.g., young versus old; middle class versus lower class) are likely to have operational definitions that differ across the available studies. Although the impact of varying operational definitions can sometimes be taken into account within a meta-analysis, complexity of this type creates interpretational problems that are not encountered by quantitative reviewers of sex differences.

Meta-analytic methods also provide a basis for relatively objective research summaries that are much less vulnerable than summaries based on traditional reviewing methods to biases stemming from reviewers' own preferences concerning the presence or absence of sex differences. This aspect of the methods no doubt is an important reason for their rapid spread, even though meta-analysis cannot completely eliminate the effects of the biases that may flow from reviewers' own beliefs about gender. Nevertheless, certain features of quantitative reviewing provide a good measure of protection against some of the more serious forms of bias. For example, the meta-analytic practice of providing a detailed statement of the procedures used for locating relevant studies guards against selection of a biased sample of studies. Even more importantly, the use of explicit statistical rules for drawing conclusions from sets of studies guards against any tendency of reviewers to allow their gender stereotypes or other beliefs to guide their generalizations about sex differences. Such features of quantitative reviews tend to hold in check the ideological biases that scholars often hold in relation to gender, which can influence their interpretation of relevant research.

Ideological biases have been problematic in scholarship on sex differences. Shields (1975) and Rosenberg (1982) have shown some of the ways in which the generalizations psychologists once offered about women's intellectual inferiority and maternal instinct reflected the ideology of patriarchy. Furthermore, the popular 1970s verdict that sex differences are typically small or nonexistent—a verdict that is being reconsidered on the basis of

---

[17]By this statement, I do not mean to argue that people are classified by sex with perfect validity in research. Ordinarily sex is operationally defined by having research participants indicate whether they are male or female or by having observers classify research participants based on observable external indicators of sex. Yet the presence in the population of people whose sex chromosomes or gonads are not congruent with their socially identified gender or their personal gender identity raises questions about the sufficiency of any single operational definition (see Kessler & McKenna, 1978).

meta-analytic scholarship—may have reflected the liberal feminist ideology held by many psychologists who worked on gender during that particular period in history. It was not possible to evaluate the accuracy of any diagnosis of sex-difference research with a desirable degree of rigor until meta-analysis provided relatively objective methods of synthesizing findings.

New Generalizations about Sex Differences

The view of sex differences in social behavior that is emerging from the new meta-analytic scholarship departs from the conclusions of many 1970s narrative reviews in numerous specific respects that will be discussed in relation to particular social behaviors. Of general importance are some noteworthy overall lessons that are emerging from quantitative reviews. As already noted, quantitative reviewers are more likely to find evidence favoring an overall sex difference. Yet, sex differences in social behaviors are typically found to be inconsistent across studies so that the value of overall verdicts about the presence or absence of sex differences is somewhat reduced.[18] Accordingly, the mean effect sizes reported in meta-analyses of sex differences in social behaviors generally aggregate some effect sizes that are small, others that are larger, and some that are quite large. In reporting such an outcome, reviewers mislead readers by only informing them about the overall magnitude of a sex difference or its reliability in the research literature as a whole. Instead, reviewers should seek to explain why reported sex differences vary in magnitude and usually in direction as well.

The problem that reviewers face when findings are inconsistent is similar to the problem that researchers interpreting data from a single study face when deciding how to regard a main effect of a variable (i.e., an overall effect) in the presence of an interaction (i.e., evidence that this effect is contingent upon the effect of a second variable). Given a statistically significant interaction, the main effect is generally of less interest, particularly if the interaction is large compared with the main effect. A related perspective regards inconsistencies between studies as analogous to individual differences in a single study (see Harris & Rosenthal, 1985). Such individual differences may reverse the direction of the effect of an experi-

---

[18]Sex differences in cognitive abilities may well be more consistent, as suggested by Linn and Peterson's (1985) findings. The relatively small amount of meta-analytic research available on sex differences in personality (see Hall's, 1984, overview) has not addressed these homogeneity issues. Like tests of cognitive abilities, personality tests also involve a limited number of instruments, usually administered under controlled conditions. Moreover, personality-test items typically require that respondents generalize across a range of situations. For these reasons, sex differences in personality should also be more consistent across studies than are sex differences in social behaviors.

mentally manipulated variable or, less seriously, may merely influence the magnitude of the effect.

If inconsistencies between sex-difference findings are substantial, the reviewer should adopt a contextualist view (McGuire, 1983), by which the sex difference is regarded as true in some contexts and untrue in others. Reviewers' most important task is the identification of these contexts. The usual method involves relating study attributes to effect-size estimates in order to discover moderating variables. Although such relations are correlational, they can still be examined for their agreement with theories of sex differences.

As shown in detail in later chapters of this book, quantitative reviews have also established that any general statements about average sex differences must now acknowledge that, overall, numerous social behaviors are to some degree sex-typed along stereotypic lines. Yet a sex difference that is reliable in the sense that a mean effect size departs significantly from the null hypothesis of no difference may nevertheless be quite small on the average. In considering this question of the magnitude of sex differences, one should keep in mind the point that I have already made—namely, that mean sex differences computed over studies deserve reduced emphasis in the face of evidence that findings are extremely inconsistent across studies. Yet reviewers quite legitimately continue to present and comment on aggregated sex-difference findings, because they provide the best prediction for a given sex difference, in the absence of knowledge of the specific characteristics of the situation that are responsible for between-study variability in the findings. Although the magnitude of sex differences is analyzed in detail in the last chapter of this book, it is worthwhile noting at this point that it is becoming far less tenable for reviewers to claim that sex differences typically are unimportant because effects are small.

2

Sex Differences
in Helping Behavior

A review of social psychological research on helping behavior provides the first application of the role theory of sex differences and quantitative methods of research synthesis. As shown in this chapter, the literature on helping behavior provides a particularly vivid example of the following aspects of scholarship on sex differences in social behavior:

1. Quantitative reviewing practices—in contrast to those of traditional, narrative reviewing—provide a firm basis for aggregating and integrating sex-difference findings. These summaries of research differ in important ways from those offered by narrative reviewers.

2. Consideration of the social roles that underlie sex differences in a class of social behaviors can yield effective prediction of the inconsistencies in these sex differences across studies as well as the overall trend.

3. The information that the psychological literature yields about sex differences in social behaviors is limited by the tendency of investigators to study behaviors in settings in which research subjects interact with strangers in brief encounters.

A SOCIAL–ROLE ANALYSIS OF
SEX DIFFERENCES IN HELPING BEHAVIOR

The giving of aid or succor to people in need, commonly known as helping behavior, has been the focus of considerable research in social psychology for more than fifteen years (see Dovidio, 1984; Piliavin, Dovidio, Gaertner,

& Clark, 1981). The determinants of helping were first examined systematically by social psychologists in the late 1960s. The well-known Darley and Latané (1968) study was an early experiment addressing the issue of why people often fail to help. This study examined helpful interventions in a laboratory simulation of an emergency situation—a person apparently suffering an epileptic fit. In the 1970s, helping behavior became one of the most active research areas in social psychology. Many different helping behaviors were examined (see Pearce & Amato, 1980; Smithson & Amato, 1982) in a great variety of field and laboratory settings. Although many of these studies, like the Darley and Latané experiment, presented subjects with an emergency situation that was staged for the purpose of examining helpful interventions, many other experiments presented subjects with less urgent needs (e.g., a person dropping a bag of groceries) or with direct requests for help (e.g., a person asking for a charity donation or blood donation).

Maureen Crowley and I (Eagly & Crowley, 1986) undertook a systematic review of the sex differences reported in this research literature. Following the social-role analysis, we regarded helping other people as role behavior and therefore viewed it as being regulated by the social norms that apply to individuals based on the roles they occupy. To account for sex differences in helping from this perspective, it is necessary to understand the ways in which helping is sustained and inhibited by the social roles occupied mainly or exclusively by one sex versus the other. Following from the assumption that conformity to gender roles often underlies sex differences observed in research settings, the implications that gender roles have for helping should be emphasized.

Specific social roles, if they are occupied mainly by a single sex (e.g., firefighter, homemaker), can also underlie sex differences in helping. Because the occupants of many specific roles must engage in helping in order to enact their roles, in natural settings many helping behaviors are more common to one sex because that sex disproportionately occupies such a role. However, as explained in Chapter 1, social psychologists rarely study sex differences in situations in which specific roles provide the main structure for social interaction. Therefore, conformity to specific roles is unlikely to result in sex differences in the helping behaviors reported in the research literature. Nevertheless, prior enactment of specific roles may impart skills and beliefs that affect helping behavior even when these specific roles are not salient. In view of these several considerations, I discuss in some detail the implications that gender roles and various specific roles have for sex differences in helping behavior.

Gender Roles and Helping

Because conformity to gender roles is likely to be one major determinant of sex differences in helping, it is important to examine the norms relevant to helping that apply to individuals based on their socially identified gender. Although the term *helping* may primarily connote caring and nurturant behavior compatible with the female role's communal emphasis, helping is more usefully regarded as a broader set of acts, of which some serve communal goals and others have the assertive and controlling characteristics of agentic behaviors. From this perspective, the helping consistent with the communal focus of the female role may be quite different from the helping consistent with the agentic focus of the male role.

The Female Gender Role.   According to the analysis presented in Chapter 1, the female gender role should foster those aspects of helpfulness that are consistent with the communal qualities that women are expected to embody. Thus, women might be expected to care for the personal and emotional needs of others, to deliver routine forms of personal service, and, more generally, to facilitate the progress of others toward their goals. Consistent with the communal theme of connectedness with other people, the demand for women to serve others in these ways should be especially strong within the family and in other close relationships such as friendships, although the caring and nurturing aspect of the female role may also be extended to some extent to the problems of the larger community.

For some years, there has been considerable consensus in the social science literature that the female gender role does include norms encouraging certain forms of helping. In the past decade, a number of social scientists have analyzed the female gender role, and often a major theme of these analyses is that women are expected to be helpful to others. For example, Bernard (1981), Chodorow (1978), and Miller (1976) have argued that women are expected to place the needs of others, especially those of family members, before their own. Gilligan (1982) has identified this theme as women's orientation toward caring and responsibility.

Because gender stereotypes function as normative expectations (see Chapter 1), research on stereotypes should be examined to determine if helpfulness or related attributes are among the communal qualities stereotypically associated with women. Indeed, such research (e.g., Bem, 1974; Ruble, 1983; Spence & Helmreich, 1978) has shown that women were rated more favorably than men, not only on helpfulness, but also on kindness, compassion, and the ability to devote oneself completely to others.

Several investigators have claimed that women's consideration for others underlies their altruism (e.g., Piliavin & Unger, 1985; Staub, 1978; Underwood & Moore, 1982). In addition, many psychologists have argued that females are generally more empathic or sympathetic than males (e.g., Feshbach, 1982; Hoffman, 1977). Yet, consistent with the social-role approach, Eisenberg and Lennon (1983) have shown that this empathy sex difference has been obtained in research primarily when gender-role obligations or demand characteristics were especially salient.

To the extent that the female gender role prescribes a communal or nurturant helpfulness for women, such behavior should be characteristic of women in a variety of contexts in addition to those that appear in the social psychological literature specifically on helping behavior. Most germane to a discussion of gender roles are those contexts in which specific roles are either not strong determinants of behavior or are equated for women and men. Thus, in a laboratory experiment, Bem, Martyna, and Watson (1976) showed that, even with subjects' level of androgyny controlled, women were rated as more nurturant than men in a conversation with an apparently lonely student of the same sex. In addition, studies of friends and room-mates have found that women, to a greater extent than men, reported providing personal favors, emotional support, and informal counseling about personal problems (Aries & Johnson, 1983; Berg, 1984; Johnson & Aries, 1983; Worell, Romano, & Newsome, 1984). Finally, suggesting that the caring orientation of the female role can extend beyond family and close relationships, women's attitudes have been shown to be somewhat more favorable than men's on a variety of compassion issues involving economic policies to help poor and oppressed groups (Shapiro & Mahajan, 1986).

The Male Gender Role.   According to the analysis given in Chapter 1, the male gender role should encourage other forms of helping—specifically, those forms of helping that are consistent with the overall expectation that men behave agentically. One such form of helpfulness would be heroic behavior, especially altruistic acts of saving others from harm that are performed at some risk to oneself. Thus, *hero* is defined in the *Oxford English Dictionary* (1971) as "a man distinguished by extraordinary valour and martial achievements; one who does brave or noble deeds." Although the culture also offers a parallel concept of *heroine,* it is not included in the analysis of the female gender role because heroine is a much less widely accepted ideal for women than hero is for men.[1]

Research on gender stereotypes provides only limited support for the claim that men are expected to behave heroically. Agentic attributes such

---

[1]Thus, few women strive for or attain heroism of the sort described in the ordinary agentic definitions of the term. However, the meaning of the term is occasionally transformed to give the heroic label to women, such as Mother Teresa, who achieve in a decidedly communal mode.

as willingness to take risks, adventurousness, calmness in a crisis, and the ability to stand up well under pressure are ascribed to men more than women (Bem, 1974; Broverman et al., 1972; Ruble, 1983; Spence, Helmreich, & Stapp, 1974). Norms favoring such tendencies may foster behaviors that predispose people to act heroically, yet heroism itself is evidently not a quality stereotypically ascribed to men as a group, because heroic acts are believed to occur only in quite extreme and unusual circumstances not commonly encountered in daily life.

To the extent that the male gender role includes the expectation that men behave heroically when appropriate situations do occur, some evidence of men's heroic behavior might be found in locations in addition to the social psychological literature on helping. Along these lines, some support for an association between heroism and the male role comes from noting that almost all of the people who have been singled out as heroic by scholars and other writers are men (e.g., Hook, 1943; Kerenyi, 1960; Thomas, 1943). However, the implications of this evidence for the male gender role are not clear-cut because some of these heroes occupied specific roles (e.g., military leader) that strongly encourage heroic behavior.

Additional information relevant to the claim that the male role supports heroic behavior can be found in the records of the Carnegie Hero Fund Commission, which since 1904 has given awards to people who perform acts (in the United States or Canada) in which they risk or sacrifice their lives "in saving, or attempting to save, the life of a fellow being" (Carnegie Hero Fund Commission, 1907, p. 21). It is convenient for determining whether heroism is linked with the male gender role (and not merely with certain specific roles) that the Carnegie Hero Fund Commission has excluded from consideration acts such as those of firefighters that are carried out as an aspect of one's regular vocation. Because parental roles may require that heroism be displayed when one's children are in danger, it is also convenient that the Carnegie Hero Fund Commission has excluded from awards persons who rescue family members, "except in cases of outstanding heroism where the rescuer loses his life or is severely injured" (Carnegie Hero Fund Commission, 1983, p. 4). Women are explicitly included: "Whenever heroism is displayed by man or woman in saving human life, the Fund applies" (Carnegie, 1907, p. 11). Yet classification of the 6,955 Carnegie medalists according to their sex revealed that only 616 (8.86%) were women (W. F. Rutkowski, Secretary, Carnegie Hero Fund Commission, personal communication, February 18, 1986).

The idea that heroic forms of helping are prescribed by the male gender role suggests that men are more helpful than women under certain circumstances. For example, because heroism implies that the helper takes risks, the amount of danger inherent in helping may affect sex differences in helping. Women may perceive many classes of situations as more dangerous than men do—for example, when giving aid entails the risk of physical injury to the helper. In the absence of pressures to behave heroically, women may not feel as obligated as men do to risk injury to themselves in order to provide help.

The presence of an audience and the availability of other helpers may also be relevant to heroic helping. Thus, bystanders might elicit greater helping from men than women because bystanders are presumed to support prevailing gender-role norms. Moreover, heroic status is achieved only if there is public recognition for one's exploits. In the words of Hoffer (1951), "There is no striving for glory without vivid awareness of an audience" . . . (p. 65). The availability of other potential helpers may also increase men's helping behavior because heroism is achieved by being the one person among many who is willing to take the risks involved in helping.

Related to heroism is chivalry, a syndrome of behaviors that includes many helpful acts. Chivalry, like heroism, is consistent with the agentic aspect of the male gender role. Behaviors labeled as *chivalrous* are "characterized by pure and noble gallantry, honor, courtesy, and disinterested devotion to the cause of the weak or oppressed" (*Oxford English Dictionary,* 1971). The helpfulness inherent in chivalry is illustrated by several of the chivalric vows taken by medieval knights: (a) "to protect the weak and defenseless," (b) "to respect the honor of women," (c) "to live for honor and glory, despising pecuniary reward," and (d) "to fight for the general welfare of all" (Hearnshaw, 1928, p. 24). The continuing influence of chivalry on conceptions of ideal male behavior in Western society is well documented (e.g., Aresty, 1970; Fraser, 1982; Girouard, 1981). Furthermore, rules consistent with the chivalric code, especially rules prescribing that men protect women, are common in Twentieth Century etiquette books (e.g., Post, 1924; Vanderbilt, 1963). Yet as Walum (1974) has shown, many people have become ambivalent about chivalrous behavior since the advent of the Women's Movement.

Because gender-role expectations are represented in stereotypes about women and men, research on stereotypes was examined to see whether attributes such as civility are ascribed to men. There was no suggestion in this research that civility and related qualities are ascribed to men as a group. Yet chivalry, with its quality of *noblesse oblige,* may be stereotypically associated primarily with men of relatively high social status rather than men in general. More generally, chivalrous behavior is not synonymous with polite or civil behavior because chivalry describes only certain forms of politeness carried out in relation to certain targets in appropriate social contexts.

To develop a thorough understanding of chivalry's implications for sex differences in helping, particularistic aspects of gender roles (see Chapter 1) would have to be examined in detail, and unfortunately, research of this type has not been carried out for helpful behavior. Nonetheless, some predictions can be offered, based on common knowledge of social norms pertaining to chivalrous behavior. Thus, to the extent that chivalry continues to influence behavior, men would be more helpful than women in situations that allow chivalrous protectiveness or civility. Examples include a man carrying a heavy package for a woman or helping a woman put on her coat. Such behaviors, like heroic behaviors, would be directed toward strangers as well as intimates, and at least some courtesies, such as assisting a woman with her coat, probably occur more commonly among people who do not know one another well than among people who are well acquainted.

Women probably receive more chivalrous help than men do. The chivalric code stipulates that men direct their courteous and protective acts toward women, who constitute one class of "weak and oppressed" people whom chivalrous men are supposed to help. Indeed, women are regarded as weaker and more dependent than men (e.g., Broverman et al., 1972), although this perception of weakness may elicit victimization as well as helping. Also important in insuring that chivalrous helping is directed toward women is women's fulfillment of their chivalric duty to welcome and, moreover, to inspire men's courtesies and protection. Ventimiglia's (1982) finding that women for whom a man held a door displayed more gratitude than men for whom a woman held a door is consistent with this portrayal of women but also allows other interpretations (e.g., men's surprise or puzzlement at unexpected behavior).

Even though my discussion has emphasized the support gender roles provide for helping, prohibitions against helping may also be included in these roles. In particular, parents and other socializers may teach girls about the potential dangers of dealing with strangers. Rules of avoidance, primarily intended to lessen the possibility that girls and women will be victims of sexual assault (e.g., U.S. Department of Justice, 1979), may lead them to judge many helping behaviors as dangerous. Thus, norms enjoining women to avoid strangers, especially male strangers, may be as important in accounting for help given (and not given) to strangers as norms encouraging men to lend assistance to strangers.

Gender Roles and Social Status.   As discussed in Chapter 1, gender functions as a status cue because of the widespread power and status differences between men and women. These differences are directly reflected in the gender-stereotypic perception of men as dominant and influential and women as submissive and easily influenced. The belief that women and men should differ in these qualities is one aspect of gender roles.

The status analysis of gender roles has important implications for helping behavior. Because the fact that an individual is male conveys power and

importance, assistance in attaining longer-term goals may be disproportionately directed toward men and delivered by women. This pattern
contrasts with that predicted for minor courtesies, which by chivalric rules
should be directed by men toward women.

The status analysis of gender roles has additional implications when
efforts to elicit help are viewed as forms of social influence. From this
perspective, a direct request for aid is one type of influence attempt.
Helping in response to such an appeal can be regarded as compliant
behavior. In contrast, the mere portrayal of a need, as in bystander intervention studies (e.g., Piliavin, Rodin, & Piliavin, 1969), is an indirect appeal for
aid. Because no specific request is directed toward the potential helper,
helping in such a situation can be regarded as assertive behavior.

If women, like members of other lower-status categories, are expected to
behave in somewhat compliant and unassertive ways, the status difference
between the sexes has quite different implications for compliant versus
assertive helping behaviors. In particular, as Deaux (1976) has also argued,
when helping is elicited by the mere portrayal of a need and is therefore an
assertive act, women may be less helpful than men. In contrast, when
helping is elicited by a direct request and is therefore a compliant act,
women may be more helpful than men.

Summary of Gender-Role Analysis.   In summary, the helping behaviors
consistent with the male gender role differ both in kind and in social
context from those consistent with the female gender role. The helping
expected of men has agentic connotations. It encompasses nonroutine and
risky acts of rescuing others as well as behaviors that are courteous and
protective of subordinates. These behaviors commonly occur in relationships with strangers as well as in close relationships and may often be
directed toward women. The helping expected of women has communal
connotations. It mainly consists of caring for others, primarily in close and
long-term relationships. In addition, the female gender role may include
the prescription that women avoid many types of interactions with strangers,
including helpful exchanges. Finally, the gender-role expectations that men
be dominant and women be submissive may encourage men to help when
helping is an assertive act of intervention and encourage women to help
when helping is a compliant response to a direct request.

Other Social Roles and Helping

In natural settings, some helping behaviors may be more common in one
sex because they are aspects, not of gender roles, but of specific social
roles occupied mainly by persons of that sex. The domestic role is a case in
point. The service-oriented character of the "housewife" role has been

noted in feminist writings (e.g., Friedan, 1963) and documented in empirical research (e.g., Walker & Woods, 1976). Because this role is occupied almost exclusively by women, care-giving within the family is much more commonly carried out by women than by men.

The view that the domestic role encourages caring behavior toward family members is consistent with some of the more general views that have been expressed about women's roles in close relationships. For example, Bernard (1981) summarized evidence documenting that women supply the major emotional support, both to their husbands and to their women friends, and Belle (1982a, 1982b) documented the ways in which women's traditional roles as homemaker, friend, and neighbor often require that they provide more social support than they receive. Based on a review of the social-support literature, Vaux (1985) suggested that women provide (and receive) more emotional support than men.

Other helping behaviors are required by occupational roles other than the domestic role—for example, secretaries are expected to help bosses, nurses to help physicians, and social workers to help poor and oppressed people. Women are particularly well represented in paid occupations that focus on some form of personal service: Over half of all employed women are in clerical and service occupations, and women with professional positions are predominantly in teaching and nursing (U.S. Department of Labor, 1980). In contrast, men are especially well represented in paid occupations that may require placing one's life in jeopardy to help others (e.g., firefighter, law enforcement officer, soldier). Finally, women's traditional dedication to community service in volunteer roles is yet another source of sex differences in helping behavior in natural settings.

The status of specific roles within organizations may also influence helping. In general, subordinate status in hierarchical role relationships increases the likelihood that role occupants will be providers of services rather than recipients. Because men tend to have higher status than women in organizations of all kinds, men are more likely than women to receive aid in attaining organizationally-relevant goals, and women are more likely to provide such aid.

The absence of sex differences based on conformity to specific social roles from the empirical literature on helping behavior is consistent with the description of psychologists' research methods presented in Chapter 1. Most psychologists have preferred to study the social behavior of adults in relatively controlled contexts that are little influenced by specific social roles, such as those stemming from occupations and family life. Nevertheless, specific roles (as well as gender roles) may affect sex differences displayed in these research settings through the impact that prior enactment of such roles has on role occupants' skills and beliefs. Thus, skills relevant to helping and beliefs about the consequences of helping may become sex-typed when specific roles have been occupied primarily by persons of one sex.

Skills and Beliefs Acquired in Social Roles

Particularly as occupants of specific social roles, people often gain skills required to provide certain types of help to other people and then transfer these skills to new settings unrelated to the role in which the skills were originally learned. For example, men are more likely to have occupied roles in which they service automobiles and therefore are more likely to have gained the expertise to help people with their cars. In contrast, women are more likely to have occupied roles in which they nurture young children and therefore are more likely to have gained the expertise to help children. Consequently, possessing appropriate skills allows men to help people with their cars and women to help children, even in the absence of a contemporaneous specific role requiring these behaviors.

A preliminary examination of the helping behaviors investigated in social-psychological research suggested that such role-linked skills were sometimes required to perform these behaviors. Therefore, in the Eagly and Crowley (1986) meta-analysis, helpful acts were examined for the extent to which women or men feel more competent and comfortable engaging in them. Persons of whichever sex is more competent and comfortable in relation to a particular act should be more likely to engage in that act (see Deaux, 1976; Piliavin & Unger, 1985).

Although enactment of both specific roles and gender roles may cause women and men to differ in their beliefs about the consequences of helping, such beliefs were not examined extensively in the meta-analysis. One of the barriers to incorporating such beliefs was that few consequences appeared relevant to most behaviors because of the diversity of the behaviors that had been examined in the research literature. For example, the perceived consequences of giving blood (Zuckerman & Reis, 1978) are no doubt quite different from the perceived consequences of picking up a package dropped by someone outside of a supermarket (Wispé & Freshley, 1971).

Nevertheless, one particular consequence—danger to oneself—was deemed relevant to many of the helping behaviors examined in the research literature. If the male gender role encourages heroic behavior and the female gender role encourages avoidance of strangers, women and men should differ in their perception of whether providing aid is likely to result in danger to themselves as helpers. Particularly in situations with an element of risk, women should perceive more danger than men. The resulting sex differences in perceived danger should predict sex differences in helping— that is, women should be relatively less helpful than men when women perceive helping as more dangerous than men do.

Limitations of the Research Literature

As already noted, helping has been studied almost exclusively in brief encounters with strangers. Even though field experiments have been especially popular in helping research, studies have rarely examined providers and receivers of help who have a social relationship of long standing. Therefore, the helping fostered by the female gender role in close or long-term relationships would not be displayed in the available research. Neither would several other forms of women's helping be evident—namely, the help they provide as (a) homemakers, (b) job-holders in service and helping occupations, (c) community volunteers, and (d) occupants of lower-status roles in organizations. In contrast, the heroic and chivalrous forms of helping, which are prescribed by the male gender role, would be generously represented because they are displayed in brief encounters with strangers. Even though research on helping has not investigated extremely heroic behaviors such as those of the Carnegie medalists, even for the moderately dangerous behaviors that have been examined (e.g., changing a tire for a stranger or giving a stranger a ride), men's willingness to take risks and women's obligation to avoid them should engender more help by men than by women. Also, the analysis of the male role in terms of heroism and chivalry leads to a number of additional predictions already noted, such as a tendency for men to be especially helpful compared with women in the presence of an audience. Finally, the helping behaviors studied in the research literature should be affected by other sex-related differences that follow from the role analysis— namely, sex differences in specific skills and in compliance and assertiveness.

In conclusion, when the various components of the social-role analysis are applied to the restricted settings within which social psychologists have studied helping, the overall prediction is that men are more helpful than women. Yet according to the role analysis, the sex differences reported in research on helping would vary considerably across the studies, even in this limited range of situations. As already noted, features of social settings (e.g., the presence of other people) and helping acts (e.g., the specific skills they require) should affect the direction and magnitude of the sex differences.

METHOD FOR META–ANALYSIS[2]

Sample of Studies

Studies were located primarily through computer searches and examination of relevant bibliographies and were included in the sample if they met the following criteria: (a) the dependent measure was either a helping

---

[2]See Eagly and Crowley (1986) for a detailed description of the method as well as a list of the studies and helping behaviors included in the sample.

behavior or, in a few studies, a commitment to engage in a helping behavior, (b) the reported results were sufficient to calculate a sex-of-subject effect size or to determine the statistical significance and/or direction of the sex difference, and (c) the subjects were male and female adults or adolescents from the United States or Canada who were not sampled from specialized populations (e.g., mental hospital patients). Studies were omitted if their authors reported the sex distribution of the helpers but failed to report the sex distribution of the non-helpers or the baseline proportions of females and males in the setting (e.g., Bryan & Test, 1967; Snyder, Grether, & Keller, 1974).[3] The resulting sample of 172 studies yielded 182 sex-of-subject reports.

Variables Coded from Each Study

The following information was recorded from each report: (a) date of publication; (b) source of publication (journal; other source); (c) percentage of male authors; (d) sex of first author; (e) sample size (female, male, and total). In addition, the following variables were coded from the information provided in each report: (a) setting (laboratory; campus or school; off-campus); (b) surveillance of helping act by persons other than victim or requester (no surveillance; unclear; surveillance); (c) availability of other potential helpers (not available; unclear; available);[4] (d) type of appeal for help (direct request; presentation of need); (e) occupants of victim and requester roles (same person; different persons); (f) identity of victim/requester (male; female; sex varied; same sex as subject; collective, e.g., charity; unclear). These variables were coded by one rater, whose work was then checked by a second rater. A third rater, who independently coded 25 of the studies according to the criteria developed by the first two raters, agreed with 92%-100% of their judgments, depending on the variable. Disagreements were resolved by discussion.

---

[3]These exclusions (and others, see Eagly & Crowley, 1986) can be seen as implementing study-quality criteria. Interestingly, some studies frequently cited as indicating sex differences in helping behavior (e.g., Bryan & Test, 1967) do not meet even this minimal standard of an interpretable sex-difference report.

[4]Other helpers were regarded as available even if not physically present if it was likely that subjects believed that such helpers were potentially available to the victim or requester. For example, other helpers were coded as available to people who requested charity donations, although these other helpers were not necessarily physically present.

Variables Derived from Questionnaire Respondents' Judgments of Helping Behaviors[5]

A questionnaire study was conducted to generate measures of the extent to which each helping behavior was associated with sex differences in (a) the ability to help, (b) the belief that helping is dangerous to oneself, and (c) the perceived likelihood of helping. The likelihood measures were included to evaluate how well the respondents' beliefs about their own and others' behavior predicted the helping sex differences obtained in the research literature.

Each of the 304 respondents completed a questionnaire that contained brief descriptions of one-third of the helping behaviors investigated in the studies in the meta-analysis. For example, Darley and Latané's (1968) study was described as "Coming to the aid of a male student who is having a seizure in a nearby room; you have never met him before but you, he, and the other participants are communicating with one another via microphones as part of a psychology experiment when he suddenly becomes agitated and incoherent." Cunningham, Steinberg, and Grev's (1980) study was described as "Donating money to the World Children's Fund when someone approaches you in a shopping mall with a poster advertising this charity."

Respondents judged these helping behaviors in response to three questions assessing skills and beliefs relevant to helping: (a) How competent would you be to provide this help? (b) How comfortable would you feel when you provided this help? (c) How much danger would you probably face if you provided this help? Respondents also judged these behaviors in response to three likelihood questions: (a) How likely is it that you would provide this help? (b) How likely is it that the average woman would provide this help? (c) How likely is it that the average man would provide this help? These ratings were made on 15-point scales.

Analysis of Ratings. For the first four of the six questions just listed mean scores for each helping behavior were computed separately for female and male respondents. For each behavior, the female mean was subtracted from the male mean to yield a mean sex difference, which was then standardized by dividing it by the pooled (within-sex) standard deviation. For the questions on the average woman's and average man's likelihood of helping, the respondents' mean rating of the average woman for each behavior was subtracted from their mean rating of the average man to yield a mean stereotypic sex difference, which was then standardized by

---

[5]In this chapter (as well as in Chapter 3), the term *respondents* designates people who participated in a questionnaire study in which behaviors were rated, and the term *subjects* designates people who participated in the original experiments reviewed in these meta-analyses

dividing it by the standard deviation of the differences between the paired ratings.

Computation and Analysis of Effect Sizes

The statistical significance and/or direction of the 182 sex-of-subject differences was recorded, and an effect size, d, was calculated for the behaviors for which sufficient information was provided. Whenever possible, these procedures were also carried out for sex of victim/requester differences as well as for the simple effects of (a) sex of subject for male and female victims/requesters and (b) sex of victim/requester for male and female subjects.

The effect sizes were corrected for the bias from d's overestimate of the population effect size, especially for small samples (Hedges, 1981). Then the study outcomes were combined by averaging the effect sizes. To determine whether the studies shared a common effect size, the homogeneity of each set of effect sizes was examined (see Chapter 1). Various models for predicting the magnitude of effect sizes were tested. These model tests used statistical methods introduced specifically for the analysis of effect sizes (Hedges, 1982a, 1982b; Hedges & Olkin, 1985).

RESULTS OF META-ANALYSIS

Characteristics of Studies

As a first step, it is informative to look carefully at the characteristics of the studies from which conclusions about sex differences in helping are drawn. Table 2.1 shows these study characteristics summarized separately for (a) the studies for which effect sizes could be calculated and (b) the larger sample of studies, which included studies with calculable effect sizes and studies that reported a nonsignificant sex difference but did not provide information sufficient to compute an effect size. The first eight characteristics are called *continuous variables* because they were measured on continuous scales, and the remaining five are called *categorical variables* because each consists of discrete categories into which the studies were classified.

As shown by the central tendencies of the first three continuous variables in Table 2.1, the studies usually (a) were published relatively recently; (b) involved moderate numbers of subjects; and (c) had male authors. The means for the next three continuous variables represent overall sex differences in questionnaire respondents' judgments of (a) their competence to engage in each helping behavior; (b) their comfort in providing this help;

TABLE 2.1
Summary of Study Characteristics

Variables	Sample with known effect sizes	All reports[a]
Continuous variables[b]		
Mdn publication year	1975.46	1975.62
Mdn no. of subjects	159.88	119.94
M percentage of male authors	75.97 (69.37/82.57)	75.88 (70.89/80.86)
M sex differences in judgments of helping behaviors		
Competence[c]	0.06 (−0.02/0.14)	0.00 (−0.05/0.06)
Comfort	−0.07 (−0.15/0.00)	−0.13 (−0.18/−0.08)
Danger	0.11 (0.06/0.16)	0.09 (0.06/0.12)
Own behavior	−0.02 (−0.10/0.06)	−0.07 (−0.12/−0.02)
Stereotypic[d]	−0.09 (−0.22/0.05)	−0.21 (−0.30/−0.12)
Categorical variables[e]		
Setting[f]	16/36/47	41/58/84
Surveillance[g]	41/42/16	77/79/25
Availability of other helpers[h]	42/57	73/108
Type of appeal[i]	59/40	109/72
Identity of victim/requester[j]	24/18/34/6/15/2	48/37/55/8/26/7

Note. Table from Eagly and Crowley (1986). *n* = 99 for "Sample with known effect sizes" column. *n* = 181 for "All reports" column.

[a]Sample includes studies for which effect sizes were calculable and studies for which they were not. Studies reporting only the direction of the effect size were excluded.

[b]Values in parentheses are 95% confidence intervals.

[c]Values are positive for differences expected to be associated with greater helping by men (greater male estimates of competence, of comfort, and of own likelihood of helping; greater female estimate of danger to self).

[d]Values are positive when questionnaire respondents believed men were more helpful than women.

[e]Entries are numbers of reports found within each category. Reports that could not be classified because the attribute was varied in the study were placed in the middle category for setting and surveillance and in the first category for availability of other helpers and type of appeal.

[f]Categories are laboratory/campus/off-campus.

[g]Categories are no surveillance/unclear/surveillance.

[h]Categories are not available or unclear/available.

[i]Categories are direct request/presentation of need.

[j]Categories are male/female/sex-varied/same-sex-as-subject/collective/unclear.

and (c) the danger they would face if they provided this help.[6] As shown by the confidence intervals associated with these means, only the danger sex difference differed significantly from 0.00 (the value indicating exactly no sex difference) for the studies with known effect sizes: Women estimated they would face more danger from helping than men estimated they themselves would face. For the larger sample of studies, this danger sex difference was also significant, and in addition, women rated themselves as significantly more comfortable in helping than men did.

The last two continuous variables in Table 2.1 reflect questionnaire respondents' judgments of the likelihood that the helping behaviors would be performed. Sex differences in these judgments proved significant only for the larger sample of studies: Female respondents judged themselves more likely to help than male respondents judged themselves, and respondents of both sexes judged the average woman more likely to help than the average man.

The summaries of the categorical variables appear next in Table 2.1. The studies were more often conducted in field settings (off-campus or on) than in laboratory settings. The potential helpers usually were either not under surveillance by anyone other than the victim or requester or it was unclear whether such surveillance occurred. Studies were more evenly distributed in relation to the next two variables—availability of other helpers and type of appeal. For identity of victim or requester, common arrangements were male targets, female targets, targets who varied by sex, or collective targets (e.g., charities).

Summary of Sex-of-Subject Differences

The summary of the sex-of-subject effect sizes in Table 2.2 allows one to determine whether there is an overall sex difference in helping, based on the available reports. A mean effect size that differs significantly from the 0.00 value that indicates exactly no difference suggests an overall sex difference. The mean of the known effect sizes differed from 0.00 in the direction of greater helping by men than women. Weighting each known effect size by the reciprocal of its variance (Hedges & Olkin, 1985), a procedure that gives more weight to effect sizes that are more

---

[6]These variables can be viewed as examining the study-quality consideration of the extent to which studies utilized sex-typed tasks (e.g., changing a tire). Thus, the extent of sex-typing of experimental tasks was assessed by sex differences in respondents' beliefs about competence, comfort, and danger. Individual studies utilizing a sex-typed task can be viewed as generating findings that have limited generalizability. More importantly, whether the overall sex difference that is aggregated across studies (see Table 2.2) lacks generalizability because tasks tended to be sex-typed in the male or female direction in the literature as a whole can be estimated by the mean level of task sex-typing for the studies (see Table 2.1).

reliably estimated, yielded the largest mean effect size in the male direction.[7]

There is no completely satisfactory method for computing a mean effect size that takes into account the nonsignificant effects that could not be calculated because of a lack of sufficient information. Nevertheless, one possible solution is to give these nonsignificant effects the value of 0.00 (indicating exactly no sex difference). When this step was taken, the mean (unweighted) effect size decreased, but remained significant, again in the male direction. This mean is reported in Table 2.2, under "All reports."

As Table 2.2 shows, the conclusion that men helped more than women was supported by counting test results (see Rosenthal, 1978), demonstrating that .62, the proportion of reports indicating a sex difference in the male direction (disregarding significance) departed significantly from .50, the proportion expected under the null hypothesis. As Table 2.2 also shows, greater helping by men than by women was also consistent with a second counting test, which demonstrated that .15, the proportion of reports indicating a significant sex difference in the male direction, departed significantly from .025, the proportion expected under the null hypothesis.

Homogeneity of Effect Sizes

Although the aggregated sex differences in Table 2.2 are of interest in relation to the social-role theory predictions, their importance can be questioned in view of inconsistency of the findings across the studies. Calculation of a homogeneity statistic, Q, which has an approximate chi-square distribution with $k - 1$ degrees of freedom, where k is the number of effect sizes (Hedges, 1981; Hedges & Olkin, 1985), indicated that the hypothesis that the known effect sizes were homogeneous was rejected, $Q = 1,813.45, p < .001$. Therefore, study attributes were used to account for variability in the sex differences. Prediction was attempted only for the 99 known effect sizes, because the 0.00 values used to estimate the nonsignificant effects that could not be calculated are too inexact to warrant attempting to fit statistical models.

Tests of Categorical Models

This type of test of the relations between study attributes and the effect sizes is analogous to analysis of variance. Thus, Table 2.3 presents tests of the univariate categorical models that yielded significant between-class effects (analogous to *main effects* in an analysis of variance) for sex-of-

---

[7]Studies were thereby weighted according to one aspect of their quality—the reliability of the sex-difference finding.

TABLE 2.2
Summary of Sex-of-Subject Differences

Criterion	Values	
	Effect size analyses	
Known effect sizes ($n = 99$)		
M effect size (Md)	0.13	
95% CI for Md	0.03/0.23	
Mdn effect size	0.10	
M weighted effect size (d_+)[a]	0.34	
95% CI for d_+	0.32/0.36	
Total no. of subjects	37,308	
All reports ($n = 181$)		
M effect size (Md)	0.07	
95% CI for Md	0.02/0.13	
Total no. of subjects	48,945	
Counting methods		
	Frequencies	χ^2
Differences in the male direction[b]	63/101 (.62)	5.70*
Significant differences in the male direction[c]	28/181 (.15)	104.13[d]**

Note. Table from Eagly and Crowley (1986). When all reports were included, a value of 0.00 (exactly no difference) was assigned to sex differences that could not be calculated and were reported as nonsignificant. Effect sizes were calculated for all significant differences. Effect sizes are positive for differences in the male direction and negative for differences in the female direction. CI = confidence interval.
[a]Effect sizes were weighted by the reciprocal of the variance.
[b]Frequencies are number of differences in the male direction divided by the number of differences of known direction. The proportion appears in parentheses.
[c]Frequencies are the number of significant differences ($p < .05$, two-tailed) in the male direction divided by the total number of comparisons of known significance. The proportion appears in parentheses. Although there were 18 significant differences in the female direction, the statistical significance of this unpredicted outcome cannot be evaluated, given the one-tailed logic of these counting tests (see Rosenthal, 1978).
[d]Based on expected values of 5 and 176, or .03 and .97 of N.
*$p < .01$, one-tailed. **$p < .001$, one-tailed.

subject differences. In addition to a test of the significance of between-class effects, this approach provides a test of the homogeneity of the effect sizes within each class. If a categorical model were correctly specified (i.e., the data fit the model in the sense that the model sufficiently accounted for the systematic variation in effect sizes), it would yield a significant between-class effect and homogeneous effect sizes within each class. The between-class effect (e.g., the effect of the setting of the study) is estimated by Q_B, which has an approximate chi-square distribution with $p - 1$ degrees of freedom where p is the number of classes. The homogeneity of the effect sizes within each class (e.g., within laboratory settings) is estimated by Q_{W_i}, which has an approximate chi-square distribution with $m - 1$ degrees of freedom where m is the number of effect sizes in the class. Table 2.3 also includes (a) the mean effect size for each class, calculated with each effect size weighted by the reciprocal of its variance,[8] and (b) the 95% confidence interval for each mean.

Consistent with the significant between-class setting effect, post-hoc comparisons among the mean effect sizes for the three classes (Hedges & Becker, 1986; Hedges & Olkin, 1985) showed that the sex difference (in the male direction) in off-campus settings was larger than the sex difference in campus settings, which differed from the sex difference in the laboratory. Consistent with the significant between-class surveillance effect, the sex difference (in the male direction) with surveillance was larger than the sex

TABLE 2.3
Tests of Categorical Models for Sex-of-Subject Effect Sizes

Variable and class	Between-class effect (Q_B)	n	Weighted effect size (d_{i+})	95% CI for d_{i+} (lower/upper)	Homogeneity within each class (Q_{W_i})
Setting	587.74*				
Laboratory		16	-0.18	-0.28/0.09	40.28*
Campus		36	-0.04	-0.08/0.00	210.32*
Off-campus		47	0.50	0.48/0.53	975.11*
Surveillance	789.37*				
No surveillance		41	-0.02	-0.06/0.03	203.98*
Unclear		42	0.22	0.18/0.25	360.19*
Surveillance		16	0.74	0.70/0.77	459.90*
Availability of other helpers	93.74*				
Not available or unclear		42	0.20	0.17/0.24	369.55*
Available		57	0.42	0.39/0.44	1,350.15*
Type of appeal	498.20*				
Direct request		59	0.07	0.04/0.11	348.99*
Presentation of need		40	0.55	0.52/0.58	966.26*

Note. Table from Eagly and Crowley (1986). Effect sizes are positive for differences in the male direction and negative for differences in the female direction. CI = confidence interval.
[a]Significance indicates rejection of the hypothesis of homogeneity.
*$p < .001$.

---

[8]Again, studies were weighted according to one aspect of their quality—the reliability of the sex-difference finding. The model-testing procedures themselves can be viewed as exploring other study-quality considerations. For example, readers who think that laboratory studies are better than field studies (perhaps because laboratory studies are more controlled) or that field studies are better than laboratory studies (perhaps because field studies are more naturalistic) can examine the effects of the setting on the sex-difference outcomes of the studies.

difference when surveillance was unclear, which differed from the sex difference without surveillance. The remaining significant between-class effects showed that the tendency for men to help more than women was (a) greater when other helpers were available (or their availability was unclear) versus unavailable and (b) greater when the appeal was a presentation of a need versus a direct request.

Despite these highly significant between-class effects, none of these categorical models can be regarded as having fit the effect sizes. For each model, the hypothesis of homogeneity of the effect sizes was rejected within each class (see Table 2.3). In addition, the confidence intervals of the mean effect sizes showed that all of the category means indicating a sex difference in the male direction (a positive number), but none of the means indicating a sex difference in the female direction (a negative number), differed significantly from 0.00 and thus indicated a significant sex difference.

Tests of Continuous Models

Univariate and multivariate tests of continuous models for the sex-of-subject differences were also conducted (Hedges, 1982b; Hedges & Olkin, 1985). These models are least squares regressions, calculated with each effect size weighted by the reciprocal of its variance.[9] Each such model yields a test of the significance of each predictor as well as a test of model specification, which evaluates whether significant systematic variation remains unexplained by the regression model. The error sum of squares statistic, Q_E, which provides this test of model specification, has an approximate chi-square distribution with $k - p - 1$ degrees of freedom, where k is the number of effect sizes and p is the number of predictors (not including the intercept).

As Table 2.4 shows, univariate tests indicated that six of the continuous variables were significantly related to the sex-of-subject differences. The first of these variables, publication year, was related negatively to the magnitude of the effect sizes: Effect sizes were larger (i.e., greater tendency for men to help more than women) in the studies published at earlier dates. Effect sizes also were larger to the extent that the following sex differences were obtained in questionnaire respondents' judgments of the helping behaviors: Male (compared with female) respondents (a) rated themselves more competent to help; (b) rated themselves more comfortable in helping;

---

[9]This weighting takes study quality, defined as reliability of the sex-difference finding, explicitly into account in the model-testing procedure. Also, the tests of continuous models, like the tests of categorical models, can be viewed as explorations of other types of study-quality considerations because they estimate relationships between sex-difference findings and study attributes often considered to be quality-relevant.

TABLE 2.4
Tests of Continuous Models for Sex-of-Subject Effect Sizes

Variable	Univariate models		Multivariate model		Multivariate model with interactions	
	b	$b*$	b	$b*$	b	$b*$
Continuous variables						
1. Publication year	−.05***	−.34	−.01*	−.06		
2. Competence sex difference[a]	.58***	.45	.13**	.10		
3. Comfort sex difference	.27***	.28				
4. Danger sex difference	.72***	.39	.54***	.29		
5. Own behavior sex difference	.49***	.42				
6. Stereotypic sex difference[b]	.32***	.49				
Categorical variables						
7. Off-campus setting[c]			.34***	.34		
8. Laboratory setting[d]			−.16**	−.08		
9. Surveillance[e]			.06	.06		
10. No surveillance[f]			−.16***	−.15		
11. Availability of other helpers[g]			−.01	−.01		
12. Type of appeal[h]			.24***	.27		
Interaction terms						
13. Competence Sex Difference × Availability of Other Helpers					.54***	.3
14. Danger Sex Difference × Availability of Other Helpers					.55***	.2
Additive constant			.52		.44	
Multiple R			.80***		.83***	
SE of estimate			.27		.25	

Note. Table from Eagly and Crowley (1986). Models are weighted least squares regressions calculate with weights equal to the reciprocal of the variance for each effect size. b = unstandardized regressi coefficient. $b*$ = standardized regression coefficient. Effect sizes are positive for differences in male direction and negative for differences in the female direction. $n = 99$.
[a]Values are positive for differences expected to be associated with greater helping by men (greater m estimates of competence, of comfort, and of own likelihood of helping; greater female estimate of d ger to self).
[b]Values are positive when questionnaire respondents believed that men were more helpful than wom
[c]0 = campus or laboratory; 1 = off-campus.
[d]0 = campus or off-campus; 1 = laboratory.
[e]0 = no surveillance or unclear; 1 = surveillance.
[f]0 = surveillance or unclear; 1 = no surveillance.
[g]0 = not available or unclear; 1 = available.
[h]0 = direct request; 1 = presentation of need.
*$p < .05$. **$p < .01$. ***$p < .001$.

(c) estimated they faced less danger from helping; and (d) judged themselves more likely to help. Effect sizes also were larger to the extent that respondents of both sexes judged the average man more likely to help than the average woman. Despite highly significant relations, none of these models was correctly specified ($ps < .001$).

To examine the simultaneous impact of the continuous and categorical variables that were significant univariate predictors of effect sizes, various multivariate models were explored. For purposes of these analyses, the categorical variables were dummy-coded. The continuous variables constructed from questionnaire respondents' likelihood judgments were excluded from these models because they assessed, not study attributes, but respondents' abilities to predict helping behaviors. In addition, the sex difference in the respondents' comfort ratings was excluded because of its high correlation with the sex difference in their competence ratings, $r(97) = .81, p < .001$.

The first multivariate model in Table 2.4 entered publication year, competence sex difference, danger sex difference, and all of the categorical variables significant on a univariate basis. All of these predictors were significant, with the exception of surveillance and the availability of other helpers. The most substantial predictor in this model was the danger sex difference. As reflected in the multiple R of .80, this model was quite successful in accounting for variability in the magnitude of the effect sizes, although the test of model specification showed that it cannot be regarded as correctly specified, $Q_E = 665.35, p < .001$.

Further exploration showed that the sex differences in questionnaire respondents' ratings of competence, comfort, and danger predicted the effect sizes considerably better at some levels of the categorical variables than at others. Prediction from these ratings was especially effective when the setting was off-campus, the helper was under surveillance, other helpers were available, and the appeal to the helper was the presentation of a need. The effects of the resulting interactions are illustrated by the inclusion of the two largest interactions in the second multivariate model in Table 2.4.

This second model included the interactions of the competence and the danger sex differences with the availability of other helpers. Consistent with these interactions, when other helpers were available there was a strong tendency for effect sizes to be larger (i.e., more helping by men than women) to the extent that male (vs. female) respondents rated themselves more competent to help or as facing less danger from helping. When other helpers were not available, these relations between the effect sizes and the competence and the danger sex differences were considerably weaker. Consistent with the hierarchical analysis of interactions (see Cohen & Cohen, 1983), in this second model the main effects were partialed from the interactions but the interactions were not partialed from the main effects. Therefore, for this second model, regression coefficients for the main effects are not reported because they are not interpretable. The second model proved very successful in accounting for variability in the effect sizes, as shown by its multiple R of .83, although it also cannot be regarded as correctly specified, $Q_E = 568.10, p < .001$. Additional interaction terms were not added to this model because of the large number of predictors and the multicollinearity that resulted.

Additional Analyses

Additional analyses (see Eagly & Crowley, 1986) pertain to the subset of the studies that varied the sex of the victim or requester and reported a test of the impact of this manipulation on helping. The weighted mean of the 36 sex-of-victim/requester effect sizes that were available was −0.46 (95% CI = −0.49/−0.44), indicating that greater helping was received by women than by men. Because the hypothesis that these effect sizes were homogeneous was rejected, $Q = 761.09, p < .001$, study attributes were evaluated as predictors of the effect sizes. In general, the relations demonstrated between the various predictors and the sex-of-subject effect sizes also tended to be significant for the sex-of-victim/requester differences but opposite in sign. Thus, to the extent that men helped more than women, women received more help than men. In various models predicting the sex-of-victim/requester effect sizes, surveillance by persons other than the victim or requester emerged as the most substantial predictor: The tendency for women to be helped more than men was larger if the helper was under surveillance.

Twenty-five of the studies reported enough information to calculate sex-of-victim/requester effect sizes separately for male and female subjects and sex-of-subject effect sizes separately for male and female victims or requesters. These findings (see Eagly & Crowley, 1986) indicated that the men were significantly more likely to help women than other men, whereas the women were about as likely to help women or men. Also, the men were equally likely to receive help from women and men, whereas the women were more likely to receive help from men than women. In general, these findings showed that men helping women is an especially prevalent form of helping in this research literature.

DISCUSSION

Overall Sex Difference

Because social psychological studies of helping have been confined to short-term encounters with strangers, the social-role theory predicted that men should help more than women. This prediction followed from the contention that the male gender role fosters agentic forms of helping—

namely, chivalrous acts and nonroutine acts of rescuing, both of which are often directed toward strangers, whereas the female gender role fosters communal forms of helping—namely, acts of caring for others and tending to their needs, primarily in close or long-term relationships. Therefore, in general, the research literature on helping that has been constructed by social psychologists would tend to examine the kinds of helping that men display more than women and to omit many of the kinds of helping that women display more than men.

Consistent with this prediction, the mean weighted sex-of-subject effect size based on the known effect sizes was 0.34, or approximately one-third of a standard deviation in the direction of greater helping by men than women. Because the additional sex differences reported as nonsignificant that could not be estimated were no doubt smaller on the average than the known differences, 0.34 should be regarded as an upper bound of the aggregated sex-of-subject differences in the sample of studies.

Whether this mean effect size, which is one of the outcomes of the meta-analysis, yields a valid conclusion about the relative helpfulness of women and men is an issue that should be approached with considerable care. As explained in Chapter 1, such overall summaries warrant reduced emphasis when sex difference findings are inconsistent across studies, as very clearly is the case for helping behavior. Furthermore, the overall mean should be interpreted in the context of various possible threats to the validity of the sex difference it suggests. As explored in more depth in Chapter 5, threats to construct validity and external validity (i.e., generalizability) are of special concern. The findings of the helping meta-analysis suggest that the validity of the overall sex-difference findings was not compromised by disproportionate selection of helping behaviors congenial to men's skills (see Table 2.1). Instead, the overriding validity issue is the exclusive focus of the helping literature on interactions with strangers in short-term encounters. The elevation of women's danger ratings relative to those of men (see Table 2.1) no doubt reflects the use of these contexts. Because of the omission of helping in close and long-term relationships, no general conclusion can be drawn about the relative helpfulness of women and men.

In summary, one major finding of this meta-analysis is that the overall tendency in the helping-behavior literature is for men to be more helpful than women. This finding is fascinating because it seems counterstereotypic—women are believed to be more helpful than men. Although the discrepancy between this finding and the overall stereotype is understandable in terms of the very specialized selection of social contexts in helping research, the counterstereotypic quality of the overall trend seems to have prevented it from being discovered by narrative reviewers. Maccoby and Jacklin (1974) and Piliavin and Unger (1985) provided partial reviews of research on sex differences in helping behavior yet did not report a general tendency for either sex to be especially helpful.

Although narrative reviewers might be faulted for failing to note the overall sex-difference trend, they should be praised for emphasizing other considerations, in view of the great variability of findings in helping research. Because the effect sizes in the present meta-analysis were extremely heterogeneous, mean effect sizes implying an overall sex difference are much less important than successful prediction of variability in the magnitude of the effect sizes. Helping is a behavior for which a relatively small mean sex-difference effect size can be created by averaging very heterogeneous effect sizes, some of which are in fact quite large.

Social Roles and the Prediction of Sex Differences in Helping

The social-role theory of sex differences yielded a number of hypotheses that were tested meta-analytically. The success of these predictions provides an index of the value of approaching sex differences in terms of social-role concepts.

The Male Gender Role.   The observation that the social-psychological literature has focused on the kinds of chivalrous and heroic acts supported by the male gender role suggested not only that men should be found more helpful than women on the average but also that this sex difference should be larger to the extent that (a) women perceived helping as more dangerous than men did; (b) an audience witnessed the helping act; and (c) other potential helpers were available. On a univariate basis, all three of these predictions were confirmed, although the availability of other helpers remained significant only as an interaction in the multivariate models.

The chivalry analysis suggested in addition that men should direct their helping acts toward women more than men. The sex-of-victim/requester effect sizes showed that in general, women received more help than men. More relevant to our chivalry prediction was the examination of these effect sizes separately for male and female subjects. These findings revealed that men helped women more than men, whereas women helped women and men to approximately the same extent.

Also relevant to chivalry is the finding that surveillance by on-lookers emerged as by far the strongest predictor of the sex-of-victim/requester effect sizes. Because an audience of on-lookers would generally be regarded as potential reinforcers of acts supportive of prevailing social norms, it is not surprising in terms of our chivalry analysis that women elicited an especially large amount of help under such conditions. Indeed, to the extent that the tendencies for men to be more helpful than women and for women to receive more help than men are enhanced by the presence of an audience, chivalrous and heroic behavior may be largely a product of social norms rather than ingrained motives or dispositions.

S ex Differences in Compliance and Assertiveness.   In terms of another aspect of the gender-role analysis, men's higher status in society leads people to expect them to be somewhat more dominant and assertive than women. As a consequence, when helping is assertive, men should help more than women. This status analysis also suggested that, when helping is compliant, women might help more than men. Yet, because in many studies other conditions favored helping by men (e.g., stranger relationships), the general tendency for men to help more than women merely decreased for compliant helping. Men were considerably more helpful than women when helping was elicited by the presentation of a need (and was therefore assertive) and only slightly more helpful than women when helping was elicited by a direct request (and was therefore compliant).

Sex Differences in Skills.   The role theory of sex differences also suggested that sex differences in skills should influence the sex-of-subject effect sizes. Consistent with this hypothesis, men helped more than women to the extent that male respondents believed themselves more competent and more comfortable in helping than female respondents believed themselves to be. It is also noteworthy that these skill-related factors as well as the sex difference in danger emerged as considerably more important predictors under some conditions than others. Most strikingly, these sex-typed determinants of helping were more important if other helpers were available. In contrast, if a potential helper was the only individual available to help, he or she tended to overcome limitations of sex-typed skills and vulnerability to danger. Similarly, sex-typed skills and vulnerability to danger tended to be important to the extent that the setting was off-campus, the helper was under surveillance, and the appeal was the presentation of a need. These findings suggest that in many natural settings, especially those with onlookers and multiple potential helpers and without direct appeals for help, people behave in ways that are markedly sex-typed, with men helping considerably more than women when sex-typed masculine skills are called for and when potential dangers are more threatening to women. Thus, these interaction findings also support the generalization that sex differences are quite large in some social contexts.[10]

Success of Predictions.   The success of the prediction of sex differences in helping behavior is striking. The study attributes were able to account for approximately 70% of the variability in the available findings.

---

[10]Also, sex differences in helping favored men less strongly in later publication years. However, publication year was itself correlated with various study attributes and was not a major predictor in the multivariate analyses (see Table 2.4). The effects of date of publication in this and other meta-analyses of sex differences are discussed further in Chapter 5.

In evaluating this figure, one should keep in mind that the tendency to help was typically assessed by single-act criteria of low reliability and that the research paradigms were extremely heterogenous, varying on many dimensions not represented by our predictor variables. In addition, the majority of the studies were conducted in field settings where it is difficult to control extraneous variables. These factors no doubt placed a ceiling on prediction.

The prediction achieved by the multivariate models can be compared with that achieved by the questionnaire respondents. For each helping behavior, these respondents estimated their own response as well as those of the average woman and man. The mean sex differences in these judgments, aggregated across all of the helping behaviors (see Table 2.1), were in the female direction and thus were inconsistent in direction with the overall sex difference in helping behavior (see Table 2.2). Perhaps the general stereotype that women are helpful biased these judgments somewhat in favor of women. Nevertheless, *across studies* the magnitude of sex differences in these judgments predicted moderately well the effect sizes that estimated sex differences in helping (see Table 2.4). Although it should be recalled that these judgments were aggregated over the respondents, the fact that these judgments predicted study-level sex differences as well as they did suggests that people have reasonably good implicit theories of the conditions under which men and women help (see Chapter 5). In making intuitive predictions about helping, people are quite adept at taking into account the particular features of the situation and the helping act. The implicit theories that allow people to make these predictions no doubt would have fared even better if the respondents had access to a full range of cues instead of short descriptions of the helping acts. Still, consistent with the literature on statistical and intuitive prediction (e.g., Meehl, 1954), these implicit theories fared less well than the multivariate models, which excluded respondents' estimates of their own and others' behavior.

Conclusion

The social psychological literature on helping behavior has been limited almost exclusively to supererogatory helping of strangers in brief encounters that often hold potential dangers for helpers. This narrow focus is restrictive with respect to drawing conclusions about sex differences in helping because many of the types of helping excluded from this literature are carried out primarily by women, within the family and other close or long-term relationships. Thus, the care that researchers have taken to study behavior in situations that are relatively uncontaminated by the specific roles that regulate helping in natural settings constricts the lens through which helping behavior is seen so that only helping between strangers can be viewed. Whether an agentic bias is present in social psychologists' construction of helping primarily as acts of rescuing and civility that take place between strangers is an issue that I explore in a wider context in Chapter 5 of this book.

Finally, this meta-analysis demonstrates the value of social-role theory in accounting for variability in sex differences in social behavior. Hypotheses concerning the effects of several variables on sex differences in helping strangers were derived from the role framework, and most were supported. Although numerous other approaches have been proposed for explaining altruism, including biological theories (e.g., Hoffman, 1981; Trivers, 1971), it is doubtful that they can account for the extraordinary variability of sex differences in helping as successfully as these social psychological variables.

3 Sex Differences in Aggressive Behavior

The existence in social psychology of a large research literature on aggressive behavior makes it possible to examine sex differences in another important class of social behaviors. Aggression has been defined by psychologists as behavior intended to inflict harm or injury on other people (e.g., Baron, 1977; Berkowitz, 1964), whereas helping, as explained in Chapter 2, has been regarded as behavior intended to provide aid or succor to others. Thus, because the intended effect of aggression is the opposite of that of helping, aggressive behavior provides an instructive contrast to helping behavior.

Together with Valerie Steffen, I undertook a quantitative review of the sex differences reported in the aggression literature (Eagly & Steffen, 1986a). Although these sex differences had been reviewed previously, most reviewers (e.g., Hyde, 1984, 1986; Maccoby & Jacklin, 1974, 1980) had focused primarily on children's aggressive behavior. Yet the tendency for males to be more aggressive than females is larger among children than adults in both psychological (Hyde, 1984) and the ethnographic (Rohner, 1976) research. Furthermore, the methods used to study aggression are quite different in the child and adult literatures. Therefore, reviews containing a substantial proportion of child studies not only provide larger estimates of sex differences in aggression than are valid for adults but also may emphasize determinants of aggression that are valid primarily for children. Our review, like Frodi, Macaulay, and Thome's (1977) narrative review, was limited to sex differences in adult aggression.

To insure comparability with other meta-analyses of sex differences in social behavior, we limited our sample to studies with behavioral measures and omitted studies that assessed aggressiveness by means of projective and other self-report measures. In the studies in this literature, adult subjects were exposed to a standardized situation designed to elicit aggressive behavior. Most such studies were conducted in experimental laboratories, although a substantial minority were conducted in field settings. In the laboratory-experimental tradition, there has been heavy reliance on a "teacher-learner" paradigm (e.g., Buss, 1963) in which college-student subjects take the role of a teacher who is required to deliver electric shock or other aversive stimuli to punish a learner for apparent errors. Within the field-experimental tradition, aggression has been elicited by exposing people to a mildly frustrating event such as someone cutting into line in front of them (e.g., M. B. Harris, 1974) or a driver not moving when a traffic light turns green (e.g., Doob & Gross, 1968). Similar to helping behavior, aggressive behavior has not been investigated in close personal relationships or organizational contexts, in either the laboratory or the field research tradition. Rather, aggression occurred during relatively brief encounters between strangers.

A SOCIAL-ROLE ANALYSIS OF SEX DIFFERENCES IN AGGRESSIVE BEHAVIOR

Like other social behaviors, aggression can be viewed as role behavior and therefore as regulated by the social norms that apply to people based on the roles they occupy (see also Lubek, 1979). To account for sex differences in aggression from this perspective, it is necessary to understand the ways in which aggression is sustained or inhibited by the social roles that are occupied mainly or exclusively by persons of each sex. Following from the theoretical analysis in Chapter 1, gender roles are one important class of social roles in this discussion. Yet other roles, if they are occupied primarily by one sex (e.g., military roles; homemaker role), can also underlie sex differences in aggressive behavior in a variety of natural settings and, through the mediation of sex-typed skills and beliefs, can underlie sex differences in research settings as well.

Gender Roles and Aggression

Because the social-role analysis suggests that gender roles often underlie sex differences manifested in research settings, it is important to determine whether expectations about aggressiveness are included in gender roles. First I consider the implications of the male role for aggressiveness, and then the implications of the female role.

The Male Gender Role.   The male gender role includes norms encouraging many forms of aggression. Psychologists and popular writers who have analyzed the male gender role have claimed that men are expected to be tough, violent, and aggressive. To validate this idea, some writers (e.g., Fasteau, 1974) have pointed to the prevalence of aggressiveness among male heroes in literature and the popular culture. Following from Chapter 1's theoretical analysis, it is relevant to note that psychologists' studies of stereotypes about men have documented more systematically that people expect men to be aggressive (see the review by Cicone & Ruble, 1978). Similarly, research on gender stereotypes has shown that men are rated as more aggressive than women and as more extreme on related qualities such as assertiveness and competitiveness (e.g., Broverman et al., 1972; Ruble, 1983; Spence & Helmreich, 1978). In support of the interpretation that these beliefs about aggressiveness are normative, gender-stereotype research has also established that aggressiveness and related qualities are considered more desirable in men than women. Moreover, the more favorable attitudes that men have been shown to hold toward aggressive and violent behavior suggest that men tend to have internalized the positive value the male gender role places on aggression. Thus, Smith's (1984) review of public opinion findings showed that men hold more positive attitudes than women concerning aggression in realms as diverse as international relations and war, social control and law enforcement, interpersonal relations, and the portrayal of violence on television (see also Shapiro & Mahajan, 1986).

Despite evidence suggesting that aggressiveness is a component of the male gender role, this role may also include norms that foster some behaviors incompatible with aggression. Specifically, as argued in Chapter 2, the traditional male role encompasses norms of chivalry as well as aggressiveness. The ideology of chivalry stipulates that men should protect the weak and defenseless and be courteous and protective to subordinates. Rules of chivalry temper male aggressiveness, at least toward subordinates, within certain social contexts. Furthermore, despite little empirical evidence for overall change in gender-role norms about communal and agentic behavior (see Chapter 1), it is worth noting that some psychologists (e.g., Pleck, 1981) have argued for the importance of less traditional forms of the male gender role that de-emphasize aggressiveness and support communal qualities such as sensitivity to other people and emotional expressiveness.

The Female Gender Role.   The traditional female gender role places little emphasis on aggressiveness. Also, the primacy that this role gives to caring and other communal qualities (see Chapter 2) may favor behaviors incompatible with aggressiveness toward other people. In addition, as also noted in Chapter 2, the female gender role emphasizes avoiding physical harm to oneself. In particular, rules of caution and avoidance of strangers, intended in part to lessen the possibility that girls and women will be victims of sexual assault (e.g., see U.S. Department of Justice, 1979), may lead women to be less aggressive than men in situations in which physical retaliation is likely.

Although the lack of empirical evidence for general change in gender roles must again be noted, it is probably important that less traditional forms of the female gender role include an emphasis on assertiveness, a quality advocated by feminists. Assertiveness, although popularly regarded as synonymous with aggressiveness, has often been distinguished from it by proponents of assertiveness training (e.g., Bloom, Coburn, & Pearlman, 1975; Fensterheim & Baer, 1975). Advocates of assertiveness have emphasized the lack of harmful intent underlying assertive behaviors versus the presence of such intent underlying aggressive behaviors. Nevertheless, the support for women's assertiveness in recent years suggests that the female gender role, like the male gender role, conveys complex messages about aggression and related behaviors. This complexity could be explored in terms of the particularistic aspects of gender roles discussed in Chapter 1. For example, a possible hypothesis is that the assertive, feminist woman, and perhaps the gentle, sensitive man as well, are gender subtypes admired in some subcultures in American society, but regarded unfavorably by a majority of Americans.

Other Social Roles and Aggression

In natural settings, some aggressive behaviors are more common in one sex because they are aspects, not of gender roles, but of specific social roles occupied primarily by that sex. Yet such specific roles may affect sex differences displayed in research settings through the impact that prior enactment of such roles has on role occupants' skills and beliefs. Particularly important are military and athletic roles, because a substantial proportion of all males occupy such roles sometime during their lives and therefore receive important socialization in aggressiveness in these contexts.

As Arkin and Dobrofsky (1978) argued, military roles foster a number of traditionally masculine values. Aggressiveness is central among these values. Yet military aggressiveness is supposed to be expressed only within defined limits and only toward military enemies. Nevertheless, military indoctrination may transmit an ideology that legitimizes a wide range of aggressive behaviors.

Participation in competitive sports may also promote aggressive behavior as well as an ideology that supports aggressiveness (Stein & Hoffman, 1978). Because men are more likely than women to have gained experience in competitive sports, the behavior and the values fostered in athletic roles affect more men than women. Like military roles, athletic roles require a

Occupations

controlled aggressiveness, directed in this instance primarily toward opposing players and teams.

Various occupational roles may have implications for sex differences in aggression-relevant skills and beliefs as well as for aggressive behaviors carried out in natural settings. Although, aside from the military, most occupations pursued disproportionately by men lack such clear-cut implications for aggressiveness, managerial roles in business and industry may incorporate an element of aggressiveness. The aggressive behavior typical of these roles is primarily directed externally toward rival companies, but a pattern of competitive (if not openly aggressive) behavior toward fellow employees is sometimes held to typify American managers (e.g., McClelland, 1961; Whyte, 1956).

Most occupations pursued disproportionately by women discourage aggressive behavior and emphasize some form of giving help to others. As already noted in Chapter 2, over half of all women in the paid labor force are in clerical and service occupations, and women with professional positions are predominantly teachers and nurses (U.S. Department of Labor, 1980). In addition, the domestic role emphasizes care-giving and other forms of personal service, although it does foster aggressive behavior in defense of one's children—a form of aggression that is very directly in the service of dependent others.

Finally, consistent with the analysis of status provided in Chapter 1, one aspect of social roles that may have general relevance to sex differences in aggressiveness is the distribution of the sexes into higher and lower status roles. On the average, men have higher status than women in organizations of all kinds and in the family (see Chapter 1). Although high status does not necessarily imply that an individual should behave aggressively, subordinate status enjoins many types of aggression, particularly aggression directed toward people of higher status.

Predictions about Overall Sex Differences and Variability Due to Contextual Variables

Overall Sex-of-Subject Difference.   The several aspects of the social-role analysis all suggest that the overall aggression sex difference would tend to be in the male direction, and past reviews have found such a difference. Nevertheless, as I have argued, both the female and the male gender roles incorporate norms that encourage and norms that discourage aggressiveness, even though the two roles very clearly differ in their emphasis. Consequently, sex differences in adult aggressive behavior may not be any larger than those established for other social behaviors. Furthermore, the magnitude of aggression sex differences should vary considerably across studies because of the complexities already noted in the ways social roles regulate aggression.

Effect of Contextual Variables on Sex Differences in Aggression.   The social-role framework directed attention to certain contextual features of studies of aggression. Most importantly, the hypothesis was tested that sex differences are larger for aggression causing pain or physical injury in the target person than for aggression causing psychological or social harm.[1] Interest in this hypothesis stemmed from its consistency with aspects of the social-role analysis. For example, the claim that the female role includes norms that discourage placing oneself in physical jeopardy suggests that women would avoid physical aggression, because of its greater likelihood of provoking physical retaliation. Also supporting the prediction of larger sex differences with physical versus psychological aggression is the argument that military and athletic roles emphasize primarily physical aggression.

Frodi et al. (1977) suggested that sex differences in aggression were little affected by whether aggression has physical or psychological effects. Yet Hyde (1986) found that the tendency for males to be more aggressive than females was nonsignificantly larger for physical than psychological aggression. Because Hyde's sample included few studies assessing psychological aggression, Valerie Steffen and I sought a larger sample to test the hypothesis of larger sex differences for physical than psychological aggression.

On an exploratory basis, the meta-analysis also examined several other situational variables as correlates of sex differences in aggression. One such variable distinguishes whether subjects exercised freedom of choice about aggressing or were required to deliver an aggressive behavior (and therefore merely chose the intensity of the act). The amount of provocation or frustration that subjects faced was also examined. Strong external pressures in terms of either reduced freedom of choice or extreme provocation might outweigh gender-related normative factors and therefore lessen any sex differences.

Studies were also classified according to whether the aggressor was

---

[1]The distinction between physical and psychological aggression has appeared in more than one variant in the aggression literature. Some investigators (e.g., Buss, 1961) have distinguished between these two types of aggression based on the overtly physical versus vocal nature of the aggressor's act. Following Frodi et al. (1977), Valerie Steffen and I preferred to focus on the type of harm to the target. Yet Frodi and her collaborators labeled aggression causing psychological or social harm (e.g., hurt feelings, lowered self-esteem, damage to one's reputation) as *verbal aggression,* not psychological aggression. The term *psychological aggression* is preferable because it refers to type of harm and, unlike verbal aggression, it encompasses the nonverbal aggressive behaviors assessed in some of the studies that were reviewed. In the research literature on aggression, experimental situations typically allowed either psychological or physical aggression—not both.

likely to have been under surveillance by other people. An audience of onlookers might often increase the magnitude of sex differences in aggression, because it would make gender-role obligations salient (Richardson, Bernstein, & Taylor, 1979). In contrast, the possibility that surveillance by onlookers might reduce the likelihood of retaliation by the target suggests that the sex difference may be lessened by an audience, if it is true that women often avoid aggression that may lead to retaliation. Furthermore, the *absence* of surveillance by the *target* could also reduce the likelihood of retaliation and thereby lessen the sex difference, because a target cannot retaliate against an unknown or absent aggressor. The complexity of these considerations underscores the exploratory status of the surveillance variable in our meta-analysis.

Studies were also classified according to their laboratory or field setting, even though the variability of the field-experimental paradigms makes it difficult to predict the impact of this situational variable. Finally, the number of behaviors aggregated in the aggression measure was recorded for each study. For example, a "teacher-learner" experiment (e.g., Buss, 1963) in which the teacher is supposed to shock the learner for each of 36 mistakes provides an aggression measure aggregated over 36 behaviors. To the extent that measures were based on multiple observations over occasions or situations, they should yield more reliable estimates of sex differences.[2] The logic underlying this relation between the number of observations and the reliability of the sex difference is analogous to the relation between the number of items in a test and the reliability of the total test (e.g., Ghiselli, 1964). Reliable indicators of aggression should be more strongly related to subjects' sex and should yield more stable estimates of sex differences in aggression.

Effect of Sex Differences in Skills and Beliefs on Sex Differences in Aggression

To illuminate the psychological processes that may mediate the impact that prior participation in social roles has on the sex differences found in research settings, both the skills and the beliefs that roles impart should be considered. An analysis of aggression from the standpoint of skills suggests that people are able to behave aggressively to the extent that they have acquired the relevant skills. The skills needed to aggress effectively are often acquired primarily by one sex because people of this sex are more

---

[2]Because measures based on multiple observations should be more reliable, assessment of the number of behaviors aggregated in the aggression measure can be viewed as taking study quality into account. Methods of assessing study quality that duplicate those explained in the footnotes of Chapter 2 are not explained again in the present chapter.

likely to have occupied roles in which such skills are learned. For example, skills relevant to physical aggression may be more common in men than women because these skills are imparted in both military and athletic roles. However, despite the probable importance of aggressive skills in natural settings, sex differences in skills were not assessed in the meta-analysis because the particular behaviors examined in aggression research required very little in the way of specialized skills (see Eagly & Steffen's, 1986a, descriptions of these behaviors), and none of the aggressive behaviors involved strenuous physical combat.

An analysis of aggression from the standpoint of beliefs suggests that people behave aggressively to the extent that their beliefs about the consequences of aggression legitimize aggression and that people behave unaggressively to the extent that their beliefs inhibit aggression. In particular, the male gender role's emphasis on aggression may decrease the perceived likelihood of the negative outcomes of (a) guilt and anxiety about causing people to suffer and (b) harm to others. In contrast, the female gender role's emphasis on caring and concern for others' welfare may increase the perceived likelihood of (a) guilt and anxiety about causing people to suffer and (b) harm to others. These differing reactions may stem from specific social roles as well. For example, military and athletic roles may foster beliefs that support aggression, whereas caring roles such as homemaker and nurse foster beliefs that inhibit aggression.

Consistent with this reasoning about sex differences in the perceived consequences of aggression, research has repeatedly demonstrated that women report more guilt and anxiety about behaving aggressively than men do (see Frodi et al., 1977). This sex difference in guilt and anxiety may underlie a sex difference in aggression, if, as Frodi et al. argued, guilt and anxiety about aggression are negatively associated with the tendency to aggress. Therefore, in the meta-analysis, the magnitude of sex differences in aggression was expected to be positively associated with the tendency for women (vs. men) to view an aggressive behavior as causing themselves more guilt and anxiety.

Beliefs about harming others are usually discussed in terms of empathy with the targets of aggression. As already noted in Chapter 2, several scholars have argued that females are generally more empathic or sympathetic than males (e.g., Feshbach, 1982; Hoffman, 1977), yet Eisenberg and Lennon (1983) showed that this sex difference has been obtained primarily when demand characteristics or gender-role obligations are salient. With respect to the specific hypothesis that women's greater empathy mediates sex differences in aggressiveness, Frodi et al. (1977) reported mixed empirical support. This mixed support may well be consistent with the role-theory assumption that only some situations elicit more empathy in women than men, and in these situations men are more aggressive than women. Such an interpretation suggests that the magnitude of sex differences in aggression should be positively associated with the tendency for women (vs. men) to view an aggressive behavior as causing more harm to others.

Another likely sex difference in beliefs about the consequences of aggression is a tendency for women to believe that their aggressive behaviors pose dangers to themselves, for example, from retaliation by the target. As discussed in Chapter 2, the female gender role may include norms discouraging women from placing themselves in physical jeopardy. In contrast, in various male-dominated roles, especially in the military and in athletics, people may learn to disregard possible harm to themselves. As a result, the magnitude of aggression sex differences would be correlated with the tendency of women to perceive their aggressive behaviors as more dangerous to themselves than men do. Consistent with this logic, the review of helping behavior reported in Chapter 2 showed that men were more helpful than women to the extent that women perceived their helping behaviors as more dangerous to themselves than men did.

In summary, the overall prediction for the research literature on aggression is that men are more aggressive than women. Yet, the social-role analysis suggests that this sex difference should be quite variable across studies. As explained, features of social settings as well as differences between women's and men's beliefs about the consequences of aggressive acts should predict the magnitude of the sex differences.

METHOD FOR META-ANALYSIS[3]

Sample of Studies

Studies were located primarily through computer searches and examination of relevant bibliographies and were included in the sample if they met the following criteria: (a) the dependent variable was an aggressive behavior directed toward another person; (b) the reported results were sufficient to calculate a sex-of-subject effect size or to determine the statistical significance and/or direction of the sex difference; and (c) the subjects were female and male adults or adolescents from the United States or Canada who were not sampled from specialized populations (e.g., criminals, mental hospital patients). Studies were omitted if the process by which female and male subjects had been selected equalized their status on a personality variable that has been found to correlate with both sex and aggression. The sex difference in aggression could not be accurately esti-

---

[3]See Eagly and Steffen (1986a) for a detailed description of the method as well as a list of the studies and aggressive behaviors included in the sample.

mated in studies with such a selection process.[4] The resulting sample (see Eagly & Steffen, 1986a) consisted of 63 studies, which yielded 81 sex-of-subject reports.

Variables Coded from Each Study

The following information was recorded for each report: (a) date of publication; (b) source of publication (journal; other source); (c) percentage of male authors; (d) sex of first author; (e) sample size (male, female, and total). In addition, the following variables were coded from the information provided: (a) number of behaviors or responses aggregated in the aggression measure; (b) setting (laboratory; field); (c) type of aggression (physical, including shocking, delivering noxious noise, and hitting; psychological, including vocal, nonverbal, and written); (d) surveillance of aggressive act (private, i.e., not under anyone's immediate surveillance, e.g., questionnaire ratings; semiprivate, i.e., accessible to target and/or experimenter; public, i.e., accessible to additional onlookers); (e) freedom of choice to aggress (aggression required; free choice); (f) amount of provocation (minimal, i.e., impediment to subject's progress; greater than minimal, including insult, physical harm, violation of rights, assignment of impossible task, and blockage of opportunity to win money); (g) sex of target of aggression (male; female; varied; same sex as subject).[5] These variables were coded by two raters, who agreed on 85%–100% of their judgments, depending on the variable. Disagreements were resolved by discussion.

---

[4]This exclusion (and others, see Eagly & Steffen, 1986a) can be seen as implementing study-quality criteria.

[5]Whether aggression was direct (i.e., the target of aggression was the person who instigated anger or provoked aggression) or indirect (i.e., the target was neither instigator nor provoker) was not coded, because the exclusion of studies with self-report and projective measures removed most instances of indirect aggression. Although Frodi et al. (1977) considered negative written evaluations of instigating or provoking persons to be indirect aggression (e.g., Feshbach, 1955), such aggression was considered direct by Eagly and Steffen (1986a) because in most studies these evaluations were presumed to be available to supervisory personnel, and often to the instigator or provoker at some later point. Also, the extent to which aggression was justified was not coded because (a) most studies provided some justification for aggression, such as its value in teaching a learner; (b) justification usually did not vary with degree of aggression (e.g., magnitude and duration of shock delivered), which constituted the dependent variable in most studies; and (c) to the extent that high levels of aggression were justified, such justification usually followed from provocation of the subject, a variable included in the meta-analysis.

Variables Derived from Questionnaire Respondents'
Judgments of Aggressive Behaviors

A questionnaire study was conducted to generate measures of the extent to which each aggressive behavior elicited sex differences in (a) beliefs about the consequences of aggression and (b) the perceived likelihood of aggression. The likelihood measures were included to evaluate how well respondents' beliefs about their own and others' behavior predicted the aggression sex differences obtained in the research literature.

Each of the 200 respondents completed a questionnaire that contained brief descriptions of half of the aggressive behaviors investigated in the studies used in the meta-analysis. For example, Buss's (1963) study was described as "Choosing at least moderately painful electric shocks to administer to an adult pupil sitting out of view; you are a subject in a psychological experiment in which you are to choose the level of electric shock to administer for mistakes on a task that you have been assigned to teach the person." Doob and Gross's (1968) study was described as "Honking at least once at a man driving a car stopped at a traffic light in front of you on a Sunday when there is not much traffic; this car did not start moving after the light turned green."

Respondents judged these behaviors in response to three questions assessing beliefs about aggression: (a) How harmful would this act be to the person it is directed toward? (b) How much anxiety or guilt would you feel if you enacted this behavior? (c) How much danger would you probably face if you enacted this behavior? Respondents also judged these behaviors in response to three likelihood questions: (a) How likely is it that you would enact this behavior? (b) How likely is it that the average woman would enact this behavior? (c) How likely is it that the average man would enact this behavior? These ratings were made on 15-point scales.

Analysis of Ratings.   For the first four of the six questions just listed, mean scores for each aggressive behavior were computed separately for female and male respondents. For each behavior, the female mean was subtracted from the male mean to yield a mean sex difference, which was then standardized by dividing it by the pooled (within-sex) standard deviation. For the last two questions, the respondents' mean rating of the average woman for each behavior was subtracted from their mean rating of the average man to yield a mean stereotypic sex difference, which was then standardized by dividing it by the standard deviation of the differences between the paired ratings.

Computation and Analysis of Effect Sizes

The statistical significance and/or direction of the 81 reported sex-of-subject differences was recorded, and an effect size, d, was calculated for the behaviors for which sufficient information was provided. When sufficient additional information was available, these procedures were also carried out for sex-of-target differences as well as for the simple effects of (a) sex of subject for female and male targets and (b) sex of target for female and male subjects. The procedures for analyzing the effect sizes were the same as those described in Chapter 2.

RESULTS OF META-ANALYSIS

Characteristics of Studies

As a first step, it is informative to examine the characteristics of the studies from which conclusions about sex differences in aggression are drawn. Table 3.1 shows these study characteristics, summarized separately for (a) the studies for which effect sizes could be calculated and (b) the larger sample of studies, which included studies with calculable effect sizes and studies that reported a nonsignificant sex difference but did not provide information sufficient to compute an effect size. The first nine characteristics are *continuous variables,* and the remaining six are *categorical variables.*

As shown by the central tendencies of the first four continuous variables in Table 3.1, the studies usually (a) were published relatively recently, (b) involved moderate numbers of subjects, (c) were somewhat more likely to have male than female authors, and (d) assessed aggression by an index that aggregated a moderate number of behaviors. The means for the next three continuous variables in Table 3.1 represent the sex differences in questionnaire respondents' beliefs about the consequences of aggression. As shown by the confidence intervals associated with these means, for both samples of studies all of these sex differences differed significantly from 0.00 (the value indicating exactly no sex difference). Thus, women estimated that the aggressive acts would cause more harm to the target than men did. Women (compared with men) also estimated that they would experience more anxiety or guilt and would face more danger from aggressing.

The last two continuous variables in Table 3.1 reflect questionnaire respondents' judgments of the likelihood that the aggressive behaviors would be performed. For both samples of studies, female respondents judged themselves significantly less likely to aggress than male respondents judged themselves, and respondents of both sexes judged the average woman considerably less likely to aggress than the average man.

TABLE 3.1
Summary of Study Characteristics

Variables	Sample with known effect sizes	All reports[a]
Continuous variables[b]		
Mdn publication year	1974.67	1974.38
Mdn no. of subjects	84.50	90.20
M percentage of male	58.50	58.34
authors	(45.66/71.34)	(47.97/68.71)
Mdn no. of behaviors		
aggregated	10.00	7.75
M sex differences in judgments of aggressive behaviors		
Harm[c]	0.09	0.09
	(0.04/0.15)	(0.05/0.13)
Guilt/anxiety	0.34	0.33
	(0.28/0.40)	(0.28/0.38)
Danger	0.20	0.25
	(0.17/0.24)	(0.21/0.29)
Own behavior	0.31	0.31
	(0.26/0.37)	(0.27/0.35)
Stereotypic[d]	0.84	0.80
	(0.77/0.90)	(0.75/0.86)
Categorical variables[e]		
Setting[f]	13/37	26/51
Type of aggression[g]	20/30	42/35
Surveillance[h]	6/30/14	13/43/21
Freedom of choice to aggress[i]	27/23	50/27
Amount of provocation[j]	29/21	50/27
Sex of target[k]	4/14/19/13	6/22/31/18

Note. Table from Eagly and Steffen (1986a). $n = 50$ for "Sample with known effect sizes" column. $n = 77$ for "All reports" column.

[a]Sample includes studies for which effect sizes were calculable and studies for which they were not. Studies reporting only the direction of the sex difference were excluded.

[b]Values in parentheses are 95% confidence intervals.

[c]Values are positive for differences expected to be associated with greater aggression by men (greater female estimates of harm to others, of guilt and anxiety, and of danger to self; greater male estimate of own likelihood of aggressing).

[d]Values are positive when questionnaire respondents believed men were more aggressive than women.

[e]Entries are numbers of reports found within each category.

[f]Categories are field/laboratory.

[g]Categories are psychological/physical.

[h]Categories are private/semiprivate/public.

[i]Categories are free choice/aggression required.

[j]Categories are greater-than-minimal/minimal.

[k]Categories are female/male/varied/same-as-subject.

The summaries of the categorical variables appear next in Table 3.1. The studies were more often conducted in laboratory than in field settings. Psychological and physical aggression were both commonly assessed. Subjects usually were under surveillance either by only the target and/or experimenter (semiprivate), or by additional onlookers (public). Somewhat more studies allowed subjects to choose freely between aggressive and other types of behaviors versus required them to engage in an aggressive behavior. Somewhat more studies involved greater-than-minimal versus minimal amounts of provocation of the aggressor. Designs rarely included only female targets.

Summary of Sex-of-Subject Differences

The summary of the sex-of-subject effect sizes in Table 3.2 allows one to determine whether there is an overall sex difference in aggression, based on the available reports. A mean effect size that differs significantly from the 0.00 value that indicates exactly no difference suggests an overall sex difference. The mean of the known effect sizes differed from 0.00 in the direction of more aggression by men than women. Weighting each known effect size by the reciprocal of its variance (Hedges & Olkin, 1985), a procedure that gives more weight to effect sizes that are more reliably estimated, yielded a significant mean effect size in the male direction that was smaller than the unweighted mean.

As also noted in Chapter 2, there is no completely satisfactory method to compute a mean effect size that takes into account the nonsignificant effects that could not be calculated because of a lack of sufficient information. When these nonsignificant effects were given the value of 0.00 (indicating exactly no sex difference), the mean (unweighted) effect size became smaller but remained significant in the male direction. This mean is reported in Table 3.2, under "All reports."

As Table 3.2 shows, the conclusion that men aggressed more than women was supported by counting test results (Rosenthal, 1978) demonstrating that .89, the proportion of reports indicating a sex difference in the male direction (disregarding significance) departed significantly from .50, the proportion expected under the null hypothesis. As Table 3.2 also shows, greater aggression by men than women was also consistent with a second counting test, which demonstrated that .34, the proportion of reports indicating a significant sex difference in the male direction, departed significantly from .025, the proportion expected under the null hypothesis.

TABLE 3.2
Summary of Sex-of-Subject Differences

Criterion	Values
Effect size analyses	
Known effect sizes ($n = 50$)	
M effect size ($M\,d$)	0.40
95% *CI* for $M\,d$	(0.28/0.51)
Mdn effect size	0.43
M weighted effect size $(d_+)^a$	0.29
95% *CI* for d_+	(0.24/0.34)
Total no. of subjects	4,879
All reports ($n = 77$)	
M effect size ($M\,d$)	0.26
95% *CI* for $M\,d$	(0.17/0.34)
Total no. of subjects	6,524

Counting methods		
	Frequencies	*Exact p*
Differences in the male direction[b]	50/56 (.89)	< .001
Significant differences in the male direction[c]	26/77 (.34)	< .001

Note. Table from Eagly and Steffen (1986a). When all reports were included, a value of 0.00 (exactly no difference) was assigned to sex differences that could not be calculated and were reported as nonsignificant. Effect sizes were calculated for all significant differences. Effect sizes are positive for differences in the male direction and negative for differences in the female direction. CI = confidence interval.
[a]Effect sizes were weighted by the reciprocal of the variance.
[b]Frequencies are the number of differences in the male direction divided by the number of differences of known direction. The proportion appears in parentheses. Exact p (one-tailed) is based on the binomial distribution with $p = .5$ (Harvard University Computation Laboratory, 1955).
[c]Frequencies are the number of significant differences ($p < .05$, two-tailed), in the male direction divided by the total number of comparisons of known significance. The proportion appears in parentheses. Exact p (one-tailed) is based on the binomial distribution with $p = .025$ (Robertson, 1960). There was 1 significant difference in the female direction.

Homogeneity of Effect Sizes

Although the aggregated sex differences given in Table 3.2 are of interest in relation to the predictions, their importance can be questioned in view of the inconsistency of the findings across the studies. Calculation of a homogeneity statistic Q, which has an approximate chi-square distribution with $k - 1$ degrees of freedom where k is the number of effect sizes (Hedges, 1982a; Hedges & Olkin, 1985), indicated that the hypothesis that the known effect sizes were homogeneous was rejected, $Q = 202.44$, $p < .001$.

Therefore, study attributes were used to account for variability in the sex differences. Prediction was attempted only for the 50 known effect sizes.

Tests of Categorical Models

Table 3.3 presents tests of the univariate categorical models that yielded significant between-class effects (see Chapter 2 for a description of this type of analysis). Significant between-class effects showed that the tendency for men to aggress more than women was greater in laboratory than in field settings and for physical versus psychological aggression. Consistent with the significant between-class surveillance effect, post-hoc comparisons among the mean effect sizes for the three classes showed that the sex difference in semiprivate contexts (target and/or experimenter present) was larger than the sex difference in public contexts (additional onlookers present), and marginally larger than the sex difference in private contexts. Also, the tendency for men to aggress more than women was significantly larger when aggression was required rather than freely chosen.

Despite these significant between-class effects, none of these categorical models can be regarded as having fit the effect sizes. For each model, the hypothesis of homogeneity of the effect sizes was rejected within each

TABLE 3.3
Tests of Categorical Models for Sex-of-Subject Effect Sizes

Variable and class	Between-class effect (Q_B)	n	Weighted effect size (d_{i+})	95% CI for d_{i+} (lower/upper)	Homogeneity within class $(Q_{W_i})^a$
Setting	7.89**				
Field		13	0.21	0.13/0.28	99.18***
Laboratory		37	0.35	0.28/0.42	95.37***
Type of aggression	19.27***				
Psychological		20	0.18	0.10/0.25	112.51***
Physical		30	0.40	0.33/0.47	70.66***
Surveillance	11.96**				
Private		6	0.17	0.00/0.34	8.01
Semiprivate		30	0.38	0.31/0.45	82.23***
Public		14	0.21	0.14/0.29	100.25***
Freedom of choice to aggress	5.62*				
Free choice		27	0.24	0.18/0.30	145.39***
Agression required		23	0.37	0.28/0.45	51.42***

Note. Table from Eagly and Steffen (1986a). Effect sizes are positive for differences in the male direction and negative for differences in the female direction. CI = confidence interval.
^aSignificance indicates rejection of the hypothesis of homogeneity.
*$p < .05$. **$p < .01$. ***$p < .001$.

class, except for one category containing only six effect sizes (the private category of the surveillance variable, see Table 3.3). With the exception of this same category, all of the category means differed from 0.00 and thus indicated a significant sex difference in the male direction. No category mean was positive, which would indicate a difference in the female direction.

Tests of Continuous Models

Univariate and multivariate tests of continuous models (see Chapter 2) for the sex-of-subject differences were also conducted. As Table 3.4 shows, univariate tests indicated that six of the continuous variables were significantly related to the sex-of-subject differences. The first of these variables, the number of behaviors aggregated in the aggression measure, was related positively to the magnitude of the effect sizes: Effect sizes were larger (i.e., a greater tendency for men to aggress more than women) for aggression measures that aggregated larger numbers of behaviors. Effect sizes were also larger to the extent that the following sex differences were obtained in questionnaire respondents' judgments of the aggressive behaviors: Female (compared with male) respondents (a) estimated that aggressing would cause more harm to the target; (b) estimated they would experience more guilt or anxiety from aggressing; (c) estimated they would face more danger from aggressing; and (d) judged themselves more likely to aggress. Effect sizes were also larger to the extent that respondents of both sexes judged the average man more likely to aggress than the average woman. Despite these significant relations, none of these models was correctly specified (ps < .001).

To examine the simultaneous impact of the continuous and categorical variables that were significant univariate predictors of effect sizes, we explored various multivariate models. For purposes of these analyses, the categorical variables were dummy-coded. As in the helping review (Chapter 2), the continuous variables constructed from questionnaire respondents' likelihood judgments were excluded from these models because they assessed, not study attributes, but respondents' abilities to predict aggressive behaviors. In addition, the sex difference in respondents' estimates of harm was excluded because of its substantial correlation with the sex difference in their guilt/anxiety estimates, $r(48) = .61$, $p < .001$. Furthermore, the surveillance variable (dummy-coded to reflect the larger effect sizes obtained in semiprivate versus public and private situations) was excluded because of its high correlation with type of aggression, $r(48) = .83, p < .001$, as well as setting, $r(48) = .83, p < .001$.

The first multivariate model in Table 3.4 entered number of behaviors aggregated, guilt/anxiety sex difference, danger sex difference, setting, type of aggression, and freedom of choice to aggress. The two significant

TABLE 3.4
Tests of Continuous Models for Sex-of-Subject Effect Sizes

Variable	Univariate models		Multivariate model		Multivariate model with interactions	
	b	b^*	b	b^*	b	b^*
Continuous variables						
1. Number of behaviors aggregated	0.00*[a]	.14	0.00	.13		
2. Harm sex difference[b]	0.40**	.18				
3. Guilt/anxiety sex difference	0.68***	.38	0.54***	.30		
4. Danger sex difference	1.17***	.41	1.08***	.38		
5. Own behavior sex difference	0.92***	.47				
6. Stereotypic sex difference[c]	0.40***	.27				
Categorical variables						
7. Setting[d]			− 0.03	− .05		
8. Type of aggression[e]			0.10	.13		
9. Freedom of choice to aggress[f]			0.01	.01		
Interaction term						
10. Danger Sex Difference × Freedom of Choice to Aggress					− 1.88***	− .56
Additive constant			− 0.15		− 0.23	
Multiple R			0.56		0.62	
SE of estimate			0.30		0.29	

Note. Table from Eagly and Steffen (1986a). Models are weighted least squares regressions calculated with weights equal to the reciprocal of the variance for each effect size. b = unstandardized regression coefficient. b^* = standardized regression coefficient. Effect sizes are positive for differences in the male direction and negative for differences in the female direction. $n = 50$.
[a] $b = 0.0037$, $SE(b) = .0019$.
[b] Values are positive for differences expected to be associated with greater aggression by men (greater female estimates of harm to others, of guilt and anxiety, and of danger to self; greater male estimate of own likelihood of aggressing).
[c] Values are positive when questionnaire respondents believed that men were more aggressive than women.
[d] 0 = field; 1 = laboratory.
[e] 0 = psychological; 1 = physical.
[f] 0 = free choice; 1 = aggression required.
*$p < .05$. **$p < .01$. ***$p < .001$.

predictors in this model were the sex differences in guilt/anxiety and in danger. As reflected in the multiple R of .56, this model was moderately successful in accounting for variability in the magnitude of the effect sizes, although the test of model specification showed that it cannot be regarded as correctly specified, $Q_E = 137.72, p < .001$.

Further exploration showed that the sex differences in questionnaire respondents' estimates of harm, guilt/anxiety, and danger predicted the effect sizes considerably better at some levels of the categorical variables than at others. Prediction was especially effective (a) from harm ratings when the setting was laboratory and aggression was physical; (b) from guilt/anxiety ratings when aggression was not required; and (c) from danger ratings when the setting was field and aggression was not required. The effects of the resulting interactions are illustrated by the inclusion of the largest of the interactions in the second multivariate model in Table 3.4.

This second model included the Danger Sex Difference × Freedom of Choice to Aggress interaction. Consistent with this interaction, only when subjects were not required to aggress were effect sizes larger to the extent that male respondents estimated that they faced less danger from enacting an aggressive behavior. Consistent with the hierarchical analysis of interactions (see Cohen & Cohen, 1983), the main effects were partialed from the interaction but the interaction was not partialed from the main effects. Therefore, for this second model, regression coefficients for the main effects are not reported because they are not interpretable. This second model proved moderately successful in accounting for variability in effect sizes, as shown by its multiple R of .62, although it also cannot be regarded as correctly specified, $Q_E = 125.75, p < .001$. Additional interaction terms were not added to this model because of the large number of predictors and the multicollinearity that resulted.

Additional Analyses

A number of additional analyses were carried out (see Eagly & Steffen, 1986a). Some of these analyses pertained to the subset of the studies that varied the sex of the target and reported a test of this manipulation's impact on aggression. The weighted mean of the 20 sex-of-target effect sizes that were available was 0.13 (95% CI = 0.05/0.20), indicating that greater aggression was directed toward men than women. Because the hypothesis that the known sex-of-target effect sizes were homogeneous was rejected, $Q = 198.79, p < .001$, study attributes were evaluated as predictors of the effect sizes. However, because the number of effect sizes was relatively small, these analyses were more limited than those for the sex-of-subject differences. Unfortunately, even smaller numbers of studies reported information sufficient to calculate sex-of-target differences separately for female and male subjects and sex-of-subject differences separately for female and male targets.

DISCUSSION

Overall Sex Difference

As predicted, men were more aggressive than women. The mean weighted sex-of-subject effect size based on the known effect sizes was 0.29—less than one-third of a standard deviation in the direction of greater aggression by men than by women. Because the additional sex differences reported as nonsignificant that could not be estimated were no doubt smaller on the average than the known differences, 0.29 should be regarded as an upper bound of the aggregated sex-of-subject differences in the sample of studies.

Although this mean sex-of-subject effect size is smaller than the mean of 0.50 reported by Hyde (1986), the preponderance of studies with child subjects in Hyde's review probably accounts for this discrepancy. On the average, aggression sex differences are apparently not especially large among adult subjects, compared with sex differences in other social behaviors such as helping (see Chapter 2) and nonverbal behaviors (see Chapter 4). Although Maccoby and Jacklin (1974) concluded that aggression is the only social behavior for which there is clear-cut evidence of a sex difference, quantitative reviewing suggests that aggression is not one of the larger sex differences among adult research subjects.

As in the case of helping behavior, the mean effect size produced by the meta-analysis does not in itself necessarily yield a valid general conclusion about the relative aggressiveness of men and women. The fact that sex-difference findings proved to be inconsistent across studies reduces the value of such overall summaries. Moreover, the focus of the social psychological aggression literature on interactions with strangers in only a few types of short-term encounters (see also Krebs & Miller, 1985) raises questions about the construct validity and external validity of the overall sex-difference findings. For helping behavior, this limitation appeared to be very serious because of evidence suggesting that the typical direction of the helping sex difference in stranger relationships probably reverses in close and long-term relationships. For aggressive behavior, the direction of the sex difference outside of research settings is somewhat less clear.

Some information concerning aggression sex differences in natural settings in which specific roles are important can be gleaned from certain applied literatures. For example, men's greater participation in crime (Bowker, 1978), especially violent crime, might be relevant to sex differences in aggression. Also of possible relevance are women's and men's apparently similar rates of violent behavior toward their spouses, although women are more likely to be injured in such encounters (e.g., Straus, Gelles, & Steinmetz, 1980). Yet feminist analyses of family violence (see Breines & Gordon, 1983) assert that spouse abuse is asymmetric because it is generally initiated by husbands and functions to maintain male dominance in the marriage. Moreover, women's violence toward their husbands is more likely to be in self-defense than is men's toward their wives (Straus, 1980). Research on family violence also suggests that mothers and fathers participate about equally in child abuse (Breines & Gordon, 1983). However, in interpreting this finding, women's greater responsibility for child care should be taken into account because it exposes them to greater provocation and opportunity to aggress. Sex differences in psychological aggression have been studied relatively little in close or long-term relationships, although investigations of conflict in couples have suggested that in seeming contrast to the typical direction of aggression sex differences, women tend to confront conflict and men tend to avoid it (Peplau, 1983). Yet, based on several self-report studies, Frost and Averill (1982) concluded that despite few differences in women's and men's everyday experience of anger, women may be less overtly aggressive when expressing their anger. Although the implications of these diverse findings for sex differences in aggression require further exploration, the absence of an obviously consistent sex difference suggests caution in drawing firm conclusions about the relative aggressiveness of women and men outside of the relatively narrow band of settings used in the aggression research reviewed in this meta-analysis.

Related to these concerns about the limited social contexts of social psychological aggression research are the questions that a number of scholars have raised about the construct validity of the findings generated by the popular laboratory research paradigms. This meta-analysis included in its sample of studies nearly all studies that researchers regarded as investigating adult aggression (provided that these studies also met criteria for an interpretable sex difference, see the Method section). As other commentators have pointed out (Bertilson, 1983; Geen, 1976; Rajecki, 1983), there is little internal evidence in most such studies that the dependent measure is primarily an aggressive behavior motivated by the harmful intent central to most social psychological definitions of aggression (e.g., Baron, 1977; Berkowitz, 1964). For example, an ostensibly aggressive behavior may reflect demand characteristics of the experiment (Schuck & Pisor, 1974) or the perpetrator's desire to either help the target person (Baron & Eggleston, 1972) or reciprocate a hostile action (Tedeschi, 1983; Tedeschi, Smith, & Brown, 1974). Although the validity of laboratory aggression research has been defended (e.g., Berkowitz & Donnerstein, 1982), for the most part these important issues remain unresolved. Moreover, as shown by dictionary definitions of aggression, nonpsychologists consider that aggression encompasses forceful actions intended to dominate or master, regardless of their harmful intent. The resulting discrepancy between popular and social psychological definitions of aggression also suggests caution in generalizing from this meta-analysis to conclusions about sex differences in the broad range of behaviors ordinarily considered aggressive.

Social Roles and the Prediction of Sex Differences in Aggression

Generally compatible with the social-role analysis are the findings that sex differences in aggression are relatively small when averaged and quite inconsistent across studies. Recall, for example, that the male gender role, although more supportive of aggressiveness than the female gender role, was regarded as discouraging aggressiveness under certain circumstances. Because of such complexities of normative regulation of aggression, considerable variability in the magnitude of sex differences in aggression would be expected, along with a relatively small mean difference. As in the case of helping behaviors (Chapter 2), this relatively small mean was created by averaging heterogeneous effects, some of which are quite large. Given these results, mean effect sizes implying a sex difference of a certain magnitude are less important than successful prediction of variability in the effect sizes.

The social-role analysis proved moderately successful in suggesting specific predictors of sex differences in aggression. With respect to the categorical study attributes, the strongest predictor was whether aggression caused physical or psychological harm to its target. Thus, supporting the analysis, the tendency for men to aggress more than women was more pronounced when the situation provided an opportunity for physical rather than psychological aggression. Reinisch and Sanders (1986) have reported similar findings in a study of college students' retrospective reports of how they coped with conflict situations at age 13: Males reported more physical aggression than females but did not differ from females on verbal aggression (e.g., calling one's opponent a bad name or yelling at one's opponent). However, in the meta-analysis the sex difference in psychological aggression (similar to Reinisch and Sanders's verbal aggression) remained significant (see Table 3.3).

The greater aggressiveness of men than women was also more pronounced (a) in the laboratory than in the field, (b) in semiprivate (surveillance by the experimenter and/or target) versus public or private contexts, and (c) when aggression was required rather than freely chosen. Although these additional categorical variables have some relevance to the role-theoretic analysis (see the introductory section of this chapter), interpretations of these findings are not offered because these variables were confounded to varying degrees with type of aggression (physical vs. psychological) and with one another. When the categorical variables that were significantly related to the aggression sex difference on a univariate basis were simultaneously entered as dummy-coded predictors in a multiple regression model, only the type of aggression remained a significant predictor. Therefore, type of aggression warrants primary emphasis in the interpretation of the impact of the categorical variables on sex differences in aggressiveness.

Sex Differences in Beliefs about the Consequences of Aggression.   The social-role analysis suggested that (a) women's and men's beliefs about the consequences of aggression would differ in general and (b) variability in the magnitude of these differences in perceived consequences would account for the variability in sex differences in aggression. Consistent with expectancy-value theories (e.g., Fishbein & Ajzen, 1975), these hypotheses presume that aggression is cognitively controlled in terms of its expected consequences.

As expected, male (vs. female) questionnaire respondents reported that their aggressive behavior would cause them less guilt and anxiety about others' suffering and would cause less harm to others. In addition, the guilt/anxiety and harm sex differences were substantial univariate predictors of the aggression effect sizes. Moreover, women, more than men, believed that their aggressive behaviors were likely to pose dangers to themselves, and the danger sex difference was a significant predictor of the effect sizes. As in the meta-analysis of helping behavior (see Chapter 2), the sex difference in perceived danger to oneself was one of the most substantial predictors of the effect sizes.

It is noteworthy that sex differences in beliefs about the consequences of aggression emerged as more important predictors under some conditions than others. Most importantly, the guilt/anxiety and danger sex differences predicted sex differences in aggression more effectively when aggressive behavior was not required. Perhaps the optional quality of aggression in such situations favors systematic weighing of the consequences of aggressing. These and other interactions involving the predictors constructed from the questionnaire respondents' judgments suggest that in many natural settings, which typically do not require aggressive behavior, people sometimes behave in ways that are markedly sex-typed. Thus, in some circumstances, men aggress considerably more than women to the extent that women believe that an aggressive act has more strongly negative outcomes than men believe it has.

The first multivariate model showed that only the sex differences in the perceived consequences of aggression (guilt/anxiety and danger) remained significant when both the categorical and continuous variables were entered in the regression equation. Furthermore, this regression equation did not account for significantly more variation than one entering only sex differences in guilt/anxiety and danger. These outcomes are consistent with the conclusion that the impact of the contextual variables on aggression sex differences was mediated by sex differences in the perceived consequences of aggression. Supporting this interpretation, an analysis of variance partitioning the studies on type of aggression, the most important categorical predictor, found that physical (vs. psychological) aggression was associated with significantly larger sex differences in ratings of guilt/anxiety and harm to others ($ps < .001$), and with nonsignificantly larger sex differences in danger to self ($p = .13$). The sex difference in harm to self might have been more strongly related to type of aggression had the majority of the studies on physical aggression not been conducted in laboratories, which are presumed to provide protection for experimental subjects who perpetrate aggression.

Biological Theories of Sex Differences in Aggression

Aggression in general and aggression sex differences in particular have often been analyzed in terms of underlying biological mechanisms (e.g., Hamburg & Trudeau, 1981; Simmel, Hahn, & Walters, 1983). Yet the adequacy of the research evidence that human sex differences in aggression are biologically mediated has been contested by some reviewers (Bleier, 1984; Pleck, 1981) and accepted by others (e.g., Maccoby & Jacklin, 1974; Parke & Slaby, 1983). Without taking a position on the strength of the evidence for the existence of biological mediation, Valerie Steffen and I formulated a social psychological analysis for the meta-analysis because of social-role theory's assumptions that (a) social norms as well as sex-typed beliefs and abilities are the proximal determinants of sex differences in adult aggressive behavior and (b) biological causes are for the most part only indirectly relevant (see Chapter 5). Although the social-role framework should be more successful in explaining *variability* in sex-difference findings than are biological theories, the social-role account does not invalidate alternative theories, and the findings of this meta-analysis do not bear directly on the issue of biological versus environmental causation.

Despite these reservations, comparisons between the child and adult research literatures on aggression have some relevance to disentangling biological and environmental causes. Although such comparisons are perilous because of differences in research methods, the relatively small average effect size yielded by the meta-analysis of the adult literature is consistent with other reviewers' claims that the aggression sex difference is larger among children than adults (Hyde, 1984; Rohner, 1976). One may speculate whether this possible difference in the magnitude of the overall sex difference is due to a decrease in biological control of aggression and an increase in normative regulation as people develop. In particular, the social-role analysis suggested that the male gender role, despite encouraging aggressiveness overall imposes limits on aggressive behavior and that the female gender role, despite discouraging aggressiveness overall, may in its modern form encourage self-assertive behavior, at least under some circumstances. In addition, other social roles occupied by women and men encourage or discourage aggressiveness, and, even if they encourage aggression, regulate the conditions under which role occupants may behave aggressively. The consequent restraint of male aggressiveness under many circumstances and probable encouragement of female aggressiveness may result in an overall lessening of aggression sex differences in adulthood.

Conclusion

In general, this meta-analysis shows that men are more aggressive than women and finds that this sex difference is more pronounced for physical than psychological aggression. It also demonstrates that women and men think differently about aggression and suggests that these differing beliefs are important mediators of sex differences in aggressive behavior. Women reported more guilt and anxiety as a consequence of aggression, more vigilance about the harm that aggression causes its victims, and more concern about the danger that their aggression might bring to themselves. Women's and men's beliefs about the consequences of aggression diverge considerably, when, for example, the situation provides an opportunity to aggress physically rather than psychologically. In such situations, sex differences in aggression are often relatively large.

One important implication of the meta-analytic findings is that the best known and most popular methods for studying human aggression—the "teacher-learner" and related experimental paradigms (e.g., Buss, 1963)—happen to be those that are most likely to elicit greater aggression in men than women. These paradigms manifest the four conditions associated with larger sex-of-subject effect sizes: a laboratory setting, physical aggression, a semiprivate context, and required aggressive behavior. Given the positive value that the male gender role places on aggression, it is interesting to speculate on the possibility of an agentic bias in this preference for a research paradigm that maximally elicits this sex difference. This issue is explored in Chapter 5.

Success of Predictions. The overall success in predicting aggression sex differences using study attributes is best described as moderate, even though this success was greater than that of the questionnaire respondents' implicit theories, which were assessed from these respondents' estimates of the likelihood of their own and others' aggressive behaviors (see Table 3.4). Multivariate models, which excluded these likelihood measures, accounted for approximately 40% of the variability in the available findings. Given the many subtle differences between the research paradigms in this literature, it is probably unreasonable to expect to account for all of the systematic variation between effect sizes. However, the 40% of variability explained is substantially lower than the approximately 70% of variability accounted for in the meta-analysis of helping behavior (see Chapter 2). This lesser success could be due to any of several factors, possibly including (a) a less adequate social psychological analysis for this aggression review than for the helping review and (b) the limitations (discussed in this chapter) of the measures that social psychologists have devised for studying aggression. Yet this 40% figure is quite respectable among published meta-analyses on psychological topics, which have typically accounted for less variability in effect sizes.

The variability this meta-analysis demonstrated in the magnitude of aggression sex differences is challenging, especially in view of the partial success of social psychological predictors in accounting for this variability. Perhaps a framework incorporating additional predictors will account for more variability. If it is correct that adult social roles have the important function of channeling and regulating aggression so that it is expressed primarily in socially approved ways, future research could well investigate in more detail the differing normative environments that surround women's and men's aggressive behavior.

4

Sex Differences in
Other Social Behaviors

In Chapters 2 and 3, a theory based on social roles and the methods of quantitative reviewing were applied to research on sex differences in helping behavior and aggressive behavior. The findings of these two reviews have implications that are worth exploring in relation to other social behaviors. In general, these reviews suggested that quantitative methods produce descriptions of sex differences that differ in substance from the descriptions typically produced by traditional, narrative methods. For sex differences in helping behavior, quantitative methods revealed a different verdict for the overall trend than narrative reviewers had offered. For aggression and especially for helping, quantitative methods indicated considerable variability of the sex differences across studies. Although prior reviewers were not unaware of inconsistencies, this heterogeneity of research findings was documented in the meta-analyses by a statistically appropriate method and followed by systematic testing of hypotheses about the sources of these inconsistencies. As the outcome of this process of testing hypotheses, sex-difference findings were shown to be related to several variables suggested by the social-role theory of sex differences. However, despite these interesting findings, these reviews did not necessarily yield valid *general* conclusions about the relative helpfulness or aggressiveness of women and men. Reservations about validity, which are considered more fully in Chapter 5, stem from psychologists' tendency to investigate relatively narrow sets of helpful and aggressive behaviors, pertaining to giving help and causing harm in brief encounters with strangers.

In this chapter, I discuss the extent to which similar descriptions are appropriate for research findings on other social behaviors. I confine this discussion to behaviors that have been examined using the methods of quantitative reviewing. Each of the available reviews has produced an overall generalization about sex differences in a given class of social behaviors and to some extent has examined inconsistencies across studies. These reviews concern sex differences in influenceability, nonverbal behaviors, and group behaviors. When the outcomes of these meta-analyses are considered, along with the outcomes of the helping and aggression reviews, the range of social behaviors that have been scrutinized with quantitative methods is considerable. I will therefore be able to address the question of whether, in typical research settings, women's social behavior has an especially communal emphasis and men's has an especially agentic emphasis.

SEX DIFFERENCES IN INFLUENCEABILITY

Because social influence is a classic research area in social psychology, the available literature is large and offers an attractive opportunity to examine whether the sexes differ in how easily they are influenced by other people. The major research paradigms within this literature are *persuasion* and *conformity.* In persuasion experiments, an individual, or *influencing agent,* gives a position on one or more issues and presents arguments supporting the position(s). In conformity experiments, influencing agents take positions but provide no arguments to support these positions. In the classic *group pressure* conformity experiments made famous by Sherif (1935) and Asch (1956), the influencing agents are the other members of a group in which the research subject participates. In another conformity paradigm, sometimes known as "fictitious norm" studies, positions on issues are ascribed to one or more influencing agents who are not present. In all of these paradigms, the influencing agents' positions typically are discrepant from those of the subjects, and the dependent variable is change in the subjects' positions toward the positions taken by the influencing agents. A sex difference in influenceability indicates the extent to which women and men differ in the amount they change.

A Social-Role Analysis of
Sex Differences in Influenceability

The role framework suggests that gender roles may be one source of a sex difference in influenceability. As Eagly and Wood (1985) argued, the relevance of gender roles to social influence stems from both the agentic focus of the male role and the communal focus of the female role. As I explain in the following discussion, the two roles allow the same prediction—that men are less easily influenced than women.

Suggesting the importance of the male role in relation to social influence are studies of gender stereotypes (e.g., Bem, 1974; Broverman et al., 1972; Spence & Helmreich, 1978) documenting that most stereotypic attributes pertaining to influencing and being influenced (e.g., independence and dependence, dominance and submission) are components of the agentic dimension of gender roles. From this viewpoint, the demand that men be agentic may be manifested in their resistance to being influenced.

Another form of the idea that the male role implies resistance to influence links social influence to the chronic status difference between the sexes (Eagly, 1983; Lockheed & Hall, 1976; Meeker & Weitzel-O'Neill, 1977). As explained in Chapter 1, because men are ordinarily observed in higher-status positions than women, sex functions as a status cue in new situations and thereby conveys information about the agentic qualities of the women and men who are encountered. The consequent perception of men as more assertive, independent, competitive, and self-confident than women results in a tendency for people to weigh men's comments more heavily than women's in forming opinions and for men to be less accepting than women of others' opinions.

The female gender role's emphasis on communal qualities may also affect influenceability. People who are communal in their orientation toward people should be committed to preserving group harmony and enhancing positive feelings among group members. Agreeing with other group members can be a means of attaining these communal outcomes (Buss, 1981; Eagly, 1978; Hansson, Allen, & Jones, 1980). Consistent with this idea, Bales (1950) classified agreement as a positive social-emotional act in his system for content-analyzing small-group interaction. Empirically supportive of a link between communion and agreeing with others is the association of some influence-relevant attributes with the communal dimension of gender stereotypes (e.g., Bem's, 1974, inclusion of "yielding" and "gullible" on this dimension). More compelling evidence is provided by Santee and Jackson's (1982) finding that observers ascribed more highly communal identities to conforming than non-conforming people. Thus, a tendency for women to agree more readily with others may be a product of the female role's demand to manifest communal qualities as well as the male role's demand to manifest agentic qualities.

Specific social roles may also be relevant to sex differences in influenceability, to the extent that they encourage either dominant or submissive qualities and are occupied disproportionately by one sex. Certain male-dominated occupations, particularly managerial roles and high-status positions more generally, may require at least moderate levels of dominance and resistance to influence, whereas many female-dominated job categories, especially in service and caring occupations, likely require a greater emphasis on acceding to others' wishes. The skills and beliefs learned in such specific roles may carry over to research settings and foster sex differences.

Findings of Influenceability Meta-Analyses

These social-role considerations suggest that, in general, women should be more easily influenced than men. Meta-analyses by Cooper (1979), Eagly and Carli (1981), and Becker (1986) have all found this overall tendency. Table 4.1 presents a summary of the sex-of-subject effect sizes reported by Eagly and Carli. Note that the mean effect sizes differed from the 0.00 value that indicates exactly no sex difference. As the lower section of Table 4.1 shows, the conclusion that women were more influenceable than men was supported by two counting tests as well. Yet, as Becker found in a reanalysis of Eagly and Carli's findings that used newer statistical methods (Hedges & Olkin, 1985), these sex differences were inconsistent across studies. Some aspects of these inconsistencies have been explored (see discussion below in this section).

TABLE 4.1
Summary of Sex-of-Subject Effect Sizes for Effect Sizes

Criterion	Values	
Effect size analyses		
Known effect sizes (n = 90)		
M effect size (Md)	0.26	
95% CI for Md	0.19/0.33	
Mdn effect size	0.26	
All reports (n = 148)		
M effect size (Md)	0.16	
95% CI for Md	0.11/0.21	
Total no. of subjects	21,141	
Counting methods		
	Frequencies	χ^2
Differences in the female direction[a]	84/111 (.76)	28.30*
Significant differences in the female direction[b]	35/148 (.24)	180.14*

Note. Table from Eagly and Carli (1981). When all reports were included, a value of 0.00 (exactly no difference) was assigned to sex differences that could not be calculated and were reported as nonsignificant. Effect sizes were positive for differences in the female direction and negative for differences in the male direction. CI = confidence interval.
[a]Frequencies are number of differences in the female direction divided by the number of differences of known direction. The proportion appears in parentheses.
[b]Frequencies are number of significant differences (p < .05, two-tailed) in the female direction divided by the total number of comparisons of known significance. The proportion appears in parentheses. There were 4 significant differences in the male direction.
[c]Based on expected values of 5 and 143, or .03 and .97 of n.
*p < .001, one-tailed.

The history of psychologists' descriptions of the state of the evidence on sex differences in influenceability is particularly instructive. Prior to the 1970s analyses, psychologists had long believed that women are more easily influenced than men (see Eagly, 1978). Yet in the mid-1970s the existence of this sex difference as a reliable phenomenon was discounted by Maccoby and Jacklin (1974). In a narrative review, I also expressed skepticism about this sex difference and emphasized that, even though most of the significant sex differences were in the direction of female influenceability, only a minority of studies obtained a significant difference (Eagly, 1978). These descriptions offered by narrative reviewers failed to recognize that the pattern of mainly nonsignificant effects (in the female direction) based on studies with moderate-sized samples of subjects is consistent with a reliable but not especially large sex difference. Cooper (1979) was the first to show that the conclusions based on narrative reviews were excessively conservative with respect to an overall sex difference. Linda Carli and I then carried out a quantitative reanalysis of the sample of studies that I had used in my narrative review and concurred with this aspect of Cooper's verdict (Eagly & Carli, 1981).

Despite their conservatism about the overall sex difference, the narrative reviewers (Eagly, 1978; Maccoby & Jacklin, 1974) were correct in their observation that findings are inconsistent across studies, and some of their speculations about factors that account for these inconsistencies have received support. In particular, quantitative reviewers (Becker, 1986; Eagly & Carli, 1981) have shown that the tendency for men to be more resistant to influence than women is clearest in group-pressure conformity studies (e.g., the Asch, 1956, paradigm).

This tendency for the magnitude of the sex differences to be related to type of social-influence study is consistent with the social-role analysis. As noted in Chapter 1, the presence of an audience should ordinarily heighten self-presentational concerns and encourage gender-role consistent behavior, which for women tends to be agreeing with other people and for men tends to be remaining independent in the face of social pressure. Surveillance by an audience is present only in group-pressure conformity studies, in which the audience consists of the other group members. In both persuasion and fictitious-norm conformity studies, subjects usually respond privately on a questionnaire and thus their agreement is not under the immediate surveillance of the influencing agent or any other audience. Moreover, the generalization that surveillance by an audience establishes a social context that increases the influenceability sex difference has been confirmed experimentally by Eagly, Wood, and Fishbaugh (1981) and Eagly and Chrvala (1986) in studies that manipulated surveillance by other group members over subjects' opinions.

To account for additional variability in study outcomes, Linda Carli and

I tested one aspect of the role-theory proposition that prior enactment of social roles imparts skills relevant to responding to influence attempts (Eagly & Carli, 1981). We operationalized skill as knowledge and interest pertaining to the topic on which influence was attempted. This aspect of skill was investigated because research had repeatedly demonstrated that people are more readily influenced to the extent that they lack information about a topic or regard it as trivial and unimportant (e.g., Allen, 1965; Endler, Wiesenthal, Coward, Edwards, & Geller, 1975; McGuire & Papageorgis, 1961; Rhine & Severance, 1970). Thus, lack of expertise or interest ordinarily leaves one vulnerable to influence, whereas possession of expertise and interest generally aids resistance to influence. As hypothesized, we found that topics for which men were relatively more knowledgeable and interested than women tended to be associated with greater female influenceability. However, because we could implement this analysis only for the persuasion studies, the sample of studies available for testing the hypothesis was relatively small. Neither the knowledge nor the interest sex differences significantly predicted the effect sizes, and the conclusion that these relations arose by chance could not be rejected.

Averaging over all of the topics used in the persuasion studies included in our meta-analysis, we found no overall tendency for men to be more knowledgeable or interested than women. This finding is inconsistent with the popular interpretation (e.g., Baron & Byrne, 1977; Jones, Hendrick, & Epstein, 1979), based on Sistrunk and McDavid's (1971) conformity study, that the overall tendency for women to be more conforming than men is explained by an overall tendency for men to be more knowledgeable and interested in relation to the stimulus materials typically used in social-influence studies. Thus, the argument that the overall influenceability sex difference is an artifact of biased selection of stimulus materials did not fare well in this empirical test.

Finally, Becker (1986), in a reanalysis of Eagly and Carli's (1981) findings, has shown that several methodological attributes of the studies are significant predictors of sex-difference outcomes. In particular, the type of outcome measure used for assessing influence (e.g., posttest only, pretest vs. posttest, covariance-adjusted posttest) as well as the number of items contained in the outcome measure proved to be substantial predictors of sex differences, for some of the experimental paradigms. These findings are provocative from a methodological standpoint. Yet they are not relevant to the social-role analysis, except insofar as these study attributes covary with theoretically-relevant variables and therefore provide alternative explanations for their effects. Indeed, Becker explored just such a possibility by showing that these methodological attributes of the studies were correlated with the sex of the authors of the research articles—a variable of some theoretical interest that Eagly and Carli had found was related to the magnitude of the influenceability sex differences (see Chapter 5).

In summary, quantitative reviews have established an overall tendency for women to be more influenced than men. Yet the variability of the findings across the studies suggests that accounting for the inconsistencies in these sex differences is a more important matter than describing this overall trend. Some features of social-influence studies that proved to be correlated with the effect sizes are interpretable in terms of the social-role theory. Yet my own meta-analytic work on influenceability (Eagly & Carli, 1981) was completed several years ago, before the introduction of the newer statistical methods for analyzing effect sizes (e.g., Hedges & Olkin, 1985). As a consequence, this work emphasized aggregating effect sizes more than accounting for their inconsistencies, which became the primary emphasis of my more recent meta-analyses (see Chapters 2 and 3). To account more fully for the inconsistencies in influenceability sex differences, further study is warranted. It would be appropriate to pursue Becker's (1986) methodological insights and possibly to incorporate additional predictors and a broader sample of social-influence research paradigms (see Lockheed, 1985). Also warranting investigation is the unresolved issue of the extent to which the influenceability sex difference represents a difference in willingness (a) to change internalized attitudes and beliefs or (b) merely to deliver a superficial agreement response. Additional research may allow more definitive verdicts concerning both this depth-of-change issue and the issue of the relative importance of various predictors of sex differences in this class of social behaviors.

Research on conformity and persuasion, like research on helping and aggression, has been carried out almost exclusively in the context of short-term encounters with strangers. Yet for conformity and persuasion, it is doubtful that the sex comparison would ordinarily have a different outcome outside of such contexts, unless the men and women who were compared occupied constraining specific roles (e.g., jobs in organizations) that were equated. In natural settings, specific roles are generally not equated. In fact, the specific roles disproportionately occupied by women, compared with those occupied by men, tend (a) to have lower status within organizational hierarchies and (b) to be defined by more communal and less agentic norms (see Chapter 1). These differences in occupancy of specific roles suggest that the sex difference found in social psychological research would be accentuated in many aggregate comparisons between the sexes outside of typical research contexts, because of the impact of these specific roles. For example, in an encounter between a male executive and a female secretary or between a male physician and a female nurse, the man would generally be less influenced than the woman, because of the hierarchy by which these roles are related and qualitative differences in role expectations (see Eagly & Wood, 1982).

SEX DIFFERENCES IN NONVERBAL BEHAVIOR

Differences in the nonverbal behavior of women and men have been extensively researched. Psychologists' interest in this research area is matched by popular interest in the topic, as shown by the extensive coverage of presumed sex differences in "body language" in mass-market books on nonverbal communication (see Koivumaki, 1975). Because nonverbal research encompasses many subtopics (e.g., decoding nonverbal cues, gaze, touch) that utilize a diverse array of research methods, reviewing it is a formidable task. Fortunately this task has been accomplished by Judith Hall (1984), whose book, *Nonverbal Sex Differences,* provides insightful quantitative reviews of the major areas of research on nonverbal sex differences.

Table 4.2 provides an overview of nonverbal sex differences by presenting Hall's (1984) Table 11.1, with average sex differences pertaining exclusively to children deleted and effect sizes expressed in terms of the d statistic rather than the point-biserial correlations shown by Hall. The first sex difference noted in this table was also documented by Hall (1978) in a pioneering quantitative review: Women are more skilled than men at decoding nonverbal cues—in other words, better at understanding the meaning of others' nonverbal messages. Hall also found that this sex difference is larger for some nonverbal channels than others: Women's advantage is largest for decoding facial cues, next largest for decoding body cues, and smallest for decoding vocal cues. Perhaps related to women's facility at decoding facial cues is their greater skill at recognizing faces (see Table 4.2).

As Table 4.2 also shows, women are more effective than men at communicating nonverbally—that is, women are skilled at encoding or sending nonverbal messages. The fact that this sex difference is greater for visual than vocal cues suggests that women are particularly adept at communicating via the face. In fact, Hall (1984) showed that women's greater facial expressiveness has been directly confirmed in studies that assess how labile or changeable people's faces are under various conditions.

Other sex differences in Table 4.2 include the tendency for women to smile and laugh more than men in social situations. Women also gaze at other people more than men do, and, in turn, are gazed at more than men. In addition, women approach other people more closely and in turn are approached more closely by others. However, the tendency for women to approach others more closely has been obtained primarily in natural settings in which people's interaction distances were observed. This tendency

TABLE 4.2
Sex Differences for Nonverbal Skills and Behaviors

Variable	Md^a	Number of studies
Decoding skill	0.43	64
Face recognition skill	0.34	12
Expression skill[b]	0.52	35
Facial expressiveness	1.01	5
Social smiling	0.63	15
Gaze	0.68	30
Receipt of gaze	0.65	6
Distance of approach to others		
Naturalistic	−0.56	17
Staged	−0.12	8
Projective	−0.14	11
Distance approached by others		
Naturalistic	−0.95	9
Staged	−0.63	5
Projective	−0.85	7
Body movement and position[b]		
Restlessness	−0.72	6
Expansiveness	−1.04	6
Involvement	0.32	7
Expressiveness	0.58	7
Self-consciousness	0.45	5
Vocal behavior		
Speech errors	−0.70	6
Filled pauses	−1.19	6

Note. Table modified from Table 11.1 in Hall (1984).
[a]Positive effect sizes mean higher values on the named behavior by females, and negative effect sizes mean higher values by males.
[b]Studies within these categories are not independent.

was very small in studies using more reactive research methods involving (a) "staged" settings in which subjects were instructed to indicate their preferred distances vis-a-vis another person and (b) projective measures that allowed subjects to position hypothetical people. In contrast, the tendency for women to be approached more closely by other people was convincingly demonstrated with naturalistic, staged, and projective methods.

As also given in Table 4.2, women and men differ in various aspects of body movement and position. Women are less restless (less fidgeting, fewer shifts of body position, and fewer shifts of legs and feet), less expansive (knees and arms less wide; legs, arms, and body less open), yet more involved (more nodding and forward leaning) and more expressive (more expressive gestures and head movements). Although women appear in some ways to be more self-conscious than men (more self-manipulation and self-touch), they make fewer speech errors and use fewer pause-fillers in their speech (e.g., er, ah, um).

Integrating the available research on sex differences in touch proved to be an especially difficult task, in part because of many ambiguities in research methods and reporting of research findings. Hall (1984) discerned a tendency for women to initiate touch more than men and noted that this tendency appeared to be stronger in the same-sex context of women touching other women. A more detailed review of the literature on touch by Stier and Hall (1984) confirmed the tendency for females to initiate touch more than males. In addition, Stier and Hall found a tendency for females to be touched more than males, although methodological issues rendered this finding ambiguous. They also added the following generalizations concerning the effects of the sex composition of dyads: Available research supports (a) a tendency for females to engage in more same-sex touch than males; (b) a tendency for same-sex dyads to touch more than cross-sex dyads, at least when the contact is not intimate; and (c) no overall tendency for males to touch females more than for females to touch males. Inconsistencies in these trends abound, however, and Stier and Hall provided valuable discussion of possible sources of these inconsistencies. When one considers that touch has many variants (e.g., handshakes, pushes, strokes, pats, hugs, kisses) and conveys many meanings, which vary depending on the social context, it is easy to agree with Stier and Hall's view that understanding sex differences in this research area poses especially challenging theoretical issues as well as knotty meta-analytic problems.

Although Hall and her colleagues reported tests of the homogeneity of these sets of effect sizes only for smiling and gazing (see Hall & Halberstadt, 1986), the outcome of these tests and inspection of the actual values of the effect sizes (e.g., Hall, 1978; Stier & Hall, 1984) suggest that, in general, nonverbal sex differences are not consistent in magnitude. Nonetheless, many of these sex differences are impressively consistent in direction. For example, the percentage of findings favoring females was 83% for nonverbal decoding accuracy, 74% for face recognition, 94% for social smiling (adult studies only), and 83% for gazing (adult studies only). For many nonverbal behaviors, Hall and her colleagues discovered moderating variables that account for some of the inconsistencies in effect-size magnitude. In some instances, such as the impact of communication channel on the nonverbal decoding sex difference, the effects of these moderating variables have interesting theoretical implications. Hall (1984) has discussed many of these implications.

The generalizations that emerged from Hall's thorough quantitative reviews of the nonverbal literature can be compared with those that emerged from the narrative reviews of the 1970s. Both Maccoby and Jacklin (1974) and Hoffman (1977) quite firmly rejected the idea that women are more socially sensitive than men but dealt with only a portion of the available literature on the most relevant behavior—nonverbal decoding. However, Hoffman did report some evidence favoring women's greater empathy, particularly in the area of vicarious affective responding to another person's feelings. Although Maccoby and Jacklin's and Hoffman's verdicts about social sensitivity showed the bias in favor of the null hypothesis typical of 1970s treatments of sex differences, Henley (1977), who approached the analysis of nonverbal sex differences from a decidedly feminist and less eclectic perspective, did not show this bias. On the contrary, Henley argued that evidence supported the existence of many nonverbal sex differences. The sex differences that Henley regarded as established were for the most part those that could be interpreted as manifestations of men's dominance and women's oppression (see discussion in next section).

Interpretations of Nonverbal Sex Differences

The majority of the aggregated sex-difference findings reported by Hall (1984) are well matched to the social-role theory of sex differences introduced in Chapter 1. In particular, the idea that the female gender role fosters communal qualities and thereby encourages women to be pleasant, interpersonally oriented, expressive, and socially sensitive provides an interpretation of most of these nonverbal sex differences. Women's greater skill at decoding and encoding nonverbal cues would surely enhance social skills. Decoding accuracy is particularly relevant to social sensitivity. Expressiveness of personal style is maintained by women through facial movements and to some extent through bodily movement as well. Furthermore, gazing at people, showing involvement in their speech, touching them, approaching them relatively closely, and allowing them to approach closely can help women develop rapport with others in benign and friendly social contexts. Smiling and laughing in social situations ordinarily enhance the pleasantness of these situations and thereby facilitate social bonding. Less clearly interpretable in terms of gender roles are the differing ways that women and men apparently express tension—men through restless body movement, speech errors, and pause-fillers, and women through presumably self-conscious behaviors such as self-manipulation and self-touch (and probably through smiling and laughing as well, see Hall & Halberstadt, 1986).

Interpretation of nonverbal sex differences in terms of men's dominance and women's oppression have been popular in recent years (see Frieze & Ramsey, 1976; Henley, 1977; Henley & LaFrance, 1984; Weitz, 1974). The idea that the distinctive nonverbal behaviors of each sex reflect men's largely successful efforts to dominate and control women in face-to-face encounters is plausible in relation to many of these findings. For example, according to the dominant male/oppressed female interpretation, women's smiling and gazing are gestures of appeasement directed toward men rather than expressions of a friendly, affiliative interpersonal orientation, and women's skill at decoding nonverbal cues is a survival tactic learned to ferret out the intentions of dominant (and presumably threatening) men.

This oppression account of nonverbal sex differences overlaps the social-role theory to some extent because power and status differences between the sexes are emphasized in both approaches. Nonetheless, because the dominance/oppression interpretation seems to imply active domination and control by men, not necessarily mediated through gender-role norms, the theory may be at least partially distinguishable from the social-role theory presented in this book. As I explain in Chapter 5 in a more general discussion of oppression theories, the results of comparing sex differences in same-sex and cross-sex social interaction tend not to fit this active control aspect of the oppression account as well as they fit the idea that gender-role expectancies are the proximal cause of nonverbal sex differences. Also, one of the critical predictions of the dominance/oppression account— that men routinely dominate and control women by touching them—has received only very limited empirical support (see Stier & Hall, 1984). However, it is possible that this presumed tendency for men to use touch to dominate women occurs in social contexts that are underrepresented in research on nonverbal behavior (e.g., organizational contexts and long-term role relationships more generally).

Validity issues remain worrisome for the literature on nonverbal behavior, just as they are for the other research areas I have discussed. The majority of studies on nonverbal behavior were conducted in laboratories where subjects either interacted with strangers or responded to standardized stimuli (films, videotapes, etc.). Still, some nonverbal studies, such as many of those on touch, were conducted in natural settings where researchers observed social interaction among people, at least some of whom were associates, friends, or members of the same family. Yet for obvious ethical reasons, nonverbal behavior has been assessed only in relatively public settings and not in more private or intimate settings. Studies of nonverbal behavior in organizational settings are also rare.

Whether the outcomes of sex comparisons would be much different for nonverbal behaviors in the settings and social relationships that have rarely been investigated is of course difficult to determine with any reasonable degree of certainty. Because expectations of selfless, socially sensitive, and other-oriented behavior are often held for specific social roles occupied disproportionately by women (e.g., homemaker, nurse, teacher of children) as well as for women more generally, women's nonverbal repertoire might well differ even more from men's in many of the natural settings where specific roles are enacted, as long as sex and specific roles are confounded in the typical ways. It is plausible, therefore, that ecologically representative estimates of nonverbal sex-differences would be larger than those presented by Hall (1984). However, consistent with my general argument that specific roles provide relatively clear guides for appropriate conduct, nonverbal sex differences should be minimized when the women and men who are compared occupy the same specific role.

SEX DIFFERENCES IN BEHAVIOR
IN SMALL GROUPS

In view of Hall's (1984) quantitative analyses of the nonverbal behavior literature suggesting that there is a substantial element of truth to the characterization of women as more concerned than men with good inter-personal relations, relevant aspects of research on behavior in small groups also warrant close examination, especially in relation to this communal theme. There are many important questions about sex differences that can be addressed in existing group-process research, because social behavior in task-oriented groups has been studied quite extensively by social psychologists for several decades (see McGrath, 1984). Most reports of sex differences are from laboratory studies of small groups, although there are also many naturalistic studies of on-going groups. Methodologies range from observational studies of discussion groups to studies of behavior in experimental games such as the prisoner's dilemma.

Behavior in Discussion Groups

Task and Social-Emotional Behavior. One focus of small-group research, the study of task and social-emotional behavior in discussion groups, is particularly interesting from the standpoint of gender roles. This tradition derives from Bales's (1950) distinction between two types of group behavior: *Task behavior* is directly concerned with accomplishing whatever task the group has been assigned, and *social-emotional behavior* is concerned with maintaining satisfactory morale and interpersonal relations within the group. To classify behavior as task-oriented or social-emotional, Bales developed a 12-category system for content-analyzing the verbal behavior of members of discussion groups. The task-oriented classification includes the behaviors of *answering questions* (e.g., gives information, opinion, suggestion) and *asking questions* (e.g., asks for information, opinion, suggestion). The social-emotional classification includes *positive acts* (e.g., shows solidarity, gives help, shows satisfaction, agrees, understands) and *negative acts* (e.g., disagrees, withholds help, shows tension increase, shows antagonism, deflates others' status). This system of classifying small-group interaction has been widely used in the original and modified forms (see Hare, 1976; McGrath, 1984).

The distinction between task and social-emotional behavior in group settings resembles the distinction made in Chapter 1 between agentic and communal dimensions of gender stereotypes. From this perspective, agentic role-expectations should foster task behaviors, especially the answering of questions, and communal role-expectations should foster social-emotional behaviors of the positive type. Therefore, if gender-role expectations foster agentic behavior in men and communal behavior in women, sex differences should be evident in the extent to which group members engage in task and social-emotional behaviors. As I also argued in relation to group-pressure conformity studies, gender roles should be salient because group members provide one another with an audience, which should heighten self-presentational concerns. Moreover, in this research, group members generally interact without well-defined specific roles that would make competing role expectations salient.

Sex differences in task and social-emotional behavior in research on small groups have been summarized quantitatively by Anderson and Blanchard (1982) and Carli (1982). Because these two meta-analyses have similar conclusions but Carli located more studies and used more advanced meta-analytic methods than Anderson and Blanchard, I describe Carli's review, which was based on 17 studies comparing men's and women's task behavior and 15 studies comparing positive social-emotional behavior.[1] For the 10 studies that yielded an effect-size estimate for task behavior, the mean effect size was 0.59, indicating greater task contribution by men than by women. For the 9 studies that yielded an effect-size estimate for positive social-emotional behavior, the mean effect size was -0.59, indicating greater positive social-emotional contribution by women than by men. Thus, gender-stereotypic sex differences were obtained in the content of contribution to group discussions: Men tend to give and ask for opinions and suggestions and women tend to act friendly and agree with other group members. Wood and Karten (1986) again replicated these sex differences, and, consistent with the social-role perspective, found that the differences disappeared when an unambiguous indicator of subjects' task competence (supposed aptitude-test scores) was made available (see also Eskilson & Wiley, 1976).

Although neither the Anderson and Blanchard (1982) nor the Carli (1982) review of task and social-emotional specialization utilized tests of homogeneity, the findings appear to be somewhat inconsistent in magni-

---

[1]Although the exact definition of task and social-emotional behavior differed somewhat between the studies, Carli (1982) aggregated social-emotional behaviors only for measures of positive behaviors because her hypothesis was that women are more accommodative and concerned with maintaining friendly social interaction.

tude across studies. Carli was successful in discovering some variables correlated with the effect sizes. She developed measures of sex-typed abilities by obtaining respondents' ratings of their interest and knowledge in relation to the topics that the groups had discussed in the studies in this literature. Following the Eagly and Carli (1981) precedent, Carli then calculated differences between men's and women's ratings and used these sex differences to predict the effect sizes. Topics that favored the interests of one sex more than the other were associated with increased task and social-emotional behaviors in the favored sex relative to the other sex. In addition, topics that favored the knowledge of one sex were associated with increased task behavior in the favored sex. These findings suggest that the differing interests and knowledge that women and men had gained in prior social roles were responsible for some of the variation the sex differences found in contribution to group discussions.

These sex differences in task and social-emotional specialization appear to have important effects on group performance. Wood, Polek, and Aiken (1985) presented data suggesting that sex differences in task and social-emotional specialization have implications for the types of group tasks at which women and men excel: Men excel at tasks for which productivity is directly related to the volume of ideas or other output, and women excel at tasks for which productivity requires discussion and negotiation. In partial confirmation of these findings in a meta-analytic review of 52 group-performance studies, Wood (in press) compared all-female with all-male groups and obtained data supporting the hypothesis that women's repertoire of positive interpersonal behaviors contributes to superior group-level performance at tasks requiring discussion and negotiation. Yet consistent with Wood and Karten's (1986) findings, Wood and her colleagues have pointed out that these group-productivity sex differences cannot necessarily be generalized to organizations, where status cues much less ambiguous than sex are ordinarily available and likely are stronger determinants of people's interpersonal behavior than their sex.

Other Behavior in Discussion Groups.   An overall sex difference in speech production (total amount of talking) in discussion groups was not found in any of the quantitative reviews (Anderson & Blanchard, 1982; Carli, 1982; Hall, 1984), although Hall suggested a number of interacting conditions that deserve testing if more reports become available. Also, Hall examined studies reporting sex differences in interrupting other group members. Unfortunately, only two studies contained information sufficient to estimate an effect size. These two yielded a mean of 0.98 in the male direction, and 5 of the 6 studies in which the direction of the sex difference was known indicated more interruptions by men than women.

Behavior in Other Types of Groups

Behavioral sex differences in groups that are assigned very structured tasks are also of interest, although gender roles have less direct implications for these behaviors than for task and social-emotional specialization in discussion groups. For studies in which subjects are given the task of allocating rewards between themselves and other group members, Carli (1982) found that, on the average, women took smaller rewards for themselves than men did (mean effect size of -0.29 based on 11 known effect sizes). This tendency for women to underpay themselves has subsequently been replicated in several studies (e.g., Major & Forcey, 1985; Major & Konar, 1984; Major, McFarlin, & Gagnon, 1984). Taking smaller rewards for oneself can be seen as other-oriented and selfless behavior that is consistent with the female gender role.

Research on reward allocation has often focused on the rules or norms underlying these allocations: An equity rule, by which rewards are proportional to participants' inputs, is sometimes compared with an equality rule, by which all participants are rewarded equally. In her review, Carli (1982) reported that men divided rewards more equitably than women did (mean effect size of 0.20 based on 10 known effect sizes), but the sexes did not differ in the tendency to divide rewards equally. Behavior consistent with an equity rule has been interpreted as task-oriented and competitive and therefore as agentic, whereas behavior consistent with an equality rule has been interpreted as enhancing pleasant social interaction and therefore as communal (e.g., Kahn & Gaeddert, 1985; Kahn, O'Leary, Krulewitz, & Lamm, 1980). Yet, whether equity or equality would preserve pleasant interaction no doubt depends on many features of the specific situation.

Finally, Carli (1982) also examined cooperation in studies of the prisoner's dilemma game and found no sex difference in cooperation when same-sex groups were compared. Although there was a tendency for men to behave more cooperatively than women in mixed-sex games, the mean effect size of 0.28 was based on only 6 known effect sizes and did not differ significantly from 0.00. Moreover, it is difficult to know what implications cooperation in this extremely structured game situation may have for cooperative behavior in a wider range of settings.

Implications of Group Behavior Findings

Quantitative reviews of behavior in small groups have yielded clear evidence for a sex difference in social-emotional and task behavior, with women specializing in positive social-emotional behavior to a greater extent than men and men specializing in task behavior to a greater extent than women. Also, men may interrupt others more than women do. In addition, reward-allocation studies suggest that women take smaller rewards for themselves and follow an equity rule to a lesser extent than men. In general, these findings are interpretable from a gender-role perspective suggesting that women are expected to be selfless and concerned with others' welfare and pleasant social interaction whereas men are expected to be masterful and self-assertive. Sex differences in many other behaviors in the group process literature have not yet been summarized quantitatively. Perhaps Dion's (1985) stimulating narrative review of sex differences in a broad range of these behaviors will foster additional meta-analyses.

As in the case of other social behaviors, there are important questions that should be raised about the validity of generalizations about sex differences in small-group behavior. Group research, like other research in social psychology, is based primarily on behavior of initially unacquainted people who interact on a relatively short-term basis. Research on social interaction among people who know one another well or who are in organizational roles has less often been interpreted as relevant to sex differences. If analogous sex comparisons were made in groups that exist on a long-term basis, it is not clear what outcomes might be obtained. For example, with respect to sex differences in task and social-emotional behavior, it might be important to consider that in the aggregate, women spend a much greater amount of time than men do in nurturing and service-provision activities in the home, and men spend more time than women do in wage-earning activities (Robinson, 1977). This division of labor may suggest some specialization toward social-emotional goals for women and task goals for men. However, viewed at a molecular level of content analyses of behavior, the domestic chores of homemakers require considerable task-oriented activity, and paid employment sometimes requires a large component of social-emotional activity. Because of such complexities of levels of analysis, relatively simple classificatory schemes for social interaction seem insufficient to further understanding of behavior in families—or in organizations, for that matter. Perhaps more complex content analyses could take into account the relevance that behaviors have for various types of goals. Similar issues come to mind when attempting to apply to natural settings many of the research paradigms developed to study small-group interaction in experimental laboratories. Therefore, generalizing sex-difference findings from social-psychological research on small groups to a variety of natural settings raises particularly difficult questions.

CONCLUSION

In summary, quantitative reviews of sex differences in influenceability, numerous nonverbal behaviors, and several aspects of group behavior have become available in recent years. These reviews generally provide evidence of aggregate-level sex differences as well as considerable inconsistency between studies in the magnitude of these differences. Each of these reviews encompassed a complex research literature that fully challenged reviewers' theoretical and methodological skills. Indeed, this relatively brief overview chapter on these behaviors does not provide enough detail to give the many complexities of these research areas a thorough analysis. Therefore, readers interested in the patterning of sex differences in these social behaviors should pursue the original reviews that I have cited. Having stated this proviso that more information should be sought in other writings, I can now address the task of providing a general interpretation of research on sex differences in social behavior.

5 The Interpretation of Sex Differences in Social Behavior

THE MAGNITUDE OF SEX DIFFERENCES

Before exploring the theoretical implications of the sex differences reported in quantitative reviews, let us consider the magnitude or size of sex differences. To what extent can sex-difference findings be considered *small* or *large?* In this book, labels such as small and large have only occasionally been used to describe magnitude. Such terms were avoided because arriving at such interpretations of sex differences—whether these differences are expressed in terms of effect sizes or some other metric—is a matter that demands careful analysis. Judgments about size should not be delivered upon the mere inspection of a sex difference expressed in a particular metric, because meaningful judgments should take into account other known research findings, aspects of research methods, and, if possible, the evaluation of the behavior in the society.

Interpretations of the magnitude of the aggregated sex differences (mean effect sizes) produced by meta-analytic reviews have often been proposed. However, before interpreting aggregated differences, investigators should recall that, as explained in Chapter 1, whether overall sex differences warrant emphasis at all depends on their consistency across studies: Extremely inconsistent findings should be described primarily in terms of interacting conditions that account for the inconsistencies. In addition, interpretations of magnitude are sometimes given to the sex differences reported in individual studies. Yet deciding how large individual findings are involves largely the same issues as deciding how large aggregated findings are. Therefore, this discussion pertains to judging the magnitude of both individual and aggregated findings.

As also noted in Chapter 1, social scientists commonly describe the sex differences reported in the psychological literature as small. For example, in a statement that typifies overall characterizations of sex differences found in recent textbooks, Doyle (1985, p. 57) wrote, " . . . few genuine differences of any substantial nature can be found." As proof of small magnitude, aggregated sex differences reported in meta-analytic studies are sometimes expressed in terms of the overall percentage of variability in the dependent variables that is explained by sex (e.g., Deaux, 1984; Hyde, 1981).[1] Based on currently available findings, these percentages are as great as about 25% but generally below 10% and more typically below 5%. Yet such figures, in and of themselves, do not prove small magnitude.

The complexity of the magnitude issue is suggested by the disagreements it has engendered among meta-analysts. Some quantitative reviewers (e.g., Hyde, 1981) have viewed average sex differences as relatively small, and others (e.g., Hall, 1984; Rosenthal & Rubin, 1982b) have viewed them as larger and as nontrivial in their impact on everyday life. The magnitude issue is not easily settled, because it inevitably raises questions of broader outcomes and utilities. Although these questions cannot be resolved by existing research findings, I evaluate the magnitude issue in terms of several considerations:

1. Cohen's Guidelines for Small, Medium, and Large Effect Sizes.   Cohen (1977) suggested as rough guidelines for the *d* metric that 0.20 is small, 0.50 is medium, and 0.80 is large. Cohen argued that small effect sizes are often found in new areas of inquiry, because "the phenomena under study are typically not under good experimental or measurement control or both" (p. 25). He further argued that medium effect sizes are those that people would normally notice, such as the IQ difference between clerical and semi-skilled workers. Large differences are "grossly perceptible" according to Cohen, such as the IQ difference between holders of the Ph.D. degree and typical first-year college students. Although such guidelines have been sharply criticized (Glass, McGaw, & Smith, 1981), Cohen's distinctions are interesting because they are derived from his subjective average of research findings in the behavioral sciences as well as from his impressions of the discriminability of the group differences implied by these findings. By Cohen's criteria, most mean sex-difference effect sizes fall between the small and medium benchmarks (e.g., helping behavior, aggression), some

---

[1]To determine percent-variance accounted for by sex, the mean *d* produced by a meta-analytic aggregation of findings can be translated into an *r* by means of the following formula: $r = d / \sqrt{d^2 + 4}$, and this *r* is then squared. Alternatively, some reviewers (e.g., Hyde, 1981) have calculated percent-variance for each sex-difference finding and averaged these values. Although this latter method does not take direction of the sex difference into account, it provides a more accurate estimate of the average percentage of variance accounted for by sex.

fall between the medium and large benchmarks (e.g., task and social-emotional activity, social smiling, speech errors), and a few exceed the large benchmark (e.g., facial expressiveness, filled pauses). As Hall (1984) showed, nonverbal sex differences tend to be somewhat larger than other sex differences.

2. Comparisons of Sex Differences in Social Behavior with other Known Findings. Another relevant standard involves comparing mean effect sizes of various sex differences in social behaviors with mean effect sizes that estimate the impact of other variables on social behaviors. A thorough analysis from this perspective would compare the sex difference for a given class of behaviors (e.g., aggression) with the impact of other variables (e.g., amount of frustration; anticipation of interaction with victim) on this same class. This exercise would ideally be carried out on a single sample of studies. The meta-analytic work required to make these comparisons has not yet been carried out. Nonetheless, it is worth noting the few available meta-analyses on the impact of other variables on the behaviors discussed in this book, even though the samples of studies are of course different.[2]

For helping, the class of social behaviors considered in Chapter 2 of this book, a quantitative review of the effect of negative mood states found a mean effect size of 0.22 in the direction of greater helping (Miller & Carlson, 1984). A meta-analysis on one aspect of social influence examined studies on the "foot-in-the-door" phenomenon, by which a person who has complied with a small request is more likely to comply with a subsequent larger request (Beaman, Cole, Preston, Klentz, & Steblay, 1983). The mean effect size was estimated to be 0.32. Harris and Rosenthal's (1985) review of studies of processes that may mediate interpersonal expectancy effects encompassed a number of behaviors including some of the nonverbal behaviors (e.g., smiling) discussed in Chapter 4. This review yielded mean effect sizes from 0.02 to approximately 1.00, with the majority of these means falling in the small-to-medium range in terms of Cohen's (1977) criteria.

Although other available quantitative reviews in social psychology pertain to behaviors not examined in this book, the mean effect sizes they reported provide a very rough comparative standard for sex differences. For example, Bond and Titus (1983) reviewed the social facilitation

---

[2]The mean effect size reported in a quantitative review reflects numerous decisions of the reviewer—for example, whether unknown effects reported as nonsignificant are represented by the 0.00 value that indicates exactly no difference. A more extensive comparative study of mean effect sizes would take such factors into account.

literature, where the presence of others has been hypothesized to improve performance on simple tasks and impair performance on complex tasks (Zajonc, 1965). Among various comparisons between subjects performing simple or complex tasks alone and with other people, the largest of several mean effect sizes was 0.36. In the literature on interpersonal expectancy effects, mean effect sizes in research paradigms involving only human subjects ranged from 0.17 to 1.05 (Rosenthal & Rubin, 1978). Finally, in a review of research on the effects of competitive and cooperative goal structures on achievement and group productivity, the largest mean effect sizes, which compared cooperative with competitive structures and cooperative with individualistic, were 0.78 (Johnson, Maruyama, Johnson, & Nelson, 1981). In general, these and other mean effect sizes that are associated with known and widely accepted phenomena in social psychology, are in the same range as those obtained for sex differences. For this reason, textbook authors and other interpreters of the scientific literature on social behavior should be very cautious about singling out sex-difference findings and labeling only them as small. All findings should be evaluated by the same standard.

Another comparative standard is provided by Cooper and Findley's (1982) computation of mean effect sizes for the findings cited in a sample of social psychology textbooks. These findings, which pertained to extremely diverse independent and dependent variables, yielded a mean effect-size estimate of 0.92, a larger value than the mean effect sizes reported in most meta-analyses on particular hypotheses.[3] This larger size can be accounted for by the understandable tendency of textbook writers to cite, not typical or average studies, but studies that provide especially strong demonstrations of phenomena. Indeed, some individual studies also report sex-difference effect sizes that are quite large (e.g., see effect sizes listed by Hall, 1978, and Eagly & Crowley, 1986).

Finally, mean sex differences in social behavior can be compared with other known sex differences. Hall (1984) has already carried out such an analysis for numerous psychological sex differences, including cognitive abilities and some personality traits. Hall's data suggest that, aside from the tendency for nonverbal sex differences to be relatively large, sex differences in social behaviors are typical of other psychological sex differences. This conclusion has been substantiated by meta-analyses of spatial ability (Linn & Petersen, 1985), mathematical ability (Rossi, 1983), and formal operational thought (Meehan, 1984), which became available after Hall wrote her book.

---

[3]This mean effect size aggregates comparisons involving t-tests, F-tests, and correlation coefficients.

Psychological sex differences can also be compared with physical sex differences. Thomas and French's (1985) quantitative review of sex differences in motor performance reported various mean differences in the d metric, with positive values indicating superior performance by males and negative values superior performance by females. Two of these mean effect sizes were much larger than any known aggregated psychological sex difference (d = 2.18 for throw velocity and d = 1.98 for throw distance). The other mean effect sizes for motor performance were of comparable magnitude to psychological sex differences (e.g., d = −0.21 for fine eye-motor coordination, d = 0.66 for grip strength, d = 0.54 for long jump).[4] In addition, for motor activity level, Eaton and Enns (1986) reported a mean effect size of 0.49 in the direction of greater activity by males. Comparisons between psychological and physical sex differences are particularly instructive, because the relative ease with which physical behaviors can be identified and evaluated probably gives people a surer sense for whether sex differences in these behaviors are noticeable and consequential in daily life.

3. Use of Binomial Effect Size Display to Suggest Practical Importance of Sex Differences. Rosenthal and Rubin (1982c) have suggested that mean effect size findings be presented in terms of a "binomial effect size display." They argued that this metric provides an index of the practical importance of effect sizes in terms that are easily understood, even by people with little or no statistical training. In general, this binomial effect size display indicates the effect of an independent variable (e.g., a new teaching method, a new cancer treatment) on a success rate (e.g., the percentage of people who pass a course or survive cancer). Thus, a new cancer treatment might increase survival rates from 40% to 60%, for a change of 20%.

To apply this technique to the interpretation of sex differences, an investigator determines the percentage of each sex above the average response in the combined group of women and men (see tables provided by Rosenthal & Rubin, 1982c). Thus, in terms of this method, the mean

---

[4]For some motor performances (Thomas & French, 1985) and for motor activity (Eaton & Enns, 1986), effect sizes were related to subjects' age. For such behaviors (e.g., throw velocity and distance, grip strength, long jump), sex differences were larger for post-pubertal than for pre-pubertal samples of subjects. The mean effect sizes given by Thomas and French and by Eaton and Enns were averaged over these younger and older samples. It might also be noted that (a) for some motor performances, effect sizes were homogeneous and (b) for other performances, correctly specified models were obtained once age was taken into account. These outcomes are understandable in view of the standardized measures and relatively controlled research settings found in studies of motor performance.

(weighted) effect size obtained for aggressive behavior, $d = 0.29$ (see Chapter 3), can be interpreted as meaning that above-average amounts of aggression were enacted by approximately 43% of women and 57% of men. Although this effect size accounted for "only" 2% of the variance, this percentage difference suggests a non-trivial impact. For a more substantial effect size, such as the sex difference in social smiling reported by Hall (1984), $d = 0.63$, the binomial effect size display provides the interpretation that above-average amounts of smiling occurred for 65% of women and 35% of men. This description is obtained for an effect size that accounted for "only" 9% of the variability in smiling. This percent-difference metric more readily conveys the practical meaning of effect sizes than the percent-variance metric that has been more commonly favored by reviewers. Other metrics that are related to the binomial effect-size display yield percentages or ratios of females and males who exceed the 95th or 99th percentile of the combined distribution of females and males (see Hyde, 1981; Rossi, 1983) rather than the 50th percentile.

4. Considerations of Research Methodology.   A deeper understanding of the magnitude of effect sizes must take features of research methods into account. One such consideration is that effect sizes are larger to the extent that extraneous variables are controlled. Uncontrolled variables likely increase the variability of behavior and therefore inflate the standard deviation that serves as the denominator of the effect size. Thus, sex differences should tend to be larger to the extent that extraneous subject variables are controlled through the use of homogeneous samples of subjects (see Becker & Hedges, 1984). Also, because field settings are typically relatively uncontrolled, an aggregated effect size based on studies, such as those in the helping-behavior literature, that are conducted largely in the field, is more impressive than an effect size of similar magnitude based on studies conducted largely in the laboratory.

The extent to which the behavioral criteria that serve as dependent variables aggregate responses may also influence effect-size magnitude. As suggested by research on personality traits and attitudes as predictors of behaviors (e.g., Epstein, 1979; Fishbein & Ajzen, 1974), a general disposition of persons, such as a trait or general attitude, may affect the overall tendency to engage in relevant behaviors to a substantial degree, without having more than a minor impact on each of the individual behaviors that comprise the overall tendency. For example, as Fishbein and Ajzen showed, a general attitude (e.g., attitude toward religion) predicts a general behavioral tendency (e.g., the overall tendency to engage in a diverse set of religious behaviors) quite successfully but predicts single behaviors (e.g., donating money to a religious institution) much less well. If being female or male has implications for behavior similar to those of a personality trait or attitude,[5] one's gender should have considerably more impact on one's general tendency to engage in gender-stereotypic behaviors than on single stereotypic behaviors.

From this perspective, behavioral criteria should be examined for the extent to which they involve aggregations across gender-stereotypic behaviors. Some criteria, such as those that assess task and social-emotional specialization in small groups (see Chapter 4), do aggregate gender-stereotypic behaviors, whereas others do not. It should be possible to generate substantial sex differences by building composite indices of stereotypic behaviors, and, in fact, mean effect sizes for task and social-emotional activities in small groups are larger than those for most sex differences. Smaller differences should be common for research employing single-act criteria such as those more typically used in sex-difference research. In addition, measures aggregating single behaviors across occasions should yield larger sex differences than single-occasion measures (see Chapter 3 and Becker, 1986).

By a logic that takes the level of aggregation of the dependent variable into account, it can be seen that even very small-magnitude relations may have considerable practical importance. To illustrate this point, Abelson (1985) determined that in baseball for a single batting performance the percentage of variance that is explained by batting skill is about one-third of 1%. Nevertheless, he argued that people's intuition that batting skill is nontrivially predictive of success in baseball is well founded. According to Abelson's reasoning, the effects of batting skill cumulate over individual players and over occasions at bat to create a substantial relation between batting skill and team success for the season. Similarly, a relation between sex and a single-occasion behavior that appears tiny in terms of variance explained may be nontrivial in terms of its cumulative impact.

5.   *Considerations of the Utility of Behaviors.*   Finally, in a practical sense, the size of a sex difference depends on how the behavior is regarded or evaluated in natural settings (Cooper, 1984; Gallo, 1978). For example, the ability to understand nonverbal messages might be more important for some tasks than others and perhaps in some cultures than others. Thus, from the standpoint of utility, a behavioral sex difference represented by a

---

[5]Even though this argument suggests that being female or male functions as a disposition, the analogy with personality traits and general attitudes is incomplete. Thus, by the social-role account of sex differences, individuals tend to behave stereotypically across a range of behaviors because (a) gender-role expectations, which are internalized to some extent, are important in a variety of situations, and (b) abilities and beliefs are somewhat sex-typed, due to sex differences in prior role occupancy. Thus, gender does not derive its implications for behavior merely because it functions as an internalized disposition of the person but because of a more diverse set of pressures.

small effect size could be important if people value and closely monitor performance of that behavior. Similarly, a sex difference represented by a large effect size could be unimportant if little value is attached to relative performance of the behavior. Unfortunately, because little is known about how various social behaviors are evaluated, at present it is difficult to take these important utility considerations into account in judging the magnitude of sex differences.

In summary, although reviewers may be justified in labeling mean effect sizes of, say, 0.20 or less as in some sense small, such a numerical value, in and of itself, does not allow reviewers to conclude that an effect is trivial or unimportant in natural settings. Reviewers certainly should not commit the opposite error by uncritically describing sex differences as large or important. Instead, mean sex-difference effect sizes should be given careful analysis, by comparing them with other known findings and taking features of typical methodologies into account. Even relatively small sex differences could be important to groups of women and men who work together over time. Moreover, in hazarding general statements about the size of sex differences in the psychological literature, reviewers should keep in mind that, even given the usual narrow-gauge behavioral criteria that are minimally aggregative of individual behaviors, most of the mean sex differences that have been obtained, to date, in social behaviors exceed Cohen's small-effect benchmark. Thus, people's intuitions that many of these sex differences are consequential may well be correct, despite the failure of sex to explain a large percentage of variance in typical studies carried out by psychologists.

Sex Differences and Similarities.   Within the framework of the preceding discussion of the magnitude of sex differences, it is worth commenting further on some of the summary descriptions of sex differences that psychologists have provided in modern textbooks and overviews of research. In addition to labeling sex differences as small, such discussions often emphasize similarities (Hyde, 1985; Tavris & Wade, 1984). For example, Basow (1986, p. 52) wrote, "The similarities between the sexes are as notable as, if not more notable than, the differences." In informal discussions of sex differences, psychologists sometimes assert that the sexes are more similar than different or that similarities between the sexes are more common than differences.

One possible interpretation of such statements is that sex differences have been examined for many behaviors and that the mean effect sizes found for these behaviors typically do not differ significantly from the zero value that indicates no difference. However, an interpretation of this kind is not supported by the empirical literature on sex differences. Those social behaviors and cognitive abilities that have been meta-analyzed for sex differences with reasonably large samples of studies conducted on adolescent or adult subjects have usually documented overall differences in the sense that the null hypothesis of no difference was rejected. Thus, most quantitative reviews of sex differences have, to date, indicated sex differences, not sex similarities. Reviews arguing for the absence of sex differences are, for the most part, the earlier, narrative reviews, such as that of Maccoby and Jacklin (1974), which, as explained in Chapter 1, did not implement statistically justified rules of inference when drawing overall conclusions about sex differences.

In evaluating the outcomes of the quantitative reviews that are now available, psychologists should keep in mind that, not surprisingly, reviewers have examined classes of behaviors that are stereotypically thought to yield sex differences. Perhaps other behaviors, unrelated to the agentic and communal dimensions on which the social behavior of the sexes is believed to differ, would not yield sex differences. Along these lines, Hyde (1985, p. 152) speculated that tendencies such as honesty, conscientiousness, and sincerity may be unrelated to sex. Hall's (1984, p. 147, Table 11.3) mean effect-size estimates for sex differences in a diverse set of personal qualities suggested that the null hypothesis of no difference would not be rejected for areas such as self-esteem, loneliness, and extraversion, but this evidence is not definitive because these mean effect-size estimates were based on small samples of studies. In view of the uncertain state of the evidence on nonstereotypic behaviors, claims that there are more behaviors demonstrating sex similarities than sex differences at present are not justifiable, based on the empirical literature.

Another consideration in discussing sex similarities is that the apparatus of scientific investigation is appropriate for investigating the presence and absence of differences and inappropriate for investigating similarities, as numerous psychologists have noted (e.g., Grady, 1981; Maccoby & Jacklin, 1974; Wallston & Grady, 1985). Statistical tests are formulated to allow rejection of the hypothesis of no difference and thus confirmation of the hypothesis of difference. When the null hypothesis fails to be rejected, one cannot "accept the null hypothesis" by declaring the hypothesis of no difference confirmed, although one correctly concludes that there is no evidence for a difference. To the extent that similarity has the logical status of the null hypothesis, similarity cannot be proven. This problem is one source of the ambiguity of statements of the sort that women and men are similar or more similar than different.

In view of these limitations, the similar-versus-different terminology is a poor one for discussing sex differences. Abandonment of this dichotomy should bring few regrets among social scientists: Little of scientific value would be lost because the terminology yields a categorical distinction when a continuous scale is more appropriate.[6] Obviously, the sexes are not either similar or different. Instead, they differ to varying degrees, depending on the behaviors examined. Exactly no difference is one of the end-points of the scale on which these graduated distinctions can be expressed. The most useful metrics for such descriptions are the effect size and its variants such as the binomial effect size display, which have been emphasized in this book.

Sex Differences and Individual Differences.   It is also popular among interpreters of sex-difference research to argue that individual differences are more important than sex differences. Hyde (1985, p. 141) noted that " . . . even when there are average gender differences in a particular trait, there are almost always still large individual differences—differences from one female to the next and from one male to the next. Often these individual differences are more important than the average gender differences." The point that there are sources of individual differences in addition to sex is obviously true. But whether these individual differences are more important than those associated with sex is a more interesting question that raises issues of comparative standards for judging sex-difference findings.

One possible individual-difference standard for evaluating sex differences would compare the mean sex-difference effect size for a given class of behaviors with the mean effect size associated with some other individual-difference variable regarded as relevant to this same class of behaviors (e.g., self-esteem, chronic anxiety). Careful comparative analyses of this sort have yet to be conducted. Yet, given the general tendency for sex-difference effect sizes to be comparable in magnitude to those associated with other independent variables, it is unlikely that effect sizes are systematically smaller for sex differences than for other variables believed to be sources of individual differences. Indeed, personality variables, perhaps the most important type of individual-difference variable, have been thought by some psychologists (e.g., Mischel, 1968) to yield particularly small effects, at least when these variables are related to the sorts of relatively narrow-gauge dependent variables that have been common in most psychological research.

Another possible interpretation of statements of the sort that individual differences are more important than sex differences is the following: If one were to cumulate over all sources of individual differences other than sex for a given class of behaviors, these other variables would collectively account for more variability than sex. This idea is not particularly informa-

---

[6]Nevertheless, it is worth noting that, from a liberal-feminist perspective, the term *similarity* may be more politically congenial than the term *difference*.

tive because the researcher would be pitting one variable (sex) against many other variables. Ordinarily, it is a foregone conclusion that a large set of relevant variables accounts for more variability than a single relevant variable.

Still another possible meaning of the statements about individual differences is merely that there is usually a great deal of variability that is not explained by sex. This point is of course valid. As already discussed, the percentage of variance explained by sex is typically not large—nor is the percentage of variance explained by single variables other than sex typically large. The variability within sex is clearly important in all research on sex differences: It contributes to the error term for evaluating the statistical significance of sex differences in individual studies, and it provides the denominator for computing effect sizes. Variability within sex is thus an essential ingredient of all scientific interpretations of sex differences.

Sex Differences as Overlapping Distributions. Many textbook authors (e.g., Hyde, 1985; Kaplan & Sedney, 1980; Lips & Colwill, 1978) have described sex differences in terms of overlapping female and male distributions. For example, Tavris and Wade (1984, p. 41) wrote, "Men and women overlap in abilities and personality traits, as they overlap in physical attributes. Men on the average are taller than women, but some women are taller than most men." This perspective is informative, but a description in terms of overlapping distributions should be stated precisely enough to convey the extent to which the two distributions overlap. Some motor skills (Thomas & French, 1985) and physical attributes yield very large sex differences and little distributional overlap. Height, Tavris and Wade's example, provides an illustration. The mean height for Americans has been estimated to be 64 inches for women and 70 inches for men, with a standard deviation within each sex of 2.3 inches (Gillis & Avis, 1980). The effect size associated with this difference is 2.6 in d units. Of the total area covered by the female and male populations combined, only 11% is estimated to be overlapping and 89% nonoverlapping (see Cohen, 1977, Table 2.2.1).[7] A sex difference of this magnitude is, of course, profoundly noticeable in daily life, even though some women are taller than many men and some men shorter than many women. Even for such a large sex difference, it is nevertheless true that the range within either sex is much greater than the mean difference between the sexes.

Psychological sex differences, when averaged across studies, are consid-

---

[7]Various indices of the extent to which distributions are nonoverlapping have been proposed and discussed by Cohen (1977). These indices have been used in quantitative reviews (e.g., Eagly & Carli, 1981). The binomial effect size display proposed by Rosenthal and Rubin (1983c) is closely related to Cohen's indices.

erably smaller in magnitude than the height sex difference (see Chapters 2, 3, and 4). For a sex difference yielding an effect size of 0.50 in the d metric, approximately 67% of the total area covered by the combined female and male population distributions is overlapping and 33% nonoverlapping. Nonetheless, the fact that two such distributions overlap considerably does not invalidate the difference between the sexes. Cohen (1977), as already noted, maintained that differences yielding effect sizes of 0.50 are typically discriminable by observers, and, as I have argued, caution should be exercised in labeling such differences as small or unimportant.

THEORETICAL IMPLICATIONS OF QUANTITATIVE REVIEWS OF SEX DIFFERENCES

Although only a limited number of quantitative reviews of sex differences in social behavior are available, they have yielded a considerable amount of high-quality information. As summarized in Chapter 2, such a review established an overall tendency for men to be more helpful than women in the kinds of short-term interactions with strangers that have been widely studied by social psychologists. Yet these sex differences were particularly inconsistent across studies. It is noteworthy that much of this inconsistency was accounted for by a number of predictors suggested by the social-role theory of sex differences. As summarized in Chapter 3, men were also found to be more aggressive than women, and this sex difference was larger for aggression that produced physical harm or pain than for aggression that produced psychological or social harm.

Reviews of other social behaviors were summarized in Chapter 4. Women, compared with men, were shown to agree more with other people in conformity and persuasion studies, although evidence for this sex differ-ence was strongest in group-pressure conformity studies, which allow group members to have surveillance over one another's behavior. Women were also found to be more skilled than men at nonverbal communication—that is, better nonverbal decoders and encoders, especially with respect to the face. In social situations, women smile and laugh more than men, use their faces and bodies more expressively, show more involvement with others' behavior, touch other people more, and approach them more closely. In group discussions, women, more than men, act friendly and agree with other group members. In contrast, men, more than women, contribute behaviors that are strictly oriented to accomplishing the task that the group was assigned. Men are probably more likely to interrupt other people than women are. When allocating rewards, men take more for themselves than women do and are somewhat more likely to allocate via an equity rule.

Evidence for the Social-Role Theory of Sex Differences

The relevance of findings in each of these areas to the social-role theory of sex differences has already been noted. This theory implicates conformity to gender-role expectations as a major source of the sexes' differing behavior. Therefore, one prediction from the theory is that, on the whole, social behavior is gender-stereotypic, at least in situations in which gender roles are salient. Recall that at a molar level, much of the information in gender roles can be summarized in terms of expectations that women be communal—that is, manifest social sensitivity, selflessness, and concern with others' welfare, and that men be agentic—that is, manifest mastery, control, and independence from other people. The behavioral tendencies suggested by the aggregated sex-difference findings produced by quantitative reviews usually do correspond to this description of gender roles.

A seeming discrepancy from this correspondence between gender roles and behavior was encountered in the helping-behavior literature (see Chapter 2): The stereotypic expectancy that women are especially helpful did not correspond to the overall finding of greater helpfulness among men. This discrepancy was explained by what might be termed the peculiarities of the research endeavor—namely, the particular types of helping behaviors and settings selected for investigation. These types may be so unrepresentative of daily life (in which much helping occurs in close and long-term relationships) that the direction of the aggregated sex difference would reverse were the unrepresented behaviors and settings included in research in proportion to their actual occurrence. This speculation about the unrepresented behaviors and settings is supported by research in areas such as social support and friendship suggesting that females give more help and support than males do (see Chapter 2). Therefore, the tendency for men to be found more helpful than women in helping-behavior research does not necessarily invalidate the stereotype of women as more helpful than men. In fact, as shown by Eagly and Crowley's (1986) detailed exploration of stereotypic beliefs about helping, people do regard certain types of helping behavior (e.g., potentially dangerous behaviors) as more typical of men than women. Such behaviors happen to be overselected in social psychological research on helping.

The inconsistency among effect sizes that was shown in those reviews that included tests of homogeneity is also supportive of the social-role theory. In general, stereotypic sex differences are expected to occur in settings in which gender roles are relatively more salient than any competing role expectations with counterstereotypic impact. Traditional research settings fit this description, not because they have cues that forcefully bring gender to subjects' attention, but because they usually do not bring into play the specific roles such as family and occupational roles that guide behavior in most natural settings. In the absence of such specific roles, behavior is guided by more diffuse roles such as gender roles and age-based roles. Especially in a group of college student subjects who are strangers to one another, sex is in fact one of the few available bases of social differentiation.

Despite the general tendency of research settings to promote the display of gender-stereotypic behavior, gender roles should become especially salient when certain additional conditions are in place. Among these conditions is the presence of an audience, because surveillance by other people should ordinarily increase the salience of their expectations. In the reviews of helping behavior (Chapter 2) and influenceability (Chapter 4), surveillance by an audience was associated with larger sex differences.

Also consistent with the social-role framework are numerous other predictions that were made for specific social behaviors. For example, for helping behavior (Chapter 2), it was argued based on the status analysis of gender roles that the tendency for men to help more than women should be especially large when helping is an assertive intervention rather than a compliant response to a request. The confirmation of this and other predictions that are consistent with the role analysis lends credence to the approach.

Sex Differences in Skills and Beliefs.   As causes of behavioral sex differences, the social-role theory also implicates sex-typed skills and sex-typed beliefs about the consequences of behaviors. The prior experience that women and men have had in social roles is assumed to underlie these skill and belief differences. To the extent that the sexes have not been proportionally represented in specific social roles, they should differ in the skills and beliefs that they have acquired.

These skill and belief sex differences as well as gender-role expectancies may underlie overall sex-difference findings (i.e., mean effect sizes) for social behaviors. Also, skills and beliefs can account for inconsistencies between studies in the extent to which female and male behaviors differ. Thus, for some particular behaviors of a class such as aggressive behaviors, men's and women's skills and beliefs diverge considerably and thereby foster sex differences in behavior. For other behaviors, these skills and beliefs do not diverge nearly as much.

As shown in the helping, aggression, and influenceability meta-analyses (Chapters 2, 3, and 4), the extent to which women and men differ in skills and beliefs relevant to each behavior can be assessed empirically. Respondents rated the behaviors (or stimulus materials) examined in the available studies, to determine whether female and male respondents differed in self-reported skills and beliefs relevant to each of the behaviors. Although this approach of obtaining ratings from a panel of respondents has not yet been applied as systematically as it might be, the applications described in this book have yielded correlational findings consistent with the operation of skill and belief factors. For example, sex differences in helping (Chapter 2) were significantly related to sex differences in two skill-related factors (competence and comfort in relation to the helping behaviors) and one belief factor (beliefs about the danger one faces as a helper). More thorough exploration of sex-typed skills and beliefs is warranted in primary research as well as in quantitative reviews. Among other issues, such research might examine the important assumption that sex differences in skills and beliefs are caused by prior role occupancy.

Date of Publication. The social-role analysis may be thought to have implications for secular trends in the magnitude of sex differences in social behaviors. Yet it is not clear whether the role analysis would predict change in the magnitude of sex differences during the period in which psychologists have been systematically comparing women and men. One consideration is that gender-role expectancies concerning communion and agency have apparently been relatively stable in the past three decades (see Chapter 1). Consequently, on the basis of gender roles, little change in sex differences should have occurred during this time period. It is more difficult to know whether the role occupancy of women and men has changed substantially enough to decrease sex differences in skills and beliefs related to the classes of behaviors examined in this book.

Quantitative reviewers have observed whether date of publication of studies is related to the magnitude of the sex differences they reported. A number of these analyses yielded no significant relation between publication year and sex-difference magnitude (Carli, 1982; Eagly & Carli, 1981; Eagly & Steffen, 1986a; Eaton & Enns, 1986; Thomas & French, 1985, for all motor tasks except sit-ups). Other analyses yielded (a) a tendency for sex differences to become smaller over time (Eagly & Crowley, 1986; Rosenthal & Rubin, 1982b, for all cognitive abilities except verbal ability; Thomas & French, 1985, for sit-ups), or (b) a tendency for sex differences to become larger over time (Hall, 1978, 1980; Rosenthal & Rubin, 1982b, for verbal ability; Wood, in press).[8] Interpretation of these findings is difficult because of their inconsistency across the various research areas.

---

[8]Rosenthal and Rubin (1982b; see also Becker & Hedges, 1984) reported a gain in cognitive performance for females relative to males in the time period for which data were available. Presumably this trend implies a decrease in magnitude for the sex differences in the male direction (quantitative ability, visual-spatial ability, field articulation) and an increase for the difference in the female direction (verbal ability). These trends over time appear to be stronger for cognitive abilities than for social behaviors, perhaps because cognitive abilities are more strongly affected by a single underlying social change—the equalization of educational opportunity for women and men.

Adding additional ambiguity to these findings are the relationships obtained between various study attributes and publication year within the meta-analyses, presumably because of changes that occurred in the research methods that were popular for various topics. Publication year would have to be disentangled from its methodological correlates before it could be interpreted in terms of change in the status of women. In general, although the matter warrants much more detailed study, there is at present no overall evidence that sex differences reported in the scientific literature have become generally smaller in the last decades.

Alternative Theories of Sex Differences

There are many theories of sex differences that provide alternatives to the role theory I have presented, and these other frameworks are not necessarily inconsistent with the account based on social roles. Role expectations as well as sex-typed skills and abilities may be causally linked to other factors such as childhood socialization pressures and biological predispositions.

Social Psychological Oppression Theories.   As Henley (1977) has argued in relation to nonverbal behavior, sex differences in a given situation may reflect conscious or non-conscious efforts of men to dominate and oppress women in that situation. This perspective has a somewhat different emphasis from the social-role approach. Most importantly, the role account, although it also emphasizes power and status differences between the sexes, regards these differences as leading people to have contrasting expectations about appropriate female and male behavior and treats these expectations as a proximal cause of sex differences in social behaviors. Women's prior experience in lower-status roles and men's in higher-status roles may also cause women and men to differ in the skills and beliefs that they bring to current situations. Thus, in the role framework, men's dominance and women's oppression are treated as remote or distal causes of adult sex differences and not proximal causes.

As Hall (1984) has also argued, the oppression hypothesis leads one to predict that sex differences are more pronounced when both women and men are present than when women and men are with members of their own sex only. Although some impact of oppressors on the oppressed likely carries over to same-sex contexts, active oppression of women by men should have its strongest impact in face-to-face cross-sex interaction. In view of this prediction, it should be noted that the hypothesis that sex differences are larger in cross-sex than same-sex settings has not fared well for some social behaviors. Hall (1984) showed that this pattern was generally not obtained for nonverbal behavior, and, in the case of touch, interpersonal distance, gazing, and perhaps other nonverbal behaviors, the sex difference is probably greater in same-sex than cross-sex contexts (see also Vrugt & Kerkstra, 1984). Also, Carli's (1982) meta-analysis did not find that the sex-composition of groups affected task and social-emotional specialization. For helping behavior, more aid or succor was given in the one cross-sex combination of male helper and female recipient than in the other cross-sex combination and the same-sex combinations (Eagly & Crowley, 1986). For aggressive behavior, people of both sexes tended to aggress somewhat more against men than women (Eagly & Steffen, 1986a). Although several social-influence studies have examined cross-sex and same-sex contexts, these findings have not been appropriately aggregated with a view to comparing these contexts (see Eagly's, 1978, review; also Ward, Seccombe, Bendel, & Carter, 1985). Overall, in the research reviewed in this book, there is little support for the notion that social behaviors are systematically more stereotypic in cross-sex than same-sex contexts. Yet the theoretical implications of the available findings warrant exploration, and more empirical attention is needed as well. In general, much remains to be learned about differences in the norms that govern cross-sex and same-sex interaction (see discussions by Hall, in press, and Maltz & Borker, 1982).

A major caveat must be stated when considering the implications of research findings for oppression theories: The types of behaviors that researchers examine by direct observation are limited by ethical constraints that quite understandably place severely coercive behaviors off-limits. As a result, in research settings, sex differences may tend to be mediated by relatively subtle communication of gender-role expectancies as well as by sex-typed skills and beliefs. In contrast, some natural settings allow the overtly coercive pressures that more typically come to mind when thinking about the oppression of women. For example, men may oppress women in organizations through sexual harassment (Tangri, Burt, & Johnson, 1982) and in intimate relationships through physical abuse (Breines & Gordon, 1983). Severely oppressive behaviors of these types are indeed more common in cross-sex than same-sex contexts.

Personality Theories. Theories emphasizing personality traits have provided popular approaches to the study of gender-stereotypic behavior. Socialization pressures that differ for girls and boys are presumed to bring about sex differences at the level of ingrained traits or dispositions, and these sex differences in personality, in turn, bring about corresponding sex differences in social behavior. Yet the major emphasis in these approaches is on individual differences in these traits within each sex. For example, both Bem (e.g., 1975; Bem, Martyna, & Watson, 1976) and Spence and Helmreich (1978) maintained that (a) people acquire masculine and feminine traits or dispositions to varying degrees, and (b) these dispositions then regulate gender-stereotypic behaviors, at least to some extent (see Taylor & Hall's, 1982, review).

This personality approach is distinguished from the social-role theory in two major respects:

1. According to the social-role account, sex-typed behavior flows from several causes—namely, gender-role expectancies and sex differences in abilities and beliefs. Because gender-role expectancies may be internalized to some degree, tendencies to be communal (called "feminine" in the personality approach) and agentic (called "masculine" in the personality approach) may indeed exist at the level of ingrained traits. However, social-role theory reserves judgment concerning the importance of such traits, in comparison with other causes of sex-typed behavior.

2. Whereas the personality approach stresses individual differences within each sex, the social-role approach stresses group differences between the sexes and variability in these group differences across situations.

Socialization Theories.   Socialization theories come in many variants, emphasizing, for example, social-learning (Mischel, 1966), cognitive developmental (Kohlberg, 1966), and psychoanalytic (Chodorow, 1978) accounts of the acquisition of sex-typed behavior. One obvious link between the social-role theory of sex differences and socialization theories is provided by the assumption that children and teenagers learn the content of gender roles. Presumably this content is conveyed by direct and indirect tutoring from parents, teachers, peers, and other socializers. More importantly, according to the social-role account of sex differences, mere observation of women and men enacting their roles and of the distributions of the sexes into these roles is an important source of sex-typed expectancies (see also Perry & Bussey, 1979). In addition, parents and other socializers may encourage or discourage girls and boys from entering the various specific training roles where important skills and beliefs are acquired. Such agents of socialization may very often promote occupancy of specific social roles that lead to sex-typed skills and beliefs.

The communality between the social-role theory and aspects of Chodorow's (1978) revisionist psychoanalytic theory deserves special mention. Chodorow also implicated the traditional division of labor as the source of the sex-typing of personality and behavioral tendencies. In particular, she argued that the assignment of the primary childcare role to women is the critical feature of the sexual division of labor. The fact that women perform most of the childcare was held to result in girls identifying with their mothers and developing typically feminine styles of relating to people. In contrast, boys learn that they should be different from their mothers, from whom they then separate psychologically and thereby become more involved than girls in events outside of the home and develop typically masculine styles of relating to people. Although in agreement with Chodorow's emphasis on the division of labor as the underlying source of sex differences, the social-role account developed in this book regards the assignment of childcare responsibilities to women as only one of several critical aspects of the division of labor. Also consequential is the disporportionate assignment to men of the paid employee role as well as high-status roles more generally. Additionally important are the types of activities that women and men carry out as employees (see Chapter 1). People observe all of these aspects of the division of labor and generally are participants in this system to some degree as well. From this broader social-role perspective, the learning that transpires in the mother-child dyad, although important, is only one source of the pressures that lead to gender-role expectations and sex differences in skills and beliefs, which then function as the proximal causes of sex-typed behavior.

From the role perspective, socialization pressures influence adult social behavior through the mediation of the role-related processes. Thus, parental socialization pressures have a systematic impact on adult sex differences only if these pressures affect adults' gender-role expectations or influence their prior role experiences in ways that affect their skills and beliefs. Although childhood socialization is bound to have considerable impact, learning role expectations and acquiring role-relevant skills and beliefs occur continually throughout the life cycle. Consequently, better prediction of adult sex differences can be achieved by focusing on the contemporaneous causes active in adult life rather than on childhood socialization. Early learning is but one contributor to these contemporaneous causes.

Biological Theories.   Similar points can be made with respect to biological causes. To the extent that biological sex differences exist, they may affect gender-role expectations and sex-typed skills and beliefs. For example, as argued in Chapter 3, men's greater height and upper-body strength may be reflected in many societies by encouragement for men to enter roles such as soldier that require physically aggressive behavior, and, by this mechanism, these male physical attributes probably promote formation of a social norm that men ought to be physically aggressive. If male sex hormones create a predisposition in men to behave aggressively in threatening situations, this factor would likely have similar effects on role occupancy and gender-role expectations. The proximal cause of men's greater aggressiveness would be largely social norms associated with the male gender role and some specific roles disproportionately occupied by men. As explained in Chapter 3, societies develop norms to regulate the expression of male aggressiveness, in a (sometimes unsuccessful) effort to channel male aggression in directions considered socially productive. Complementing the causal impact of social norms and role expectations, the sex-typed abilities and beliefs that result from prior occupancy of roles requiring aggression would favor a sex difference in aggressive behavior. Thus, from the role-theoretic viewpoint, biological sex differences are mainly remote or distal causes of adult sex differences.

Possible Compatibility of Role Theory with Alternative Theories.   Although it should not be assumed that adult sex differences necessarily are linked to childhood socialization and biological factors, indirect causes of these types are certainly not discounted merely by evidence favoring the social-role interpretation of sex differences. Instead, an open-minded viewpoint consistent with the social-role approach is that the causes of sex differences in adult social behavior are sequentially (or hierarchically) arranged: The best prediction is achieved by adult roles, skills, and beliefs, which are related to the distribution of women and men into specific social roles, which is, in turn, related to an unknown extent to more distal factors such as childhood socialization and biological predispositions.

In contrast to this sequential view of the causes of sex differences, alternative theories often treat differences between male and female behavior as directly under the control of ingrained dispositions arising from biology or early experience. Such analyses have difficulty accounting for the inconsistencies demonstrated in adult sex differences, because, under the influence of dispositional differences, women and men should behave differently to about the same degree in a wide range of circumstances. In other words, these analyses favor "main effect" predictions and do not readily lend themselves to predicting interactions between sex and situational variables. However, quantitative reviews have demonstrated, not invariant sex differences, but considerable variability across studies.

THE VALIDITY OF GENDER STEREOTYPES
AND OF SCIENTIFIC GENERALIZATIONS
ABOUT SEX DIFFERENCES

The Validity of Gender Stereotypes
and Their Societal Functions

As shown in Chapter 1, communion and agency comprise the majority of the qualities in which most people think that women and men differ and ought to differ. These stereotypes could well be termed an *implicit theory* (Ashmore, 1981; Schneider, Hastorf, & Ellsworth, 1979) or *naive psychology* (Heider, 1958) of sex differences because they provide both descriptions and explanations of the sex differences that people observe in daily life. Terms such as implicit theory have the fortunate connotation that lay persons' beliefs about women and men probably validly represent social reality to some extent and also distort it to some extent. As in the case of other implicit theories of personality and behavior, an appropriate attitude for social scientists to hold toward these popular beliefs about the sexes might be cautious respect, based on the potential validity of these beliefs. Not only do these implicit theories gain some validity because they have a causal role in relation to actual sex differences, but also these theories probably have substantial accuracy merely as representations of observed sex differences. As discussed in Chapter 1, gender stereotypes have been shown to reflect the distribution of women and men into the social structure and are thus anchored to social reality in this respect. Furthermore, extreme inaccuracy is unlikely merely on the ground that everyday life offers people many opportunities to obtain information about women and men. Even though some of this information, such as that derived from the mass media, may be inaccurate to some extent, people have ample opportunity to correct biased presentations through information gleaned from their own direct encounters with women and men (see Swann, 1984) as well as from their own past histories as women or men. Research has suggested that the accuracy of stereotypes is greater to the extent that people are in frequent contact with members of a stereotyped group (Triandis & Vasilliou, 1967).

The meta-analytic research presented in Chapters 2 and 3 addressed aspects of these validity issues and showed that implicit theories of sex differences have moderate accuracy for helping behavior and aggressive behavior. Thus, in both of these meta-analyses, respondents were given brief descriptions of the behaviors investigated in each of the studies in the relevant research literature. Among other judgments, respondents indicated the likelihood that the average woman and the average man would engage in each behavior. Stereotypic sex-difference scores formed by differencing ratings of the average woman and man were significantly related to the magnitude of the sex-difference effect sizes. In other words, respondents' stereotypic judgments were related to the actual behavioral sex differences obtained in the studies. The ability of these respondents to predict female and male behavior with some success based only on short written descriptions of behaviors testifies to the validity of their implicit theories of sex differences.

The fact that gender stereotypes to some extent represent genuine sex differences in social behaviors does not deny the tendency for these stereotypes to maintain and justify the existing social order (e.g., Tajfel, 1981). Indeed, the argument that gender stereotypes, which are themselves derived from the sexual division of labor, constitute normative beliefs to which people then tend to conform (or are induced to conform) describes a social psychological process by which stereotypes maintain the social order. This justifying function has been discussed in detail by Huici (1984) and O'Leary (1974). These analyses assert that the ascription to women of communal qualities and a relative lack of agentic qualities serves as an obstacle to the promotion of women to management and other high-power positions in organizations.[9] These stereotypic beliefs are also thought to favor occupational segregation by which women are encouraged to enter occupations perceived to require communal qualities and discouraged from entering occupations perceived to require agentic qualities. Once occupational segregation is established, it, in turn, intensifies stereotypic perceptions of the sexes. In fact, Hoffman's (1985) research suggested that merely assigning roles to individuals, even on the basis of traits not relevant to role performance, fosters the perception that these individuals have personality characteristics congruent with their role assignment.

The view that gender stereotypes are at least partially valid also does not deny the negative implications that these stereotypes may have for individual women and men. Individuals are of course often misperceived when viewed stereotypically and they rightfully object to such categorizations. When misperceived, individuals may choose to counter normative expectations and may sometimes be successful in effecting change in them, particularly if they act in concert with even a small number of like-minded people (Maass & Clark, 1984; Moscovici & Faucheux, 1972). Social psychological research suggests that, although it is often difficult to change other people's expectations about one's behavior (e.g., Ross, Lepper, & Hubbard, 1975), it may not be so difficult to counter others' expectations at least to the extent that one does not behaviorally confirm them (Hilton & Darley, 1985; Swann & Ely, 1984).

It is noteworthy in terms of the social-role analysis that in times of social change affecting the status or social position of a group, their members commonly attack the pervasive stereotypes by which they are described. Thus, the Women's Movement has been associated with wide-ranging challenges of stereotypic portrayals of women in the media, children's textbooks, etc. Attack on these stereotypes is politically correct, in view of their causal role in the chain of processes by which traditional relations between the sexes are maintained. Furthermore, from the perspective of social-role theory, it is precisely during a time of social change affecting women's position in social and economic institutions when existing gender stereotypes should be perceived as problematic, because their content is inconsistent with women's emerging social position and aspirations for equality. Thus, the activist's attitude toward gender stereotypes is under-

---

[9]Yet, according to Eagly and Steffen's (1984) findings suggesting little relation between status in organizations and the ascriptions of communal qualities to role occupants, belief in women's lesser agency may be the main barrier to mobility within organizations.

standably often one of implacable opposition, although this opposition does not necessarily extend to the characterization of women as more communal than men. In fact, many feminist activists have reacted enthusiastically to psychological analyses that have emphasized and endorsed women's communal qualities (e.g., Gilligan, 1982; Miller, 1976).

The Validity of Scientific Generalizations about Sex Differences

Cautious respect is also an appropriate attitude for social scientists to hold in relation to the scientific literature on sex differences. On the one hand, scholars should cherish this literature because it is a large repository of relatively objective reports of behaviors, most of which are described in convenient metrics that make possible statistical tests of sex-difference hypotheses. In its greater objectivity, this information is qualitatively different from that contained in gender stereotypes or, for that matter, in novels, biographies, and other sorts of personal and subjective accounts of gender-related experience. On the other hand, scholars should be extremely vigilant about the hazards of drawing general conclusions from sets of research findings. Considerable bias may be injected into social scientific knowledge when research findings are interpreted. Bias has been particularly problematic in the interpretation of large research literatures because, until recently, drawing conclusions from these literatures has been an impressionistic and intuitive process (see Chapter 1). The result was that such conclusions, even when offered by research psychologists, were inaccurate, often to a considerable extent, and certainly vulnerable to biases stemming from reviewers' own attitudes about gender-related issues. Conclusions drawn with the aid of appropriate quantitative methods provide substantially more accurate and replicable summaries of available findings. Nevertheless, even for these better summaries, generalizability to other subject populations and settings is by no means guaranteed.

Feminist Critique of Sex-Difference Research.   In the feminist critical scholarship of the 1970s, the attitude toward the scientific literature on sex differences was not one of cautious respect but of distrust. For example, Sherif (1979) criticized research on sex differences as exemplifying the narrow research paradigms characteristic of mainstream psychology. According to Sherif, investigators of sex differences usually examine behavior in contrived and carefully controlled laboratory contexts and, as a consequence, deal only with "selectively chosen data" (p. 108). She argued that the findings of such research are not only frequently unrepresentative of daily life, but also vulnerable to researchers' attitudinal biases, which often include implicit sexism. Even more pointedly, Bernard (1974, p. 13) stated that scientists' demonstrations of sex differences have acted as "battle weapons against women" by portraying them as inferior and justifying their low status. Parlee (1979) further argued that findings about sex differences, because they are stripped of their natural context, are misleading and cannot form the basis of valid generalizations about women and men. Similar points have been made by other social scientists (e.g., Block, 1976; Grady, 1981; Kaplan & Sedney, 1980; Mednick, 1978; Shields, 1975; Unger, 1983).

The feminist critique has provided a salutary challenge to sex-difference research. The two major issues raised by these critics are important in my own analysis—namely, possible ideological biases affecting conclusions about sex differences, and possible biases resulting from the limited social contexts in which research has generally been conducted. To protect against ideological bias, quantitative reviewers' adoption of statistical decision rules for drawing conclusions is a decided advantage, as already noted. The use of limited contexts for research creates problems that are difficult, although more amenable to partial solution in meta-analyses than in primary research. These problems are best discussed in terms of construct validity and external validity (see Eagly, 1986).

Construct Validity of Generalizations about Sex Differences. Construct validity refers to the approximate validity with which generalizations can be made about higher-order constructs on the basis of research operations (Cook & Campbell, 1979). Researchers and reviewers do desire to draw conclusions about sex differences in terms of general constructs such as aggressiveness and influenceability. Difficulties arise when there is lack of correspondence between (a) the constructs on which women and men are compared and (b) the operational definitions of these constructs. Operationalizations are often inadequate because of the condition that Cook and Campbell (1979) labeled "construct underrepresentation," which follows from relying on one or a very few operational definitions of a construct.

Relying on a single method of assessing a variable is problematic because this method likely contains irrelevant and extraneous sources of variation— "surplus construct irrelevancies" in Cook and Campbell's (1979) terminology. For example, if aggression were measured only by the amount of shock subjects deliver in the "teacher-learner" situation, aggression, as thus measured, might reflect, not only aggressiveness, but also uncertainty or concern about electric shock and the type of injury it might inflict. In general, because it is unlikely that any one operational definition can represent a construct in pure form, adequate construct validity is achieved only when investigators have utilized at least several different operations to define a construct (Campbell & Fiske, 1959).

External Validity of Generalizations about Sex Differences.   External validity is the approximate validity with which conclusions can be drawn about the generalizability of a relationship to and across populations (Cook & Campbell, 1979). As far as generalizability to and across populations of people is concerned, difficulties arise because it is rare that studies have utilized systematic samples of subjects representative of the target populations about which researchers desire to draw conclusions. In sex-difference research, these target populations might be women and men in general or in a particular culture. This issue also arises with respect to populations of settings and occasions. Investigators typically wish to generalize to a wide range of settings and occasions. The use of limited samples of settings and occasions in research makes it difficult to insure that conclusions about sex differences are externally valid.

Meta-Analysis and Validity.   As a general rule, both construct validity and external validity are greater for findings based on meta-analytic aggregations of studies than for findings of single studies. For construct validity, this superiority stems from the derivation of a meta-analytic generalization from a set of studies, which most often have utilized differing operational definitions of the dependent variable of interest. If these operationalizations are contaminated by different irrelevant sources of variation, these irrelevant sources tend to cancel one another when findings are aggregated and consequently the aggregated finding has more satisfactory construct validity. Similarly, the superior external validity of conclusions based on aggregated findings arises from the broader range of persons, settings, and occasions on which these conclusions are based. Nevertheless, validity may be threatened when a literature offers few operational definitions and few types of subject populations, settings, and occasions.

Some solutions to these potential invalidity problems can be found within the technology of meta-analysis (see Chapters 2 and 3). Quantitative reviews allow scholars to assess the effects of operational definitions, subject populations, contexts, and occasions, to the extent that these have varied in the relevant research literature. For example, even though most helping studies were conducted in the field, some were conducted in the laboratory. The reviewer can then examine whether the finding that men help more than women in social psychological helping research is intact in the laboratory as well as in the field and whether the magnitude of the sex difference is affected by the setting of the research (see Chapter 2).

However useful it is to address validity issues by relating study characteristics to the sex-difference outcomes of studies, sometimes this solution cannot be implemented because the available studies have entirely (or almost entirely) omitted certain variants. As I have pointed out for several social behaviors, the context of psychologists' research on sex differences has been primarily short-term interactions with strangers or with structured stimulus materials such as videotapes. Given this limitation, one cannot examine whether sex differences in these behaviors vary depending, for example, on the depth or length of acquaintance with other people.

Finally, in addition to limited social contexts in research, another potential source of external invalidity of meta-analytic generalizations is known as "publication bias"—a tendency for journals to publish primarily statistically significant findings. Such a tendency would bias findings toward larger effects (Greenwald, 1975; Lane & Dunlap, 1978). Yet, as Hall (1984) has also argued, such a bias is less likely to occur for sex-difference hypotheses than for many other hypotheses. The reason that publication bias is unlikely to be a major problem is that sex-difference findings in most studies on social behavior were peripheral to hypotheses about the effects of other variables. Study outcomes for these other variables would test the focal hypotheses of the studies and would therefore affect publishability much more strongly than sex-difference findings.[10]

Improving the Validity of Scientific Generalizations about Sex Differences

In stating that the meta-analyst's conclusions are threatened by substantial invalidity because the research that is aggregated is often limited to short-term encounters with strangers or standardized stimulus materials, I have come full circle in my analysis. Recall the statement in Chapter 1 that this limitation has been an essential aspect of most psychological research on adult sex differences. This limitation no doubt arose from researchers' desire to rule out explanations of sex differences that do not pertain strictly to sex or gender. Psychologists therefore had little interest in studying sex differences by comparing executives and secretaries, physicians and nurses, or even husbands and wives. This decision is defensible because it rules out current differences in specific roles as a cause of the behavioral differences that are observed when women and men are compared. However, from the standpoint of construct validity and external validity, the decision is problematic. In agreement with the critical analysis of Sherif (1979), Parlee (1979), and other feminist scholars, I believe that these validity issues have been seriously neglected in most discussions of sex differences.

In partial disagreement with the feminist critical analysis, I do not

---

[10]External-validity issues stemming from the use of college-student subjects in laboratory experimentation also deserve mention. This consideration applies to research areas such as aggressive behavior that are mainly based on laboratory experimentation and is less relevant to areas such as helping behavior that are mainly based on field studies. Sears (1986) has provided a useful discussion of the effects that overuse of college students as subjects may have on understanding of social psychological processes.

believe that social psychological research on social behaviors necessarily strips these behaviors of their context. Of course, the issue is not whether behavior in typical research settings is completely deprived of context. Some sort of context is always provided. Instead, the issue is whether the contexts that are commonly used in research pose validity issues when findings are interpreted. Social psychological research usually provides a somewhat specialized yet theoretically interesting set of social contexts in which the relative unimportance of specific social roles makes gender roles relatively important. If one concern underlying the context-stripping criticism is whether these contexts are natural, it must be noted that in some research literatures, such as helping behavior (see Chapter 2), most of the social contexts of research are in fact natural field settings (e.g., street corners, supermarkets, libraries). In other research, the majority of these social contexts are constructed in experimental laboratories.

Despite external-validity issues presented by the use of artificial contexts in laboratory research, sex-difference research conducted in laboratories should not be casually dismissed on the basis of presumed triviality or artificiality. Indeed, laboratory contexts are often very involving for subjects—that is, they possess the quality Aronson and Carlsmith (1968; Aronson, Brewer, & Carlsmith, 1985) termed *experimental realism.* Although social contexts constructed in laboratory settings do not necessarily also occur in natural settings and thus possess the quality Aronson and Carlsmith termed *mundane realism,* these contexts may elicit processes that are the same as or similar to those that occur in natural settings. However, according to the analysis developed in this book, many important processes have not been examined to any great extent in either field or laboratory settings because research has been confined primarily to behavior that occurs in brief encounters with strangers.

Possible solutions to the dilemma posed by the limited social contexts of research involve broadening sex-difference research beyond its traditional contexts. A solution that would surrender considerable internal validity is to compare women and men in representative natural settings without regard to their differing specific social roles and other attributes. Such comparisons would hold some interest as descriptions of how behaviors are divided up between the sexes. One could thereby determine which sex does more helping, aggressing, smiling, laughing, etc. At various points in this book, I have speculated about what such comparisons might reveal. Although such comparisons are not devoid of interest, they would seem insufficient to most psychologists because of the confounding of sex with specific roles and other factors. It is indeed important to know whether the observed difference is due to the different specific roles or other attributes of women and men, as opposed to the gender and sex variables that underlie comparisons that psychologists have traditionally labeled as sex differences.

In natural settings in which sex is confounded with other attributes, inferring sex differences can be regarded as a multivariate problem. An investigator might choose to convert this multivariate problem into a univariate problem by finding or creating special opportunities for controlled comparisons in natural settings. These controlled comparisons require samples of women and men who are essentially equivalent in many attributes other than sex. For example, in an organizational setting, women and men in the same job category could be compared. Ideally these women and men would also be equivalent in relevant background attributes such as education and socioeconomic status. If the two samples were comparable in job-relevant respects other than sex, an investigator would probably interpret any difference in their social behavior as a sex difference.

The investigator may also create controlled comparisons in confounded-variable settings by utilizing appropriate multivariate statistics. For example, sex may be entered in a multiple regression equation along with other relevant attributes of individuals, such as their educational level. This statistical technique allows one to estimate whether sex has an impact once it is controlled for the effects of other attributes with which it may be correlated. At least in theory it is possible to use such techniques to estimate the magnitude of the difference between women and men that cannot be accounted for by extraneous variables correlated with sex. One critical issue in such applications would be deciding what constitutes an extraneous variable whose effects should be statistically controlled before a sex comparison is made. Presumably in an organization, variables such as job category, years of experience, and educational background would be considered extraneous.[11]

Such methods have been widely used to investigate sex discrimination in organizations (see Pezzullo & Brittingham, 1979). The dependent variable

---

[11]This discussion pertains to removing the effects of variables such as years of experience in a job that would be regarded as contaminants of a male-female comparison. Such variables are necessarily and legitimately related to a dependent variable within a given social context, as years of experience are related to salary. Another logic, discussed by Hall (in press), suggests entering as predictors in a multiple-regression equation, variables thought to be underlying causes of sex differences. For example, to explore prior experience in competitive athletics as a possible cause of a tendency for men to behave more dominantly than women in groups, experience in competitive athletics might be entered as a predictor of dominant behaviors (e.g., interrupting other group members). If sex failed to account for additional variability in dominant behaviors once this predictor was entered, the plausibility of athletic experience as an underlying cause of the sex difference in dominance would be increased. Potentially causal variables (e.g., prior athletic experience) that are controlled to test causal hypotheses need to be distinguished from extraneous variables (e.g., years of experience in current job) that should be controlled to allow a sex-difference comparison. Issues of this sort associated with multivariate explorations of sex differences are far from settled and will require detailed development (see Hall, in press).

in such research generally is salary, rank, or some other index of career achievement. However, caution must be exercised in interpreting such analyses, because the statistical techniques have ambiguities and serious practical limits, which are the subject of lively debate among economists and other social scientists (e.g., Birnbaum, 1979; Conway & Roberts, 1983; Kamalich & Polachek, 1982).

Such analytic techniques would allow sex differences to be investigated in a wide range of natural settings. The resulting findings could be joined with findings from traditional research settings, to generate more valid conclusions about sex differences. Scholars would be making judicious use of applied and basic research. To be sure, the task would not be easy. Many sex comparisons in applied literatures are in fact not controlled for extraneous variables whose effects probably should be removed from the dependent variable to allow a sex-difference interpretation. For example, research on crime is potentially relevant to sex differences in aggression. Yet the available comparisons between the sexes generally are not controlled with respect to extraneous variables, nor, for that matter, is it clear that crime is predominantly an aggressive behavior. Perhaps through secondary analyses of data such as crime statistics, researchers could create comparisons that approximate sex-difference comparisons. Appropriate statistical controls might be instituted, and those types of crime that are most clearly interpretable as aggressive might be chosen for analysis. More generally, to improve the validity of generalizations about sex differences, closer ties are needed between the research paradigms that psychologists have traditionally used and the applied-research paradigms that psychologists and other social scientists have employed.

Sex Differences and the Experimental Paradigm

The proposal that multivariate statistics be used to investigate sex differences in natural settings is neither surprising nor innovative. After all, multiple regression has been available for a long time and could have been used in this way. Yet applied research has rarely been joined with more traditional social psychological research to enable psychologists to draw more valid conclusions about social behaviors. In fact, applied research has generally not been explicitly concerned with the types of behavioral tendencies (e.g., aggressiveness, helpfulness, influenceability) studied in experimental research. For example, applied researchers study crime and family violence rather than aggressiveness, social support rather than helpfulness, and leadership and managerial style rather than influenceability. So the potential coordination between applied research and traditional social psychological research has not emerged, in part because somewhat different dependent variables have been of interest in research traditions that have evolved largely without benefit of cross-fertilization.

The style of social psychological research that has been brought to bear on questions of sex differences also reflects researchers' preferences about methods. As Rosnow (1981) has argued, methods in social psychology have been dominated by an *experimental paradigm*. Social psychologists in psychology departments have strongly preferred true experiments, which require manipulation of independent variables and random assignment of subjects to conditions. Therefore, most of the studies included in existing meta-analyses of sex differences in social behavior have these features. The felt necessity to conduct true experiments essentially restricted researchers to studying social behavior in the context of short-term encounters with strangers. Although a movement toward field methods began in the late 1960s and intensified in the 1970s, these field studies were predominantly experiments. Thus, these more naturalistic experiments also involved manipulated variables and random assignment of subjects to conditions. The procedures of manipulation and random assignment can ordinarily be carried out only in the context of short-term encounters with strangers. Within close or long-term relationships, experimental manipulations and random assignment are impractical and very often unethical. Moreover, behavioral measures are often difficult to implement. Instead, outcome measures (such as longevity of relationships) may be available, and subjective reports of one's own and others' behaviors can be obtained.

Social psychologists' preference for true experiments with behavioral dependent variables and their prejudice against alternative methods reflects a mode of scientific activity that might be labeled *agentic* (Bakan, 1966), because of its controlling and objectifying qualities. Several scholars, including Carlson (1972), Wallston (1981), and Keller (1985), have identified this agentic tendency and have explored it in terms of psychologists' and other scientists' placement of natural phenomena at a distance and treatment of them as objects to be manipulated and controlled. In agreement with these scholars, I believe that science in general and social psychology in particular could have been conducted with less agentic or at least more diverse methods. In fact, had the experimental paradigm not been dominant in psychology when so much of the research on sex differences in social behavior was carried out, doubts about the validity of generalizations about sex differences would not have been so troublesome.

In agreement with Wallston (1981), I am reluctant to label as *masculine* the preference for research methods that control and objectify behavior, because I believe that this preference is characteristic of the scientific culture in general. Although all science can be regarded as male-dominated, its practitioners are both women and men. Labeling certain research methods masculine suggests that they are more common or appropriate for male than for female scientists, but sex-typing of research methods is insufficiently explored. It happens that sex of researchers has been a variable of some interest in meta-analyses of sex differences, ever since Eagly and Carli (1981) found that female and male authors reported different findings for influenceability studies as well as for the nonverbal decoding studies reviewed by Hall (1978). However, sex-of-author effects have not proven to be consistent across meta-analyses. Although Carli (1982) and Wood (in press) reported some significant sex-of-author findings in their meta-analyses of group behavior and performance and Thomas and French (1985) also did for two motor tasks, reviews of sex differences in numerous nonverbal behaviors (Hall, 1984), helping behavior (Eagly & Crowley, 1986), aggressive behavior (Eagly & Steffen, 1986a), and motor activity level (Eaton & Enns, 1986) have not found such tendencies. At present it appears that male and female investigators do not necessarily report dissimilar findings, and we know little about the extent to which they use dissimilar methods (but see Becker, 1986). Thus, because the research methods typically used by psychologists to study social behavior may well be equally congenial to female and male researchers who were schooled in the experimental paradigm, these methods are better described as *agentic* than masculine.

Sex Differences in Natural Settings

There is relatively little secure knowledge about whether the kinds of stereotypic sex differences discussed in this book also occur in a range of natural settings. The role-theory prediction that social behavior is sex-typed along gender-stereotypic lines was made primarily in relation to settings in which gender roles are relatively important and specific social roles with counterstereotypic implications are relatively unimportant. In most natural settings, particularly in organizations, specific social roles are of considerable importance.[12] In general, in much of everyday life, such roles are probably much more relevant to performance than gender roles, and so the best prediction for women and men is that they behave appropri-

---

[12]There may be a few natural-setting social contexts in which gender-role expectancies are especially important because cues in these contexts do bring gender forcefully to participants' attention. In particular, gender roles might be especially salient in heterosexual dating and romantic relationships, as suggested by studies of gender-stereotypic beliefs and behaviors among dating couples (see Brehm, 1985; Huston & Ashmore, 1986; Peplau, 1983; Peplau & Gordon, 1985). In such relationships, people may strive to fulfill partners' expectations about the ideal opposite-sex partner.

ately for their specific roles.[13] However, behavior certainly could differ between women and men in the same specific roles if the two sexes differed in role-relevant skills or beliefs because of differing prior experiences. Yet for the most part, women and men who are incumbents of the same specific roles have had many of the same prior experiences, and consequently may differ little in role-relevant skills and attitudes. Therefore, the best guess is that women and men behave more equivalently in the same specific role in natural settings than they do in typical research settings. As I have repeatedly emphasized in this book, the stereotypic behavior found in social psychological research cannot be extrapolated to organizations and other settings with constraining specific roles.

Consistent with the idea that specific organizational roles override gender roles, stereotypic sex differences have been largely discounted by many psychologists who have studied leadership and other behaviors in organizations (e.g., Bartol, 1978; L. K. Brown, 1979; S. M. Brown, 1979; Butterfield & Powell, 1981; Osborn & Vicars, 1976; Terborg, 1977). Organizational psychologists have argued that, given equivalent social roles for women and men, sex differences are less pronounced in organizations than in experimental laboratories. This claim has been substantiated by a meta-analytic review of leader effectiveness that found a mean effect size of 0.25 favoring male leaders in laboratory studies and a mean effect size of 0.04 indicating no sex difference in field studies (Dobbins & Platz, 1986), although this comparison between laboratory and field studies should be viewed with extreme caution because it was based on a sample of only eleven studies.

It is worth noting that field studies have documented no or minimal sex differences even in extremely male-dominated organizations. Such situations would be likely to put women at a disadvantage because of any skill or belief differences they might manifest. A case in point is Rice, Instone, and Adams's (1984) study of West Point cadets. At West Point during basic training, the behavior and success of male and female upperclass cadets who served as leaders did not differ, even when assessed by cadets' subjective reports. Yet in a prior leadership study that examined West Point cadets in ad-hoc laboratory groups, Rice, Bender, and Vitters (1980) obtained stereotypic sex differences, presumably because in this ambiguous situa-

---

[13]Research on status generalization in small groups has investigated how people combine two status-relevant cues such as sex and task competence (e.g., Freese & Cohn, 1973; Webster & Driskell, 1978; Zelditch, Lauerdale, & Stublarec, 1980). The most general formulation of this combinatorial process is that people weight cues according to their relevance to task performance (Hembroff, 1982). My prediction that specific social roles are more important than gender roles in determining behavior in many natural settings is consistent with this formulation, if it is assumed that specific roles have more direct implications for task performance in these settings.

tion that lacked well-defined specific roles, gender roles were relatively salient.

The no sex-difference conclusion advocated by many organizational psychologists does not seem entirely secure at this point, however, because they have examined only some social behaviors and have applied primarily narrative reviewing techniques to the available studies. As we have seen, narrative reviewing methods tend to build in a bias in favor of the null hypothesis. The one available meta-analysis (Dobbins & Platz, 1986) included only a small portion of the available research.

Also suggesting caution about the generalization that sex differences are absent in role-equated comparisons in organizational settings are the arguments that have been offered about the effects of some social factors that commonly covary with sex. Tokenism is one such factor: A woman in a managerial or other high-status role in an organization is commonly a *token* — a member of a numerically small minority. Token status is believed to have a number of negative effects (Kanter, 1977), at least some of which may occur for token women and not for token men (Yoder & Sinnet, 1985).

Interference between family roles and employment roles is another factor that may affect women more than men. In fact, Staines and Libby (1986) have shown that considerable evidence supports the idea that family roles interfere more with employment roles for women. Moreover, other social scientists (e.g., Bass, 1981; Bayes & Newton, 1978; O'Leary, 1974) have argued that gender roles spill over to organizational contexts and thereby create role conflict for women (but not for men) who occupy managerial roles, because these roles call for relatively agentic behavior. Very clearly, the relative salience of organizational and other roles deserves detailed exploration. Gender roles no doubt spill over to specific roles to some extent, but relatively little is known about the extent to which gender infuses these specific roles and causes people to have different expectations for female and male role occupants. Nevertheless, exposure to the relatively clear-cut role requirements generally associated with organizational roles would surely tend to equalize female and male behavior. Therefore, differences in the social behavior of women and men who are incumbents of the *same* organizational role are probably smaller than the differences typically obtained in traditional research settings. Indeed, studies of occupational stereotypes have found that people report no differences or only small differences between women and men described as occupying the same occupational role (e.g., Eagly & Steffen, 1984; Friedland, Crockett, & Laird, 1973; Hesselbart, 1977; but see Eagly & Steffen, 1986b).

In natural settings women and men typically occupy *different* specific social roles, with women more likely than men to occupy the domestic role and to have lower-status positions and men more likely than women to occupy the employee role and to have higher-status positions. As explained in Chapter 1, on the average the domestic role apparently requires more emphasis on communal qualities than the employee role does, and the employee role requires more emphasis on agentic qualities than the domestic role does. Also, high-status roles in organizations apparently demand more emphasis on agentic qualities than lower-status roles do. Thus, because of the particular nature of the specific roles that are disproportionately occupied by women and men, comparisons between women and men that do not control or equate these roles would generally find more sharply contrasting behaviors in the two sexes than have been found in the research literatures I have reviewed. Indeed, as Eagly and Steffen (1984) argued, gender stereotypes stem from observations of these natural-setting differences between women and men who are enacting their roles. And these stereotypes function as gender-role expectations that in turn impact on actual behavior to cause it to be somewhat stereotypic when gender roles are salient.

Research on sex differences in social behavior has concentrated on those settings in which gender roles are relatively more salient than specific roles. These carefully chosen settings do yield very useful information about gender. The moderately stereotypic behavior that such research produces is understandable in terms of the role analysis provided in this book. In contrast, behavior in everyday life is probably both *more* stereotypic and *less* stereotypic than it is in these typical research settings, depending on how behavior is analyzed by social scientists or by lay observers. If sex and specific social roles are allowed to be confounded in the modal ways, with the result that women and men are compared while they enact different roles, behavior no doubt is much more stereotypic on the average than it is in typical research settings, because of the power of these roles to determine behavior. If sex and specific social roles are not confounded, with the result that women and men are observed in the same roles, behavior is probably less stereotypic than in typical research settings, also because of the power of these roles to determine behavior.

References

Abelson, R. P. (1985). A variance explanation paradox: When a little is a lot. *Psychological Bulletin, 97,* 129–133.

Ajzen, I. (1985). From intentions to actions: A theory of planned behavior. In J. Kuhl & J. Beckman (Eds.), *Action-control: From cognition to behavior* (pp. 11–39). New York: Springer-Verlag.

Ajzen, I., & Fishbein, M. (1977). Attitude-behavior relations: A theoretical analysis and review of empirical research. *Psychological Bulletin, 84,* 888–918.

Allen, V. L. (1965). Situational factors in conformity. In L. Berkowitz (Ed.), *Advances in experimental social psychology* (Vol. 2, pp. 133–175). New York: Academic Press.

Anderson, L. R., & Blanchard, P. N. (1982). Sex differences in task and social-emotional behavior. *Basic and Applied Social Psychology, 3,* 109–139.

Aresty, E. B. (1970). *The best behavior: The course of good manners—from antiquity to the present—as seen through courtesy and etiquette books.* New York: Simon & Schuster.

Aries, E. J., & Johnson, F. L. (1983). Close friendship in adulthood: Conversational content between same-sex friends. *Sex Roles, 9,* 1183–1196.

Arkin, W., & Dobrofsky, L. R. (1978). Military socialization and masculinity. *Journal of Social Issues, 34*(1), 151–168.

Aronoff, J., & Crano, W. D. (1975). A re-examination of the cross-cultural principles of task segregation and sex role differentiation in the family. *American Sociological Review, 40,* 12–20.

Aronson, E., Brewer, M., & Carlsmith, J. M. (1985). Experimentation in social psychology. In G. Lindzey & E. Aronson (Eds.), *Handbook of social psychology* (3rd ed., Vol. 1, pp. 441–486). New York: Random House.

Aronson, E., & Carlsmith, J. M. (1968). Experimentation in social psychology. In G. Lindzey & E. Aronson (Eds.), *Handbook of social psychology* (2nd ed., Vol. 2, pp. 1–79). Reading, MA: Addison-Wesley.

Asch, S. E. (1956). Studies of independence and conformity: I. A minority of one against a unanimous majority. *Psychological Monographs, 70* (9, Whole No. 416).

Ashmore, R. D. (1981). Sex stereotypes and implicit personality theory. In D. L. Hamilton

(Ed.), *Cognitive processes in stereotyping and intergroup behavior* (pp. 37-81). Hillsdale, NJ: Lawrence Erlbaum Associates.

Ashmore, R. D., & Del Boca, F. K. (1981). Conceptual approaches to stereotypes and stereotyping. In D. L. Hamilton (Ed.), *Cognitive processes in stereotyping and intergroup behavior* (pp. 1-35). Hillsdale, NJ: Lawrence Erlbaum Associates.

Ashmore, R. D., Del Boca, F. K., & Titus, D. (1984, August). *Types of women and men: Yours, mine, and ours.* Paper presented at the meeting of the American Psychological Association, Toronto.

Ashmore, R. D., Del Boca, F. K., & Wohlers, A. J. (1986). Gender stereotypes. In R. D. Ashmore & F. K. Del Boca (Eds.), *The social psychology of female-male relations: A critical analysis of central concepts* (pp. 69-119). Orlando, FL: Academic Press.

Athay, M., & Darley, J. M. (1982). Social roles as interaction competencies. In W. Ickes & E. S. Knowles (Eds.), *Personality, roles, and social behavior* (pp. 55-83). New York: Springer-Verlag.

Bakan, D. (1966). *The duality of human existence: An essay on psychology and religion.* Chicago: Rand McNally.

Bales, R. F. (1950). *Interaction process analysis: A method for the study of small groups.* Cambridge, MA: Addison-Wesley.

Bandura, A., Blanchard, E. B., & Ritter, B. (1969). Relative efficacy of desensitization and modeling approaches for inducing behavioral, affective, and attitudinal changes. *Journal of Personality and Social Psychology, 13,* 173-199.

Baron, R. A. (1977). *Human aggression.* New York: Plenum Press.

Baron, R. A., & Byrne, D. (1977). *Social psychology: Understanding human interaction* (2nd ed.). Boston: Allyn & Bacon.

Baron, R. A., & Eggleston, R. J. (1972). Performance on the "aggression machine": Motivation to help or harm? *Psychonomic Science, 26,* 321-322.

Bartol, K. M. (1978). The sex structuring of organizations: A search for possible causes. *Academy of Management Review, 3,* 805-815.

Bartol, K. M., & Martin, D. C. (1986). Women and men in task groups. In R. D. Ashmore & F. K. Del Boca (Eds.), *The social psychology of female-male relations: A critical analysis of central concepts* (pp. 259-310). Orlando, FL: Academic Press.

Basow, S. A. (1986). *Gender stereotypes: Traditions and alternatives* (2nd ed.). Monterey, CA: Brooks/Cole.

Bass, B. M. (1981). *Stogdill's handbook of leadership: A survey of theory and research* (Rev. ed.). New York: Free Press.

Bayes, M., & Newton, P. M. (1978). Women in authority: A sociopsychological analysis. *Journal of Applied Behavioral Science, 14,* 7-20.

Beaman, A. L., Cole, C. M., Preston, M., Klentz, B., & Steblay, N. M. (1983). Fifteen years of foot-in-the-door research: A meta-analysis. *Personality and Social Psychology Bulletin, 9,* 181-196.

Beck, S. B., Ward-Hull, C. I., & McLear, P. M. (1976). Variables related to women's somatic preferences of the male and female body. *Journal of Personality and Social Psychology, 34,* 1200-1210.

Becker, B. J. (1986). Influence again: Another look at studies of gender differences in social influence. In J. S. Hyde & M. C. Linn (Eds.), *The psychology of gender: Advances through meta-analysis* (pp. 178-209). Baltimore, MD: Johns Hopkins University Press.

Becker, B. J., & Hedges, L. V. (1984). Meta-analysis of cognitive gender differences: A comment on an analysis by Rosenthal and Rubin. *Journal of Educational Psychology, 76,* 583-587.

Belle, D. (1982a). *Lives in stress: Women and depression.* Beverly Hills, CA: Sage.

Belle, D. (1982b). The stress of caring: Women as providers of social support. In L. Goldberger & S. Breznitz (Eds.), *Handbook of stress: Theoretical and clinical aspects* (pp. 496-505). New York: Free Press.

Belle, D. (1985). Ironies in the contemporary study of gender. *Journal of Personality, 53,* 401-405.

Bem, S. L. (1974). The measurement of psychological androgyny. *Journal of Consulting and Clinical Psychology, 42,* 155-162.

Bem, S. L. (1975). Sex-role adaptability: One consequence of psychological androgyny. *Journal of Personality and Social Psychology, 31,* 634-643.

Bem, S. L., & Bem, D. J. (1970). Case study of nonconscious ideology: Training the woman to know her place. In D. J. Bem, *Beliefs, attitudes, and human affairs* (pp. 89-99). Belmont, CA: Brooks/Cole.

Bem, S. L., Martyna, W., & Watson, C. (1976). Sex typing and androgyny: Further explorations of the expressive domain. *Journal of Personality and Social Psychology, 34,* 1016-1023.

Berg, J. H. (1984). Development of friendship between roommates. *Journal of Personality and Social Psychology, 46,* 346-356.

Berger, J., Rosenholtz, S. J., & Zelditch, M., Jr. (1980). Status organizing processes. In A. Inkeles, N. J. Smelser, & R. H. Turner (Eds.), *Annual review of sociology* (Vol. 6, pp. 479-508). Palo Alto, CA: Annual Reviews.

Bergman, B. R. (1986). *The economic emergence of women.* New York: Basic Books.

Berk, S. F. (1985). *The gender factory: The apportionment of work in American households.* New York: Plenum.

Berkowtiz, L. (1964). Aggressive cues in aggressive behavior and hostility catharsis. *Psychological Review, 71,* 104-122.

Berkowitz, L., & Donnerstein, E. I. (1982). External validity is more than skin deep: Some answers to criticisms of laboratory experiments. *American Psychologist, 37,* 245-257.

Berkowitz, L., & LePage, A. (1967). Weapons as aggression eliciting stimuli. *Journal of Personality and Social Psychology, 7,* 202-207.

Bernard, J. (1974). *Sex differences: An overview* (Module 26). New York: MSS Modular Publications.

Bernard, J. (1981). *The female world.* New York: Macmillan.

Berninger, V. W., & DeSoto, C. (1985). Cognitive representation of personal stereotypes. *European Journal of Social Psychology, 15,* 189-211.

Bertilson, H. S. (1983). Methodology in the study of aggression. In R. G. Geen & E. I. Donnerstein (Eds.), *Aggression: Theoretical and empirical reviews* (Vol. 1, pp. 213-245). New York: Academic Press.

Birnbaum, M. H. (1979). Is there sex bias in salaries of psychologists? *American Psychologist, 34,* 719-720.

Bleier, R. (1984). *Science and gender: A critique of biology and its theories on women.* New York: Pergamon Press.

Block, J. H. (1976). Issues, problems, and pitfalls in assessing sex differences: A critical review of "The Psychology of Sex Differences." *Merrill-Palmer Quarterly, 22,* 283-308.

Blood, R. O., Jr., & Wolfe, D. M. (1960). *Husbands and wives.* New York: Free Press.

Bloom, L. Z., Coburn, K., & Pearlman, J. (1975). *The new assertive woman.* New York: Delacorte.

Bond, C. F., Jr., & Titus, L. J. (1983). Social facilitation: A meta-analysis of 241 studies. *Psychological Bulletin, 94,* 265-292.

Bowker, L. H. (1978). *Women, crime, and the criminal justice system.* Lexington, MA: Lexington Books.

Brehm, S. S. (1985). *Intimate relationships.* New York: Random House.

Breines, W., & Gordon, L. (1983). The new scholarship on family violence. *Signs: Journal of Women in Culture and Society, 8,* 490-531.

Brim, O. G., Jr. (1960). Personality development as role-learning. In I. Iscoe & H. W. Stevenson (Eds.), *Personality development in children* (pp. 127-159). Austin, TX: University of Texas Press.

Broverman, I. K., Vogel, S. R., Broverman, D. M., Clarkson, F. E., & Rosenkrantz, P. S. (1972). Sex-role stereotypes: A current appraisal. *Journal of Social Issues, 28*(2), 59-78.

Brown, L. K. (1979). Women and business management. *Signs: Journal of Women in Culture and Society, 5,* 266–288.

Brown, S. M. (1979). Male versus female leaders: A comparison of empirical studies. *Sex Roles, 5,* 595–611.

Bryan, J. H., & Test, M. A. (1967). Models and helping: Naturalistic studies in aiding behavior. *Journal of Personality and Social Psychology, 6,* 400–407.

Buss, A. H. (1961). *The psychology of aggression.* New York: Wiley.

Buss, A. H. (1963). Physical aggression in relation to different frustrations. *Journal of Abnormal and Social Psychology, 67,* 1–7.

Buss, D. M. (1981). Sex differences in the evaluation and performance of dominant acts. *Journal of Personality and Social Psychology, 40,* 147–154.

Butterfield, D. A., & Powell, G. N. (1981). Effect of group performance, leader sex, and rater sex on ratings of leader behavior. *Organizational Behavior and Human Performance, 28,* 129–141.

Campbell, D. T., & Fiske, D. W. (1959). Convergent and discriminant validation by the multitrait-multimethod matrix. *Psychological Bulletin, 56,* 81–105.

Canter, R. J., & Meyerowitz, B. E. (1984). Sex-role stereotypes: Self-reports of behavior. *Sex Roles, 10,* 293–306.

Carli, L. L. (1982). *Are women more social and men more task oriented? A meta-analytic review of sex differences in group interaction, reward allocation, coalition formation, and cooperation in the Prisoner's Dilemma game.* Unpublished manuscript, University of Massachusetts, Amherst.

Carlson, R. (1972). Understanding women: Implications for personality theory and research. *Journal of Social Issues, 28*(2), 17–32.

Carnegie, A. (1907). Deed of trust. In Carnegie Hero Fund Commission, *Annual report* (pp. 9–11). Pittsburg, PA: Author.

Carnegie Hero Fund Commission. (1983). *Annual report.* Pittsburg, PA: Author.

Chodorow, N. (1978). *The reproduction of mothering: Psychoanalysis and the sociology of gender.* Berkeley: University of California Press.

Christensen, D., & Rosenthal, R. (1982). Gender and nonverbal decoding skill as determinants of interpersonal expectancy effects. *Journal of Personality and Social Psychology, 42,* 75–87.

Cicone, M. V., & Ruble, D. N. (1978). Beliefs about males. *Journal of Social Issues, 34*(1), 5–16.

Cohen, J. (1977). *Statistical power analysis for the behavioral sciences* (Rev. ed.). New York: Academic Press.

Cohen, J., & Cohen, H. (1983). *Applied multiple regression/correlation analysis for the behavioral sciences* (2nd ed.). Hillsdale, NJ: Lawrence Erlbaum Associates.

The compact edition of the Oxford English Dictionary. (1971). New York: Oxford University Press.

Conway, D. A., & Roberts, H. V. (1983). Reverse regression, fairness, and employment discrimination. *Journal of Business and Economic Statistics, 1,* 75–85.

Cook, T. D., & Campbell, D. T. (1979). *Quasi-experimentation: Design and analysis issues for field settings.* Chicago: Rand McNally.

Cook, T. D., & Leviton, L. C. (1980). Reviewing the literature: A comparison of traditional methods with meta-analysis. *Journal of Personality, 48,* 449–472.

Cooper, H. M. (1979). Statistically combining independent studies: A meta-analysis of sex differences in conformity research. *Journal of Personality and Social Psychology, 37,* 131–146.

Cooper, H. M. (1984). *The integrative research review: A systematic approach.* Beverly Hills, CA: Sage.

Cooper, H. M., & Findley, M. (1982). Expected effect sizes: Estimates for statistical power analysis in social psychology. *Personality and Social Psychology Bulletin, 8,* 168–173.

Cooper, H. M., & Rosenthal, R. (1980). Statistical versus traditional procedures for summarizing research findings. *Psychological Bulletin, 87,* 442–449.

Crano, W. D., & Aronoff, J. (1978). A cross-cultural study of expressive and instrumental role complementary in the family. *American Sociological Review, 43,* 463–471.

Cunningham, M. R., Steinberg, J., & Grev, R. (1980). Wanting to and having to help: Separate motivations for positive mood and guilt-induced helping. *Journal of Personality and Social Psychology, 38,* 181–192.

Darley, J. M., & Fazio, R. H. (1980). Expectancy confirmation processes arising in the social interaction sequence. *American Psychologist, 35,* 867–881.

Darley, J. M., & Latané, B. (1968). Bystander intervention in emergencies: Diffusion of responsibility. *Journal of Personality and Social Psychology, 8,* 377–383.

Deaux, K. (1976). *The behavior of women and men.* Monterey, CA: Brooks/Cole.

Deaux, K. (1984). From individual differences to social categories: Analysis of a decade's research on gender. *American Psychologist, 39,* 105–116.

Deaux, K. (1985). Sex and gender. *Annual Review of Psychology, 36,* 49–81.

Deaux, K., & Kite, M. E. (in press). Gender and cognition. In B. B. Hess & M. M. Ferree (Eds.), *Women and society: Social science research perspectives.* New York: Russell Sage.

Deaux, K., & Lewis, L. L. (1983). Components of gender stereotypes. *Psychological Documents, 13,* 25. (Ms. No. 2583).

Deaux, K., & Lewis, L. L. (1984). Structure of gender stereotypes: Interrelationships among components and gender label. *Journal of Personality and Social Psychology, 46,* 991–1004.

Deaux, K., Lewis, L. L., & Kite, M. E. (1984, August). *Individual differences in gender stereotyping.* Paper presented at the meeting of the American Psychological Association, Toronto.

Deaux, K., Winton, W., Crowley, M., & Lewis, L. L. (1985). Level of categorization and content of gender stereotypes. *Social Cognition, 3,* 145–167.

Deutsch, M., & Gerard, H. B. (1955). A study of normative and informational social influence upon individual judgment. *Journal of Abnormal and Social Psychology, 51,* 629–636.

Dion, K. L. (1985). Sex, gender, and groups: Selected issues. In V. E. O'Leary, R. K. Unger, & B. S. Wallston (Eds.), *Women, gender, and social psychology* (pp. 293–347). Hillsdale, NJ: Lawrence Erlbaum Associates.

Dobbins, G. H., & Platz, S. J. (1986). Sex differences in leadership: How real are they? *Academy of Management Review, 11,* 118–127.

Doob, A. N., & Gross, A. E. (1968). Status of frustrator as an inhibitor of horn-honking responses. *Journal of Social Psychology, 76,* 213–218.

Dovidio, J. F. (1984). Helping behavior and altruism: An empirical and conceptual overview. In L. Berkowitz (Ed.), *Advances in experimental social psychology* (Vol. 17, pp. 361–427). New York: Academic Press.

Doyle, J. A. (1985). *Sex and gender: The human experience.* Dubuque, IA: Brown.

Eagly, A. H. (1978). Sex differences in influenceability. *Psychological Bulletin, 85,* 86–116.

Eagly, A. H. (1983). Gender and social influence: A social psychological analysis. *American Psychologist, 38,* 971–981.

Eagly, A. H. (1986). Some meta-analytic approaches to examining the validity of gender-difference research. In J. Hyde & M. C. Linn (Eds.), *The psychology of gender: Advances through meta-analysis* (pp. 159–177). Baltimore, MD: Johns Hopkins University Press.

Eagly, A. H., & Carli, L. L. (1981). Sex of researchers and sex-typed communications as determinants of sex differences in influenceability: A meta-analysis of social influence studies. *Psychological Bulletin, 90,* 1–20.

Eagly, A. H., & Chrvala, C. (1986). Sex differences in conformity: Status and gender-role interpretations. *Psychology of Women Quarterly, 10,* 203–220.

Eagly, A. H., & Crowley, M. (1986). Gender and helping behavior: A meta-analytic review of the social psychological literature. *Psychological Bulletin, 100,* 283–308.

Eagly, A. H., & Kite, M. E. (in press). Are stereotypes of nationalities applied to both women and men? *Journal of Personality and Social Psychology.*

Eagly, A. H., & Steffen, V. J. (1984). Gender stereotypes stem from the distribution of women and men into social roles. *Journal of Personality and Social Psychology, 46,* 735–754.

Eagly, A. H., & Steffen, V. J. (1986a). Gender and aggressive behavior: A meta-analytic review of the social psychological literature. *Psychological Bulletin, 100,* 309–330.

Eagly, A. H., & Steffen, V. J. (1986b). Gender stereotypes, occupational roles, and beliefs about part-time employees. *Psychology of Women Quarterly, 10,* 252–262.

Eagly, A. H., & Wood, W. (1982). Inferred sex differences in status as a determinant of gender stereotypes about social influence. *Journal of Personality and Social Psychology, 43,* 915–928.

Eagly, A. H., & Wood, W. (1985). Gender and influenceability: Stereotype versus behavior. In V. E. O'Leary, R. K. Unger, & B. S. Wallston (Eds.), *Women, gender, and social psychology* (pp. 225–256). Hillsdale, NJ: Lawrence Erlbaum Associates.

Eagly, A. H., Wood, W., & Fishbaugh, L. (1981). Sex differences in conformity: Surveillance by the group as a determinant of male nonconformity. *Journal of Personality and Social Psychology, 40,* 384–394.

Eaton, W. O., & Enns, L. R. (1986). Sex differences in human motor activity level. *Psychological Bulletin, 100,* 19–28.

Eisenberg, N., & Lennon, R. (1983). Sex differences in empathy and related capacities. *Psychological Bulletin, 94,* 100–131.

Endler, N. S., Wiesenthal, D. L., Coward, T., Edwards, J., & Geller, S. H. (1975). Generalization of relative competence mediating conformity across differing tasks. *European Journal of Social Psychology, 5,* 281–287.

Epstein, S. (1979). The stability of behavior: I. On predicting most of the people much of the time. *Journal of Personality and Social Psychology, 37,* 1097–1126.

Eskilson, A., & Wiley, M. G. (1976). Sex composition and leadership in small groups. *Sociometry, 39,* 183–194.

Eysenck, H. J. (1978). An exercise in mega-silliness. *American Psychologist, 33,* 517.

Fasteau, M. F. (1974). *The male machine.* New York: McGraw-Hill.

Fausto-Sterling, A. (1985). *Myths of gender: Biological theories about women and men.* New York: Basic Books.

Fazio, R. H. (1986). How do attitudes guide behaviors? In R. M. Sorrentino & E. T. Higgins (Eds.), *The handbook of motivation and cognition: Foundations of social behavior* (pp. 204–243). New York: Guilford.

Feather, N. T. (Ed.). (1982). *Expectations and actions: Expectancy-value models in psychology.* Hillsdale, NJ: Lawrence Erlbaum Associates.

Feather, N. T., & Said, J. A. (1983). Preference for occupations in relation to masculinity, femininity, and gender. *British Journal of Social Psychology, 22,* 113–127.

Fensterheim, H., & Baer, J. (1975). *Don't say yes when you want to say no: How assertiveness training can change your life.* New York: McKay.

Ferree, M. M. (1974). A woman for president? Changing responses: 1958–1972. *Public Opinion Quarterly, 38,* 390–399.

Feshbach, N. D. (1982). Sex differences in empathy and social behavior in children. In N. Eisenberg (Ed.), *The development of prosocial behavior* (pp. 315–338). New York: Academic Press.

Feshbach, S. (1955). The drive-reducing function of fantasy behavior. *Journal of Abnormal and Social Psychology, 50,* 3–11.

Festinger, L., & Carlsmith, J. M. (1959). Cognitive consequences of forced compliance. *Journal of Abnormal and Social Psychology, 58,* 203–210.

Fishbein, M. (1980). A theory of reasoned action: Some applications and implications. In H. E. Howe, Jr., & M. M. Page (Eds.), *Nebraska Symposium on motivation 1979* (pp. 65–116). Lincoln, NE: University of Nebraska Press.

Fishbein, M., & Ajzen, I. (1974). Attitudes toward objects as predictors of single and multiple behavioral criteria. *Psychological Review, 81*, 59–74.

Fishbein, M., & Ajzen, I. (1975). *Belief, attitude, intention, and behavior: An introduction to theory and research.* Reading, MA: Addison-Wesley.

Fiske, S. T., & Taylor, S. E. (1984). *Social cognition.* Reading, MA: Addison-Wesley.

Fraser, J. (1982). *America and the patterns of chivalry.* New York: Cambridge University Press.

Freese, L., & Cohen, B. P. (1973). Eliminating status generalization. *Sociometry, 36*, 177–193.

Friedan, B. (1963). *The feminine mystique.* New York: W. W. Norton.

Friedland, S. J., Crockett, W. H., & Laird, J. D. (1973). The effects of role and sex on the perception of others. *Journal of Social Psychology, 91*, 273–283.

Frieze, I. H., & Ramsey, S. J. (1976). Nonverbal maintenance of traditional sex roles. *Journal of Social Issues, 32*(3), 133–141.

Frodi, A., Macaulay, J., & Thome, P. R. (1977). Are women always less aggressive than men? A review of the experimental literature. *Psychological Bulletin, 84*, 634–660.

Frost, W. D., & Averill, J. R. (1982). Differences between men and women in the everyday experience of anger. In J. R. Averill, *Anger and aggression: An essay on emotion* (pp. 281–316). New York: Springer-Verlag.

Gallo, P. S., Jr. (1978). Meta-analysis—a mixed meta-phor. *American Psychologist, 33*, 515–517.

Geen, R. G. (1976). The study of aggression. In R. G. Geen & E. C. O'Neal (Eds.), *Perspectives on aggression* (pp. 1–9). New York: Academic Press.

Georgoudi, M., & Rosnow, R. L. (1985). Notes toward a contextualist understanding of social psychology. *Personality and Social Psychology Bulletin, 11*, 5–22.

Ghiselli, E. E. (1964). *Theory of psychological measurement.* New York: McGraw-Hill.

Gillespie, D. L. (1971). Who has the power? The marital struggle. *Journal of Marriage and the Family, 33*, 445–458.

Gilligan, C. (1982). *In a different voice: Psychological theory and women's development.* Cambridge, MA: Harvard University Press.

Gillis, J. S., & Avis, W. E. (1980). The male-taller norm in mate selection. *Personality and Social Psychology Bulletin, 6*, 396–401.

Girouard, M. (1981). *The return to Camelot: Chivalry and the English gentleman.* New Haven, CT: Yale University Press.

Glass, G. V., McGaw, B., & Smith, M. L. (1981). *Meta-analysis in social research.* Beverly Hills, CA: Sage.

Grady, K. E. (1981). Sex bias in research design. *Psychology of Women Quarterly, 5*, 628–636.

Greenwald, A. G. (1975). Consequences of prejudice against the null hypothesis. *Psychological Bulletin, 82*, 1–20.

Gurin, P. (1985). Women's gender consciousness. *Public Opinion Quarterly, 49*, 143–163.

Hall, J. A. (1978). Gender effects in decoding nonverbal cues. *Psychological Bulletin, 85*, 845–875.

Hall, J. A. (1980). Gender differences in nonverbal communication skills. In R. Rosenthal (Ed.), *Quantitative assessment of research domains* (*New Directions for Methodology of Social and Behavioral Science,* No. 5, pp. 63–77). San Francisco: Jossey-Bass.

Hall, J. A. (1984). *Nonverbal sex differences: Communication accuracy and expressive style.* Baltimore, MD: Johns Hopkins University Press.

Hall, J. A. (in press). On explaining gender differences: The case of nonverbal communication. *Review of Personality and Social Psychology.*

Hall, J. A., & Halberstadt, A. G. (1986). Smiling and gazing. In J. S. Hyde & M. C. Linn (Eds.), *The psychology of gender: Advances through meta-analysis* (pp. 136–158). Baltimore, MD: Johns Hopkins University Press.

Hamburg, D. A., & Trudeau, M. B. (Eds.). (1981). *Biobehavioral aspects of aggression.* New York: Liss.

Hamilton, D. L. (1979). A cognitive-attributional analysis of stereotyping. In L. Berkowitz (Ed.), *Advances in experimental social psychology* (Vol. 12 pp. 53–84). New York: Academic Press.

Hansson, R. O., Allen, M. M., & Jones, W. H. (1980). Sex differences in conformity: Instrumental or communal response? *Sex Roles, 6,* 207–212.

Hare, A. P. (1976). *Handbook of small group research* (2nd ed.). New York: Free Press.

Harris, M. (1974). *Cows, pigs, wars, and witches: The riddles of culture.* New York: Random House.

Harris, M. (1977). *Cannibals and kings.* New York: Random House.

Harris, M. B. (1974). Mediators between frustration and aggression in a field experiment. *Journal of Experimental Social Psychology, 10,* 561–571.

Harris, M. J., & Rosenthal, R. (1985). Mediation of interpersonal expectancy effects: 31 meta-analyses. *Psychological Bulletin, 97,* 363–386.

Hartmann, H. I. (1981). The family as the locus of gender, class, and political struggle: The example of housework. *Signs: Journal of Women in Culture and Society, 6,* 366–394.

Harvard University Computation Laboratory (1955). *Annals of the Computation Laboratory of Harvard University:* Vol. 35. *Tables of the cumulative binomial probability distribution* Cambridge, MA: Harvard University Press.

Hearnshaw, F. J. C. (1928). Chivalry and its place in history. In E. Prestage (Ed.), *Chivalry: A series of studies to illustrate its historical significance and civilizing influence* (pp. 1–35). New York: Knopf.

Hedges, L. V. (1981). Distribution theory for Glass's estimator of effect size and related estimators. *Journal of Educational Statistics, 6,* 107–128.

Hedges, L. V. (1982a). Fitting categorical models to effect sizes from a series of experiments. *Journal of Educational Statistics, 7,* 119–137.

Hedges, L. V. (1982b). Fitting continuous models to effect size data. *Journal of Educational Statistics, 7,* 245–270.

Hedges, L. V., & Becker, B. J. (1986). Statistical methods in the meta-analysis of research on gender differences. In J. Hyde & M. C. Linn (Eds.), *The psychology of gender: Advances through meta-analysis* (pp. 14–50). Baltimore, MD: Johns Hopkins University Press.

Hedges, L. V., & Olkin, I. (1980). Vote-counting methods in research synthesis. *Psychological Bulletin, 88,* 359–369.

Hedges, L. V., & Olkin, I. (1985). *Statistical methods for meta-analysis.* Orlando, FL: Academic Press.

Heider, F. (1958). *The psychology of interpersonal relations.* New York: Wiley.

Heilbrun, A. B., Jr., & Bailey, B. A. (1986). Independence of masculine and feminine traits: Empirical exploration of a prevailing assumption. *Sex Roles, 14,* 105–122.

Helmreich, R. L., Spence, J. T., & Gibson, R. H. (1982). Sex-role attitudes: 1972–1980. *Personality and Social Psychology Bulletin, 8,* 656–663.

Hembroff, L. A. (1982). Resolving status inconsistency: An expectation states theory and test. *Social Forces, 61,* 183–205.

Henley, N. M. (1977). *Body politics: Power, sex, and nonverbal communication.* Englewood Cliffs, NJ: Prentice-Hall.

Henley, N. M., & LaFrance, M. (1984). Gender as culture: Difference and dominance in nonverbal behavior. In A. Wolfgang (Ed.), *Nonverbal behavior: Perspectives, applications, intercultural insights* (pp. 351–371). Lewiston, NY: Hogrefe.

Herrnstein, R. (1973). *IQ in the meritocracy.* Boston: Atlantic Monthly Press and Little, Brown.

Hesselbart, S. (1977). Sex role and occupational stereotypes: Three studies of impression formation. *Sex Roles, 3,* 409–422.

Hilton, J. L., & Darley, J. M. (1985). Constructing other persons: A limit on the effect. *Journal of Experimental Social Psychology, 21,* 1–18.

Hoffer, E. (1951). *The true believer: Thoughts on the nature of mass movements.* New York: Harper & Row.

Hoffman, C. (1985). A descriptive bias in trait attributions following decisions favoring one role candidate over another. *Social Cognition, 3,* 296–312.

Hoffman, M. L. (1977). Sex differences in empathy and related behaviors. *Psychological Bulletin, 84,* 712–722.

Hoffman, M. L. (1981). Is altruism part of human nature? *Journal of Personality and Social Psychology, 40,* 121–137.

Holland, D., & Davidson, D. (1984, August). *The meaning of metaphors in gender stereotyping.* Paper presented at the meeting of the American Psychological Association, Toronto.

Holland, D., & Skinner, D. (in press). Prestige and intimacy: The cultural models behind Americans' talk about gender types. In D. Holland & N. Quinn (Eds.), *Cultural models in language and thought.* New York: Cambridge University Press.

Hook, S. (1943). *The hero in history: A study in limitation and possibility.* New York: John Day.

House, J. (1981). Social structure and personality. In M. Rosenberg & R. Turner (Eds.), *Social psychology: Sociological perspectives* (pp. 525–561). New York: Basic Books.

Huici, C. (1984). The individual and social functions of sex role stereotypes. In H. Tajfel (Ed.), *The social dimension: European developments in social psychology* (Vol. 1, pp. 579–602). New York: Cambridge University Press.

Huston, A. C. (1983). Sex-typing. In P. H. Mussen & E. M. Heatherington (Eds.), *Handbook of child psychology* (Vol. 4, pp. 387–467). New York: Wiley.

Huston, T. L., & Ashmore, R. D. (1986). Women and men in personal relationships. In R. D. Ashmore & F. K. Del Boca (Eds.), *The social psychology of female-male relations: A critical analysis of central concepts* (pp. 167–210). Orlando, FL: Academic Press.

Hyde, J. S. (1981). How large are cognitive gender differences? A meta-analysis using ω^2 and d. *American Psychologist, 36,* 892–901.

Hyde, J. S. (1984). How large are gender differences in aggression? A developmental meta-analysis. *Developmental Psychology, 20,* 722–736.

Hyde, J. S. (1985). *Half the human experience: The psychology of women* (3rd ed.). Lexington, MA: Heath.

Hyde, J. S. (1986). Gender differences in aggression. In J. S. Hyde & M. C. Linn (Eds.), *The psychology of gender: Advances through meta-analysis* (pp. 51–66). Baltimore, MD: Johns Hopkins University Press.

Jacklin, C. N., & Maccoby, E. E. (1983). Issues of gender differentiation. In M. D. Levine, W. B. Carey, A. C. Crocker, & R. T. Gross (Eds.), *Developmental behavioral pediatrics* (pp. 175–184). Philadelphia: W. B. Saunders.

Jackman, M. R., & Senter, M. S. (1980). Images of social groups: Categorical or qualified? *Public Opinion Quarterly, 44,* 341–361.

Janis, I. L., & King, B. T. (1954). The influence of role-playing on opinion change. *Journal of Abnormal and Social Psychology, 49,* 211–218.

Janis, I. L., & Mann, L. (1965). Effectiveness of emotional role-playing in modifying smoking habits and attitudes. *Journal of Experimental Research in Personality, 1,* 84–90.

Jensen, A. R. (1973). *Educability and group differences.* London: Methuen.

Johnson, D. W., Maruyama, G., Johnson, R., & Nelson, D. (1981). Effects of cooperative, competitive, and individualistic goal structures on achievement: A meta-analysis. *Psychological Bulletin, 89,* 47–62.

Johnson, F. L., & Aries, E. J. (1983). Conversational patterns among same-sex pairs of late-adolescent close friends. *Journal of Genetic Psychology, 142,* 225–238.

Jones, R. A. (1982). Perceiving other people: Stereotyping as a process of social cognition. In A. G. Miller (Ed.), *In the eye of the beholder: Contemporary issues in stereotyping* (pp. 41–91). New York: Praeger.

Jones, R. A., Hendrick, C., & Epstein, Y. M. (1979). *Introduction to social psychology.* Sunderland, MA: Sinauer.

Kahn, A. S., & Gaeddert, W. P. (1985). From theories of equity to theories of justice: The liberating consequences of studying women. In V. E. O'Leary, R. K. Unger, & B. S. Wallston (Eds.), *Women, gender, and social psychology* (pp. 129–148). Hillsdale, NJ: Lawrence Erlbaum Associates.

Kahn, A. S., O'Leary, V. E., Krulewitz, J. E., & Lamm, H. (1980). Equity and equality: Male and female means to a just end. *Basic and Applied Social Psychology, 1,* 173–197.

Kamalich, R. F., & Polachek, S. W. (1982). Discrimination: Fact or fiction? An examination using an alternative approach. *Southern Economic Journal, 49,* 450–461.

Kanter, R. M. (1977). *Men and women of the corporation.* New York: Basic Books.

Kaplan, A. G., & Sedney, M. A. (1980). *Psychology and sex roles: An androgynous perspective.* Boston: Little, Brown.

Keller, E. F. (1985). *Reflections on gender and science.* New Haven, CT: Yale University Press.

Kelman, H. C. (1961). Processes of opinion change. *Public Opinion Quarterly, 25,* 57–78.

Kerenyi, K. (1960). *The heroes of the Greeks* (H. J. Rose, Trans.). New York: Grove Press.

Kessler, S. J., & McKenna, W. (1978). *Gender: An ethnomethodological approach.* New York: Wiley.

Kiesler, S. B. (1975). Actuarial prejudice toward women and its implications. *Journal of Applied Social Psychology, 5,* 201–216.

Kihlstrom, J. F., & Cantor, N. (1984). Mental representations of the self. In L. Berkowitz (Ed.), *Advances in experimental social psychology* (Vol. 17, pp. 1–47). Orlando, FL: Academic Press.

Kluegel, J. R., & Smith, E. R. (1986). *Beliefs about inequality: Americans' views of what is and what ought to be.* Hawthorne, NY: Aldine de Gruyter.

Kohlberg, L. (1966). A cognitive-developmental analysis of children's sex-role concepts and attitudes. In E. E. Maccoby (Ed.), *The development of sex differences* (pp. 82–173). Stanford, CA: Stanford University Press.

Koivumaki, J. H. (1975). "Body language taught here": Critique of popular books on nonverbal communication. *Journal of Communication, 25,* 26–30.

Krebs, D. L., & Miller, D. T. (1985). Altruism and aggression. In G. Lindzey & E. Aronson (Eds.), *Handbook of social psychology* (3rd ed., Vol. 2, pp. 1–71). New York: Random House.

Lane, D. M., & Dunlap, W. P. (1978). Estimating effect size: Bias resulting from the significance criterion in editorial decisions. *British Journal of Mathematical and Statistical Psychology, 31,* 107–112.

Laws, J. L. (1979). *The second X: Sex role and social role.* New York: Elsevier North Holland.

Leik, R. K. (1963). Instrumentality and emotionality in family interaction. *Sociometry, 26,* 131–145.

Lieberman, S. (1956). The effects of changes in roles on the attitudes of role occupants. *Human Relations, 9,* 385–402.

Lifschitz, S. (1983). Male and female careers: Sex-role and occupational stereotypes among high school students. *Sex Roles, 9,* 725–735.

Light, R. J., & Pillemer, D. B. (1984). *Summing up: The science of reviewing research.* Cambridge, MA: Harvard University Press.

Linn, M. C., & Petersen, A. C. (1985). Emergence and characterization of sex differences in spatial ability: A meta-analysis. *Child Development, 56,* 1479-1498.

Lips, H. M., & Colwill, N. L. (1978). *The psychology of sex differences.* Englewood Cliffs, NJ: Prentice-Hall.

Lockheed, M. E. (1985). Sex and social influence: A meta-analysis guided by theory. In J. Berger & M. Zelditch, Jr. (Eds.), *Status, rewards, and influence: How expectancies organize behavior* (pp. 406-429). San Francisco: Jossey-Bass.

Lockheed, M. E., & Hall, K. P. (1976). Conceptualizing sex as a status characteristic: Applications to leadership training strategies. *Journal of Social Issues, 32,* 111-124.

Lubek, I. (1979). A brief social psychological analysis of research on aggression in social psychology. In A. R. Buss (Ed.), *Psychology in social context* (pp. 259-306). New York: Irvington.

Maass, A., & Clark, R. D. (1984). Hidden impact of minorities: Fifteen years of minority influence research. *Psychological Bulletin, 95,* 428-450.

Macaulay, J. (1985). Adding gender to aggression research: Incremental or revolutionary change? In V. E. O'Leary, R. K. Unger, & B. S. Wallston (Eds.), *Women, gender, and social psychology* (pp. 191-224). Hillsdale, NJ: Lawrence Erlbaum Associates.

Maccoby, E. E., & Jacklin, C. N. (1974). *The psychology of sex differences.* Stanford, CA: Stanford University Press.

Maccoby, E. E., & Jacklin, C. N. (1980). Sex differences in aggression: A rejoinder and reprise. *Child Development, 51,* 964-980.

Major, B., & Forcey, B. (1985). Social comparisons and pay evaluations: Preferences for same-sex and same-job wage comparisons. *Journal of Experimental Social Psychology, 21,* 393-405.

Major, B., & Konar, E. (1984). An investigation of sex differences in pay expectations and their possible causes. *Academy of Management Journal, 27,* 777-792.

Major, B., McFarlin, D. B., & Gagnon, D. (1984). Overworked and underpaid: On the nature of gender differences in personal entitlement. *Journal of Personality and Social Psychology, 47,* 1399-1412.

Maltz, D. N., & Borker, R. A. (1982). A cultural approach to male-female miscommunication. In J. J. Gumperz (Ed.), *Language and social identity* (pp. 196-216). New York: Cambridge University Press.

Markus, H., & Zajonc, R. B. (1985). The cognitive perspective in social psychology. In G. Lindzey & E. Aronson (Eds.), *Handbook of social psychology* (3rd ed., Vol. 1, pp. 137-230). New York: Random House.

Mason, K. O., Czajka, J. L., & Arber, S. (1976). Change in U.S. women's sex-role attitudes, 1964-1974. *American Sociological Review, 41,* 573-596.

McArthur, L. Z. (1981). What grabs you? The role of attention in impression formation and causal attribution. In E. T. Higgins, C. P. Herman, & M. P. Zanna (Eds.), *Social cognition: The Ontario Symposium* (Vol. 1, pp. 201-246). Hillsdale, NJ: Lawrence Erlbaum Associates.

McArthur, L. Z., & Baron, R. M. (1983). Toward an ecological theory of social perception. *Psychological Review, 90,* 215-238.

McClelland, D. C. (1961). *The achieving society.* New York: Van Nostrand.

McGrath, J. E. (1984). *Groups: Interaction and performance.* Englewood Cliffs, NJ: Prentice-Hall.

McGuire, W. J. (1983). A contextualist theory of knowledge: Its implications for innovation and reform in psychological research. In L. Berkowitz (Ed.), *Advances in experimental social psychology* (Vol. 16, pp. 1-47). Orlando, FL: Academic Press.

McGuire, W. J. & Papageorgis, D. (1961). The relative efficacy of various types of prior belief-defense in producing immunity against persuasion. *Journal of Abnormal and Social Psychology, 62,* 327-337.

Mednick, M. T. S. (1978). Psychology of women: Research issues and trends. *Annals of the New York Academy of Sciences, 309,* 77–92.

Meehan, A. M. (1984). A meta-analysis of sex differences in formal operational thought. *Child Development, 55,* 1110–1124.

Meehl, P. E. (1954). *Clinical versus statistical prediction: A theoretical analysis and a review of the evidence.* Minneapolis: University of Minnesota Press.

Meehl, P. E. (1978). Theoretical risks and tabular asterisks: Sir Karl, Sir Ronald, and the slow progress of soft psychology. *Journal of Consulting and Clinical Psychology, 46,* 806–834.

Meeker, B. F., & Weitzel-O'Neill, P. A. (1977). Sex roles and interpersonal behavior in task-oriented groups. *American Sociological Review, 42,* 92–105.

Mennerick, L. A. (1975). Organizational structuring of sex roles in a nonstereotyped industry. *Administrative Science Quarterly, 20,* 570–586.

Merton, R. K. (1948). The self-fulfilling prophecy. *Antioch Review, 8,* 193–210.

Merton, R. K., & Kitt, A. S. (1950). Contributions to the theory of reference group behavior. In R. K. Merton & P. F. Lazarsfeld (Eds.), *Continuities in social research: Studies in the scope and method of "The American Soldier"* (pp. 40–105). Glencoe, IL: Free Press.

Miller, J. B. (1976). *Toward a new psychology of women.* Boston: Beacon Press.

Miller, N., & Carlson, M. (1984, August). *Explanation of the relation between negative mood and helping.* Paper presented at the meeting of the American Psychological Association, Toronto.

Mischel, W. (1966). A social-learning view of sex differences in behavior. In E. E. Maccoby (Ed.), *The development of sex differences* (pp. 56–81). Stanford, CA: Stanford University Press.

Mischel, W. (1968). *Personality and assessment.* New York: Wiley.

Moscovici, S., & Faucheux, C. (1972). Social influence, conformity bias, and the study of active minorities. In L. Berkowitz (Ed.), *Advances in experimental social psychology* (Vol. 6, pp. 149–202). New York: Academic Press.

Munroe, R. L., & Munroe, R. H. (1980). Perspectives suggested by anthropological data. In H. C. Triandis & W. W. Lambert (Eds.), *Handbook of cross-cultural psychology* (Vol. 1, pp. 253–317). Boston: Allyn & Bacon.

Newcomb, T. M. (1950). *Social psychology.* New York: Dryden Press.

Newcomb, T. M., Turner, R. H., & Converse, P. E. (1965). *Social psychology: The study of human interaction.* New York: Holt, Rinehart, and Winston.

O'Leary, V. E. (1974). Some attitudinal barriers to occupational aspirations in women. *Psychological Bulletin, 81,* 809–826.

O'Leary, V. E., & Hansen, R. D. (1985). Sex as an attributional fact. In T. B. Sonderegger & R. A. Dienstbier (Eds.), *Nebraska Symposium on motivation 1984: Psychology and gender* (pp. 133–177). Lincoln, NE: University of Nebraska Press.

Osborn, R. N., & Vicars, W. M. (1976). Sex stereotypes: An artifact in leader behavior and subordinate satisfaction analysis? *Academy of Management Journal, 19,* 439–449.

Pandey, J., & Griffitt, W. (1977). Benefactor's sex and nurturance need, recipient's dependency, and the effect of number of potential helpers on helping behavior. *Journal of Personality, 45,* 79–99.

Parke, R. D., & Slaby, R. G. (1983). The development of aggression. In P. H. Mussen (Ed.), *Handbook of child psychology* (Vol. 4, pp. 547–641). New York: Wiley.

Parlee, M. B. (1979). Psychology and women. *Signs: Journal of Women in Culture and Society, 5,* 121–133.

Parlee, M. B. (1981). Appropriate control groups in feminist research. *Psychology of Women Quarterly, 5,* 637–644.

Parsons, T., & Bales, R. F. (1955). *Family: Socialization and interaction process.* New York: Free Press.

Pearce, P. L., & Amato, P. R. (1980). A taxonomy of helping: A multidimensional scaling analysis. *Social Psychology Quarterly, 43,* 363-371.

Peplau, L. A. (1983). Roles and gender. In H. H. Kelley, E. Berscheid, A. Christensen, J. H. Harvey, T. L. Huston, G. Levinger, E. McClintock, L. A. Peplau, & D. R. Peterson (Eds.), *Close relationships* (pp. 220-264). New York: Freeman.

Peplau, L. A., & Gordon, S. L. (1985). Women and men in love: Gender differences in close heterosexual relationships. In V. E. O'Leary, R. K. Unger, & B. S. Wallston (Eds.), *Women, gender, and social psychology* (pp. 257-291). Hillsdale, NJ: Lawrence Erlbaum Associates.

Perry, D. G., & Bussey, K. (1979). The social learning theory of sex differences: Imitation is alive and well. *Journal of Personality and Social Psychology, 37,* 1699-1712.

Pezzullo, T. R., & Brittingham, B. E. (Eds.). (1979). *Salary equity: Detecting sex bias in salaries among college and university professors.* Lexington, MA: Lexington Books.

Piliavin, I. M., Rodin, J., & Piliavin, J. A. (1969). Good Samaritanism: An underground phenomenon? *Journal of Personality and Social Psychology, 13,* 289-299.

Piliavin, J. A., Dovidio, J. F., Gaertner, S. L., & Clark, R. D. (1981). *Emergency intervention.* New York: Academic Press.

Piliavin, J. A., & Unger, R. K. (1985). The helpful but helpless female: Myth or reality? In V. E. O'Leary, R. H. Unger, & B. S. Wallston (Eds.), *Women, gender, and social psychology* (pp. 149-189). Hillsdale, NJ: Lawrence Erlbaum Associates.

Pleck, J. H. (1981). *The myth of masculinity.* Cambridge, MA: MIT Press.

Pleck, J. H. (1985). *Working wives/working husbands.* Beverly Hills, CA: Sage.

Post, E. (1924). *Etiquette in society, in business, in politics and at home.* New York: Funk & Wagnalls.

Rajecki, D. W. (1983). Animal aggression: Implications for human aggression. In R. G. Geen & E. I. Donnerstein (Eds.), *Aggression: Theoretical and empirical reviews* (Vol. 1, pp. 189-211). New York: Academic Press.

Reinisch, J. M., & Sanders, S. A. (1986). A test of sex differences in aggressive response to hypothetical conflict situations. *Journal of Personality and Social Psychology, 50,* 1045-1049.

Rhine, R. J., & Severance, L. J. (1970). Ego-involvement, discrepancy, source credibility, and attitude change. *Journal of Personality and Social Psychology, 16,* 175-190.

Rice, R. W., Bender, L. R., & Vitters, A. G. (1980). Leader sex, follower attitudes toward women, and leadership effectiveness: A laboratory experiment. *Organizational Behavior and Human Performance, 25,* 46-78.

Rice, R. W., Instone, D., & Adams, J. (1984). Leader sex, leader success, and leadership process: Two field studies. *Journal of Applied Psychology, 69,* 12-31.

Richardson, D. C., Bernstein, S., & Taylor, S. P. (1979). The effect of situational contingencies on female retaliative behavior. *Journal of Personality and Social Psychology, 37,* 2044-2048.

Robertson, W. H. (1960). *Tables of the binomial distribution function for small values of p* (Scandia Corporation Monograph No. SCR-143). Washington, DC: Office of Technical Services, U.S. Department of Commerce.

Robinson, J. P. (1977). *How Americans use time: A social-psychological analysis of everyday behavior.* New York: Praeger.

Rohner, R. P. (1976). Sex differences in aggression: Phylogenetic and enculturation perspectives. *Ethos, 4,* 57-72.

Rosenberg, R. (1982). *Beyond separate spheres: Intellectual roots of modern feminism.* New Haven, CT: Yale University Press.

Rosenkrantz, P. S., Vogel, S. R., Bee, H., Broverman, I. K., & Broverman, D. M. (1968). Sex role stereotypes and self-concepts in college students. *Journal of Consulting and Clinical Psychology, 32,* 287-295.

Rosenthal, R. (1978). Combining results of independent studies. *Psychological Bulletin, 85,* 185–193.

Rosenthal, R. (1984). *Meta-analytic procedures for social research.* Beverly Hills, CA: Sage.

Rosenthal, R., & Rubin, D. B. (1978). Interpersonal expectancy effects: The first 345 studies. *Behavioral and Brain Sciences, 3,* 377–415.

Rosenthal, R., & Rubin, D. B. (1982a). Comparing effect sizes of independent studies. *Psychological Bulletin, 92,* 500–504.

Rosenthal, R., & Rubin, D. B. (1982b). Further meta-analytic procedures for assessing cognitive gender differences. *Journal of Educational Psychology, 74,* 708–712.

Rosenthal, R., & Rubin, D. B. (1982c). A simple, general purpose display of magnitude of experimental effect. *Journal of Educational Psychology, 74,* 166–169.

Rosnow, R. L. (1981). *Paradigms in transition: The methodology of social inquiry.* New York: Oxford University Press.

Rosnow, R. L. (1983). Von Osten's horse, Hamlet's question, and the mechanistic view of causality: Implications for a post-crisis social psychology. *Journal of Mind and Behavior, 4,* 319–338.

Ross, L., Lepper, M. R., & Hubbard, M. (1975). Perseverance in self-perception and social perception: Biased attributional processes in the debriefing paradigm. *Journal of Personality and Social Psychology, 32,* 880–892.

Rossi, J. S. (1983). Ratios exaggerate gender differences in mathematical ability. *American Psychologist, 38,* 348.

Ruble, T. L. (1983). Sex stereotypes: Issues of change in the 1970s. *Sex Roles, 9,* 397–402.

Santee, R. T., & Jackson, S. E. (1982). Identity implications of conformity: Sex differences in normative and attributional judgments. *Social Psychology Quarterly, 45,* 121–125.

Sarbin, T. R., & Allen, V. L. (1968). Role theory. In G. Lindzey & E. Aronson (Eds.), *Handbook of social psychology* (2nd ed., Vol. 1, pp. 488–567). Reading, MA: Addison-Wesley.

Scanzoni, J. (1972). *Sexual bargaining: Power politics in the American marriage.* Englewood Cliffs, NJ: Prentice-Hall.

Scanzoni, J. (1979). Social processes and power in families. In W. R. Burr, R. Hill, F. I. Nye, & I. L. Reiss (Eds.), *Contemporary theories about the family* (Vol. 1, pp. 295–316). New York: Free Press.

Schank, R. C., & Abelson, R. P. (1977). *Scripts, plans, goals, and understanding: An inquiry into human knowledge structures.* Hillsdale, NJ: Lawrence Erlbaum Associates.

Schlenker, B. R. (1982). Translating actions into attitudes: An identity-analytic approach to the explanation of social conduct. In L. Berkowitz (Ed.), *Advances in experimental social psychology* (Vol. 15, pp. 193–247). New York: Academic Press.

Schneider, D. J., Hastorf, A. H., & Ellsworth, P. (1979). *Person perception* (2nd ed.). Reading, MA: Addison-Wesley.

Schuck, J., & Pisor, K. (1974). Evaluating an aggression experiment by the use of simulating subjects. *Journal of Personality and Social Psychology, 29,* 181–186.

Sears, D. O. (1986). College students in the laboratory: Influence of a narrow data base on social psychology's view of human nature. *Journal of Personality and Social Psychology, 51,* 515–530.

Shapiro, R. Y., & Mahajan, H. (1986). Gender differences in policy preferences: A summary of trends from the 1960s to the 1980s. *Public Opinion Quarterly, 50,* 42–61.

Sherif, C. W. (1979). Bias in psychology. In J. A. Sherman & E. T. Beck (Eds.), *The prism of sex: Essays in the sociology of knowledge* (pp. 93–133). Madison, WI: University of Wisconsin Press.

Sherif, M. (1935). A study of some social factors in perception. *Archives of Psychology, 27*(187), 1–60.

Sherif, M., & Cantril, H. (1947). *The psychology of ego-involvements, social attitudes, and identifications.* New York: Wiley.

Sherman, J. A. (1971). *On the psychology of women: A survey of empirical studies.* Springfield, IL: Charles C Thomas.

Sherman, J. A. (1978). *Sex-related cognitive differences: An essay on theory and evidence.* Springfield, IL: Charles C Thomas.

Shields, S. A. (1975). Functionalism, Darwinism, and the psychology of women: A study in social myth. *American Psychologist, 30,* 739–754.

Shinar, E. (1978). Person perception as a function of occupation and sex. *Sex Roles, 4,* 679–693.

Simmel, E. C., Hahn, M. E., & Walters, J. K. (Eds.). (1983). *Aggressive behavior: Genetic and neural approaches.* Hillsdale, NJ: Lawrence Erlbaum Associates.

Sistrunk, F., & McDavid, J. W. (1971). Sex variable in conforming behavior. *Journal of Personality and Social Psychology, 17,* 200–207.

Skrypnek, B. J., & Snyder, M. (1982). On the self-perpetuating nature of stereotypes about women and men. *Journal of Experimental Social Psychology, 18,* 277–291.

Slater, P. (1961). Parental role differentiation. *American Journal of Sociology, 67,* 296–311.

Slavin, R. E. (1984). Meta-analysis in education: How has it been used? *Educational Researcher, 13*(8), 6–15.

Smith, T. W. (1984). The polls: Gender and attitudes toward violence. *Public Opinion Quarterly, 48,* 384–396.

Smithson, M., & Amato, P. (1982). An unstudied region of helping: An extension of the Pearce-Amato cognitive taxonomy. *Social Psychology Quarterly, 45,* 67–76.

Snyder, M. (1981). On the self-perpetuating nature of social stereotypes. In D. L. Hamilton (Ed.), *Cognitive processes in stereotyping and intergroup behavior* (pp. 183–212). Hillsdale, NJ: Lawrence Erlbaum Associates.

Snyder, M. (1984). When belief creates reality. In L. Berkowitz (Ed.), *Advances in experimental social psychology* (Vol. 18, pp. 247–305). New York: Academic Press.

Snyder, M., Grether, J., & Keller, K. (1974). Staring and compliance: A field experiment on hitchhiking. *Journal of Applied Social Psychology, 4,* 165–170.

Snyder, M., & Ickes, W. (1985). Personality and social behavior. In G. Lindzey & E. Aronson (Eds.), *Handbook of social psychology* (3rd ed., Vol. 2, pp. 883–947). New York: Random House.

Spence, J. T., & Helmreich, R. L. (1978). *Masculinity & femininity: Their psychological dimensions, correlates, & antecedents.* Austin: University of Texas Press.

Spence, J. T., Helmreich, R. L., & Holahan, C. K. (1979). Negative and positive components of psychological masculinity and femininity and their relationships to self-reports of neurotic and acting out behaviors. *Journal of Personality and Social Psychology, 37,* 1673–1682.

Spence, J. T., Helmreich, R., & Stapp, J. (1974). The Personal Attributes Questionnaire: A measure of sex-role stereotypes and masculinity-femininity. *JSAS: Catalog of Selected Documents in Psychology, 4,* 43. (Ms. No. 617).

Staines, G. L., with Libby, P. L. (1986). Men and women in role relationships. In R. D. Ashmore & F. K. Del Boca (Eds.), *The social psychology of female-male relations: A critical analysis of central concepts* (pp. 211–258). Orlando, FL: Academic Press.

Staub, E. (1978). *Positive social behavior and morality: Social and personal influences* (Vol. 1). New York: Academic Press.

Stein, P. J., & Hoffman, S. (1978). Sports and male role strain. *Journal of Social Issues, 34*(1), 136–150.

Stier, D. S., & Hall, J. A. (1984). Gender differences in touch: An empirical and theoretical review. *Journal of Personality and Social Psychology, 47,* 440–459.

Straus, M. A. (1980). Victims and aggressors in marital violence. *American Behavioral Scientist, 23,* 681–704.

Straus, M. A., Gelles, R. J., & Steinmetz, S. K. (1980). *Behind closed doors: Violence in the American family.* Garden City, NY: Anchor Books.

Stryker, S. (1983). Social psychology from the standpoint of a structural symbolic interactionism: Toward an interdisciplinary social psychology. In L. Berkowitz (Ed.), *Advances in experimental social psychology* (Vol. 16, pp. 181–218). Orlando, FL: Academic Press.

Stryker, S., & Serpe, R. T. (1982). Commitment, identity salience, and role behavior: Theory and research example. In W. Ickes & E. S. Knowles (Eds.), *Personality, roles, and social behavior* (pp. 199–218). New York: Springer-Verlag.

Swann, W. B., Jr. (1983). Self-verification: Bringing social reality into harmony with the self. In J. Suls & A. G. Greenwald (Eds.), *Psychological perspectives on the self* (Vol. 2, pp. 33–66). Hillsdale, NJ: Lawrence Erlbaum Associates.

Swann, W. B., Jr. (1984). Quest for accuracy in person perception: A matter of pragmatics. *Psychological Review, 91,* 457–477.

Swann, W. B., Jr., & Ely, R. J. (1984). A battle of wills: Self-verification versus behavioral confirmation. *Journal of Personality and Social Psychology, 46,* 1287–1302.

Tajfel, H. (1981). Social stereotypes and social groups. In J. C. Turner & H. Giles (Eds.), *Intergroup behavior* (pp. 144–167). Oxford: Blackwell.

Tangri, S. S., Burt, M. R., & Johnson, L. B. (1982). Sexual harassment at work: Three explanatory models. *Journal of Social Issues, 38*(4), 33–54.

Tavris, C., & Wade, C. (1984). *The longest war: Sex differences in perspective* (2nd ed.). New York: Harcourt Brace Jovanovich.

Taylor, M. C., & Hall, J. A. (1982). Psychological androgyny: Theories, methods, and conclusions. *Psychological Bulletin, 92,* 347–366.

Tedeschi, J. T. (1983). Social influence theory and aggression. In R. G. Geen & E. I. Donnerstein (Eds.), *Aggression: Theoretical and empirical reviews* (Vol. 1, pp. 135–162). New York: Academic Press.

Tedeschi, J. T., Smith, R. B., III, & Brown, R. C., Jr. (1974). A reinterpretation of research on aggression. *Psychological Bulletin, 81,* 540–562.

Terborg, J. R. (1977). Women in management: A research review. *Journal of Applied Psychology, 62,* 647–664.

Thibaut, J. W., & Kelley, H. H. (1959). *The social psychology of groups.* New York: Wiley.

Thomas, J. R., & French, K. E. (1985). Gender differences across age in motor performance: A meta-analysis. *Psychological Bulletin, 98,* 260–282.

Thomas, L. (1943). *These men shall never die.* Philadelphia: John C. Winston.

Thornton, A., & Freedman, D. (1979). Changes in the sex role attitudes of women, 1962–1977: Evidence from a panel study. *American Sociological Review, 44,* 831–842.

Triandis, H. C., & Vassiliou, V. (1967). Frequency of contact and stereotyping. *Journal of Personality and Social Psychology, 7,* 316–328.

Trivers, R. L. (1971). The evolution of reciprocal altruism. *Quarterly Review of Biology, 46,* 35–57.

Underwood, B., & Moore, B. S. (1982). The generality of altruism in children. In N. Eisenberg (Ed.), *The development of prosocial behavior* (pp. 25–52). New York: Academic Press.

Unger, R. K. (1978). The politics of gender: A review of relevant literature. In J. Sherman & F. Denmark (Eds.), *Psychology of women: Future directions of research* (pp. 463–517). New York: Psychological Dimensions.

Unger, R. K. (1979). Toward a redefinition of sex and gender. *American Psychologist, 34,* 1085–1094.

Unger, R. K. (1983). Through the looking glass: No wonderland yet! (The reciprocal relationship between methodology and models of reality). *Psychology of Women Quarterly, 8,* 9–32.

U.S. Department of Justice, Office of Justice Assistance, Research, and Statistics. (1979). *How to protect yourself against sexual assault: Take a bite out of crime.* Washington, DC: U.S. Government Printing Office.

U.S. Department of Labor, Bureau of Labor Statistics. (1980). *Perspectives on working women: A databook* (Bull. No. 2080). Washington, DC: U.S. Government Printing Office.

U.S. Department of Labor, Bureau of Labor Statistics. (1984). *Employment and Earnings, 31*(1), 164.

Vanderbilt, A. (1963). *Amy Vanderbilt's new complete book of etiquette: The guide to gracious living.* Garden City, NY: Doubleday.

Vaux, A. (1985). Variations in social support associated with gender, ethnicity, and age. *Journal of Social Issues, 41*(1), 89–110.

Ventimiglia, J. C. (1982). Sex roles and chivalry: Some conditions of gratitude to altruism. *Sex Roles, 8,* 1107–1122.

von Baeyer, C. L., Sherk, D. L., & Zanna, M. P. (1981). Impression management in the job interview: When the female applicant meets the male "chauvinist" interviewer. *Personality and Social Psychology Bulletin, 7,* 45–51.

Vrugt, A., & Kerkstra, A. (1984). Sex differences in nonverbal communication. *Semiotica, 50,* 1–41.

Walker, K., & Woods, M. (1976). *Time use: A measure of household production of family goods and services.* Washington, DC: American Home Economics Association.

Wallston, B. S. (1981). What are the questions in psychology of women? A feminist approach to research. *Psychology of Women Quarterly, 5,* 597–617.

Wallston, B. S., & Grady, K. E. (1985). Integrating the feminist critique and the crisis in social psychology: Another look at research methods. In V. E. O'Leary, R. H. Unger, & B. S. Wallston (Eds.), *Women, gender, and social psychology* (pp. 7–33). Hillsdale, NJ: Lawrence Erlbaum Associates.

Walum, L. R. (1974). The changing door ceremony: Notes on the operation of sex roles in everyday life. *Urban Life and Culture, 2,* 506–515.

Ward, D. A., Seccombe, K., Bendel, R., Carter, L. F. (1985). Cross-sex context as a factor in persuasibility sex differences. *Social Psychology Quarterly, 48,* 269–276.

Webster, M., Jr., & Driskell, J. E., Jr. (1978). Status generalization: A review and some new data. *American Sociological Review, 43,* 220–236.

Weitz, S. (Ed.). (1974). *Nonverbal communication: Readings with commentary.* New York: Oxford University Press.

Werner, P. D., & LaRussa, G. W. (1985). Persistence and change in sex-role stereotypes. *Sex Roles, 12,* 1089–1100.

Whyte, W. H., Jr. (1956). *The organization man.* New York: Simon & Schuster.

Williams, D. G. (1985). Gender differences in interpersonal relationships and well-being. In A. C. Kerckhoff (Ed.), *Research in sociology of education and socialization* (Vol. 5, pp. 239–267). Greenwich, CT: JAI Press.

Williams, J. E., & Best, D. L. (1982). *Measuring sex stereotypes: A thirty-nation study.* Beverly Hills, CA: Sage.

Williams, J. H. (1983). *Psychology of women: Behavior in a biosocial context* (2nd ed.). New York: W. W. Norton.

Wispé, L. G., & Freshley, H. B. (1971). Race, sex, and sympathetic helping behavior: The broken bag caper. *Journal of Personality and Social Psychology, 17,* 59–65.

Wood, W. (in press). A meta-analytic review of sex differences in group performance. *Psychological Bulletin.*

Wood, W., & Karten, S. J. (1986). Sex differences in interaction style as a product of inferred sex differences in competence. *Journal of Personality and Social Psychology, 50,* 341–347.

Wood, W., Polek, D., & Aiken, C. (1985). Sex differences in group task performance. *Journal of Personality and Social Psychology, 48,* 63–71.

Worell, J., Romano, P., & Newsome, T. (1984, May). *Patterns of nurturance in same and cross-gender friendships in middle adolescence.* Paper presented at the meeting of the Midwest Society for Research in Lifespan Development, Akron, OH.

Yoder, J. D., & Sinnet, L. M. (1985). Is it all in the numbers? A case study of tokenism. *Psychology of Women Quarterly, 9,* 413–418.

Yount, K. (1986). A theory of productive activity: The relationships among self-concept, gender, sex-role stereotypes, and work-emergent traits. *Psychology of Women Quarterly, 10,* 63–88.

Zajonc, R. B. (1965). Social facilitation. *Science, 149,* 269–274.

Zanna, M. P., & Pack, S. J. (1975). On the self-fulfilling nature of apparent sex differences in behavior. *Journal of Experimental Social Psychology, 11,* 583–591.

Zelditch, M., Jr., Lauderdale, P., & Stublarec, S. (1980). How are inconsistencies between status and ability resolved? *Social Forces, 58,* 1025–1043.

Zuckerman, M. & Reis, H. T. (1978). Comparison of three models for predicting altruistic behavior. *Journal of Personality and Social Psychology, 36,* 498–510.

Author Index

F

Fasteau, M. F., 72
Faucheux, C., 135
Fausto-Sterling, A., 7
Fazio, R. H., 14, 30
Feather, N. T., 18, 30
Fensterheim, H., 73
Ferree, M. M., 33
Feshbach, N. D., 45, 77
Feshbach, S., 79
Festinger, L., 30
Findley, M., 117
Fishbaugh, L., 100
Fishbein, M., 30, 92, 119
Fiske, D. W., 137
Fiske, S. T., 3
Forcey, B., 111
Fraser, J., 47
Freedman, D., 33
Freese, L., 145
French, K. E., 118, 124, 128, 144
Freshley, H. B., 51
Friedan, B., 50
Friedland, S. J., 33, 146
Frieze, I. H., 106
Frodi, A., 70, 75, 77, 79
Frost, W. D., 90

G

Gaeddert, W. P., 111
Gaertner, S. L., 42
Gagnon, D., 111
Gallo, P. S., Jr., 120
Geen, R. G., 90
Geller, S. H., 101
Gelles, R. J., 89
Georgoudi, M., 27
Gerard, H. B., 14
Ghiselli, E. E., 76
Gibson, R. H., 33
Gillespie, D. L., 23
Gilligan, C., 44, 136
Gillis, J. S., 124
Girouard, M., 47
Glass, G. V., 34, 36, 37, 115
Gordon, L., 89, 90
Gordon, S. L., 11, 130, 144
Grady, K. E., 1, 10, 122, 137
Greenwald, A. G., 139
Grether, J., 53

Grev, R., 54
Griffitt, W., 29
Gross, A. E., 71, 80
Gurin, P., 33

H

Hahn, M. E., 93
Halberstadt, A. G., 105, 106
Hall, J. A., 9, 18, 35, 36, 40, 103, 104,
    105, 106, 107, 108, 110, 115, 116, 117,
    119, 122, 128, 129, 130, 131, 139, 141,
    144
Hall, K. P., 9, 24, 98
Hamburg, D. A., 93
Hamilton, D. L., 2
Hansen, R. D., 1
Hansson, R. O., 98
Hare, A. P., 109
Harris, M., 20
Harris, M. B., 71
Harris, M. J., 14, 40, 116
Hartmann, H. I., 33
Harvard University Computation Laboratory,
    84
Hastorf, A. H., 133
Hearnshaw, F. J. C., 47
Hedges, L. V., 35, 36, 37, 38, 55, 57, 58, 60,
    61, 83, 84, 99, 102, 119, 128
Heider, F., 133
Heilbrun, A. B., Jr., 33
Helmreich, R. L., 13, 15, 16, 18, 33, 44, 46,
    72, 98, 130
Hembroff, L. A., 145
Hendrick, C., 101
Henley, N. M., 9, 106, 129
Herrnstein, R., 4
Hesselbart, S., 33, 146
Hilton, J. L., 135
Hoffer, E., 47
Hoffman, C., 135
Hoffman, M. L., 45, 69, 77, 105, 106
Hoffman, S., 73
Holahan, C. K., 16
Holland, D., 25
Hook, S., 46
House, J., 9
Hubbard, M., 135
Huici, C., 135
Huston, A. C., 7, 11
Huston, T. L., 144

Hyde, J. S., 1, 4, 36, 70, 75, 89, 93, 115, 119, 121, 122, 123, 124

I

Ickes, W., 28
Instone, D., 145

J

Jacklin, C. N., 2, 7, 11, 35, 36, 38, 65, 70, 89, 93, 100, 105, 106, 122
Jackman, M. R., 17, 18
Jackson, S. E., 98
Janis, I. L., 30
Jensen, A. R., 4
Johnson, D. W., 117
Johnson, F. L., 45
Johnson, L. B., 130
Johnson, R., 117
Jones, R. A., 2, 101
Jones, W. H., 98

K

Kahn, A. S., 111
Kamalich, R. F., 142
Kanter, R. M., 11, 23, 146
Kaplan, A. G., 124, 137
Karten, S. J., 109, 110
Keller, E. F., 143
Keller, K., 53
Kelley, H. H., 13
Kelman, H. C., 19
Kerenyi, K., 46
Kerkstra, A., 130
Kessler, S. J., 39
Kiesler, S. B., 19
Kihlstrom, J. F., 26
King, B. T., 30
Kite, M. E., 14, 17, 26
Kitt, A. S., 29
Klentz, B., 116
Kluegel, J. R., 33
Kohlberg, L., 131
Koivumaki, J. H., 103
Konar, E., 111
Krebs, D. L., 89
Krulewitz, J. E., 111

L

LaFrance, M., 106
Laird, J. D., 33, 146

Lamm, H., 111
Lane, D. M., 139
LaRussa, G. W., 33
Latané, B., 43, 54
Lauderdale, P., 145
Laws, J. L., 20
Leik, R. K., 20
Lennon, R., 45, 77
LePage, A., 29
Lepper, M. R., 135
Leviton, L. C., 36
Lewis, L. L. 14, 15, 17, 24, 25, 32
Lieberman, S., 30
Lifschitz, S., 33
Light, R. J., 36
Linn, M. C., 2, 40, 117
Lips, H. M., 124
Lockheed, M. E., 9, 23, 24, 98, 102
Lubek, I., 71

M

Maass, A., 135
Macaulay, J., 5, 70, 75, 77, 79
Maccoby, E. E., 2, 7, 11, 35, 36, 38, 65, 70, 89, 93, 100, 105, 106, 122
Mahajan, H., 18, 45, 72
Major, B., 111
Maltz, D. N., 130
Mann, L., 30
Markus, H., 3, 26
Martin, D. C., 23
Martyna, W., 45, 130
Maruyama, G., 117
Mason, K. O., 33
McArthur, L. Z., 24, 25
McClelland, D. C., 74
McDavid, J. W., 101
McFarlin, D. B., 111
McGaw, B., 34, 36, 37, 115
McGrath, J. E., 108, 109
McGuire, W. J., 27, 41, 101
McKenna, W., 39
McLear, P. M., 25
Mednick, M. T. S., 137
Meehan, A. M., 117
Meehl, P. E., 7, 35, 68
Meeker, B. F., 9, 23, 24, 98
Mennerick, L. A., 23
Merton, R. K., 14, 29
Meyerowitz, B. E., 17, 18
Miller, D. T., 89

Subject Index

Social influence, sex differences in, *see* Influenceability
Social learning theory, 31, 131
Social norms, normative beliefs, 13–15, 44, 46, 48, 66, 72, 95, 111; *see also* Gender roles
    critical features of, 13, 14
Social position of women, of the sexes, *see* Division of labor between the sexes, Status differences between the sexes
Social roles, *see also* Gender roles
    as causes of sex differences, 4, 8–34, 42–52, 66, 67, 71–78, 91–93, 95, 97, 98, 100, 101, 106, 107, 109, 111, 112, 126–129
    in research settings, 10, 11, *see also* Social context of social-psychological research
    specific roles, 12, 13, 20–23, 28–30, 33, 34, 43, 49–51, 68, 71, 73, 74, 89, 90, 94, 98, 102, 103, 107–109, 126, 127, 131, 139, 140, 144–147
    theory of, 3, 12–15, 28, 29
Social status, *see* Status differences between the sexes
Social stereotypes, 14, *see also* Gender stereotypes
Social structure and sex differences, 3, 4, 9, 19–25, *see also* Division of labor between the sexes, Status differences between the sexes
Socialization
    anticipatory, 28, 29, 131
    theories of sex differences, 7, 31, 131, 132

Status differences between the sexes, 23, 24, 147
    and aggressive behavior, 74
    and gender stereotypes, 23, 24, 135
    and helping behavior, 48–50, 67, 127
    and influenceability, 98
Stereotypes, *see* Gender stereotypes
Structural versus cultural theories of group differences, 9

T

Task behavior in discussion groups, 108–110, *see also* Group behavior
Tokenism, 146

V

Validity of sex-difference findings, 2, 8, 37, 65, 89, 96, 107, 112, 136–144
    construct validity, 137
    external validity or generalizability, 57, 89, 138; *see also* Social context of social-psychological research
    meta-analysis and, 138, 139
    publication bias, 139
Violence, *see* Aggression
Vote-counting method of aggregating findings, 35, *see also* Narrative reviewing

W

Work, and women, *see* Division of labor between the sexes, Social roles
Work-emergent traits, 21